As pastor of Washington, D.C.'s, historic New York Avenue Presbyterian Church, Peter Marshall preached with sharp wit, sparkling imagery of words, and passionate zeal in making the "Chief" real to all who listened. Furthermore, the daily prayers he offered while chaplain of the United States Senate spoke so pungently to current topics that they were quoted widely in the press. Those prayers were so helpful to the senators that they began seeking him out as their pastor.

We share these same spiritually nourishing messages and prayers with you in **The Best of Peter Marshall.** As editor, Catherine Marshall lovingly and carefully drew from over 600 Peter Marshall sermons, plus hundreds of prayers. The result is a volume that will entertain, inspire, and edify people of all ages, from every walk of life. In short, this is a treasury of a great man's ministry. Parents and teachers, pastors and laymen will all find practical guidance, inspiration, drama, and good common sense in these pages.

Books Written or Edited by Catherine Marshall

Mr. Jones, Meet the Master
A Man Called Peter
Let's Keep Christmas
The Prayers of Peter Marshall
To Live Again
The First Easter
Beyond Our Selves
John Doe, Disciple (now Heaven Can't Wait)
Christy
Something More
Adventures in Prayer
The Helper
My Personal Prayer Diary
   (with Leonard E. LeSourd)
Meeting God at Every Turn

Children's Books

Friends with God
God Loves You
Catherine Marshall's Story Bible

The Best of PETER MARSHALL

Compiled and Edited By
CATHERINE MARSHALL

Chosen Books
A Division of Baker Book House Co
Grand Rapids, Michigan 49516

Sermons in this volume are compiled from MR. JONES, MEET THE MASTER; LET'S KEEP CHRISTMAS; A MAN CALLED PETER; HEAVEN CAN'T WAIT; THE FIRST EASTER; and THE PRAYERS OF PETER MARSHALL are used by permission.

Library of Congress Cataloging in Publication Data

Marshall, Peter, 1902-1949
    The best of Peter Marshall.

    "Culled from six books: Mr. Jones, meet the master; Let's keep Christmas; A man called Peter; Heaven can't wait; The first Easter; and The prayers of Peter Marshall" — P. vii.
    1. Presbyterian Church — Sermons.   2. Sermons, American.
3. Prayers. I. Marshall, Catherine, 1914-1983. II. Title.
BX9178.M363B47 1983   252'.051   83-7341
ISBN 0-8007-9123-1

A Chosen Book
Copyright © 1983 by Catherine Marshall LeSourd
Chosen Books are published by Fleming H. Revell
a division of Baker Book House Company
P.O. Box 6287, Grand Rapids, MI 49516-6287

Fifth printing, March 1995

Printed in the United States of America

Contents

A Note to the Reader

It seems incredible that, nearly thirty-five years after Peter
Marshall's death, volumes of his sermons and prayers (all of
them still in print) have sold more than three million copies,
and that fan mail continues to come in from all over the world.

Some of these correspondents report that Dr. Marshall was
instrumental in making the Scriptures come alive for them, or
even in enabling them to hear God's call into full-time ministry. Some write to request a copy of a particular beloved
sermon. Others ask how to obtain recordings of his preaching
(which began to be made nine months before his death). And
nearly all these correspondents share with love and gratitude
the impact that the late pastor and Senate chaplain has had on
their lives.

Thus the reason for this new compilation of Dr. Marshall's
material, culled from six books—*Mr. Jones, Meet the Master;
Let's Keep Christmas; A Man Called Peter; Heaven Can't Wait; The
First Easter;* and *The Prayers of Peter Marshall.* As she did when
each of these books was published, Catherine Marshall has
selected and edited the material, writing short new introduc-
tions where necessary, and always keeping in mind what has
the most relevance to today.

As in Dr. Marshall's other books, these sermons appear
almost exactly as his sermon notes were typed, resembling
free verse. This style, intended originally for ease in reading,
has become the hallmark of Peter Marshall's written material.
It conveys something of the force of his personality to the
printed page, and makes articulate, almost audible, the written word. We believe this style will add much to your reading
enjoyment.

—*The editors of Chosen Books*

Peter Marshall.

Here Is Peter Marshall

N ot long ago, a tall, broad-shouldered man approached me after the Sunday morning service of our Florida church. He introduced himself as a Presbyterian pastor from Pennsylvania. "I've long wanted to let you know," he told me, "that I'm in the ministry today because of Peter Marshall's influence on me through the movie and book *A Man Called Peter* and through Peter's sermons."

As I thanked him, I marveled at how many hundreds of times I have heard this same statement over the past thirty years and continue to hear it today from yet another generation.

How is it that such interest in Peter Marshall, Scottish immigrant-pastor and chaplain of the United States Senate during the last two years of his life, lives on so long after his death?

Surely, it must be because our basic human needs are much the same in any decade, no matter how the modern wrappings change. And because Peter Marshall's preaching and prayers gave answers to people—and still do. He knew that those answers would not come through any wisdom of his, but only as he introduced people, all kinds of people—Mr. Jones or Mrs. Smith—to the living Lord who always has the solution we seek.

One reason that Peter had an extraordinary ability to introduce ordinary folks, including the young, to "the Chief," as he liked to call his Lord, was that the preacher himself had been led into the ministry out of a working-class background. This included a machinist's job in Scottish iron-and-tube works, then emigration to America, and to Columbia Theological Seminary by way of digging ditches in New Jersey and newspaper work in Alabama.

Thus from the beginning this Scot with the burr to his *r*'s was more concerned with reaching those who had no notion about Christianity than he was with appealing to settled church members.

Passion and burning conviction poured out of the preacher's own experience as he told Mr. Jones how much a contemporary Lord wants to rescue us, guide our lives, heal hurting bodies, mend marriages and homes in trouble, comfort the sorrowing, challenge each one of us to rise above mediocre living, restore the joy of living to jaded, disillusioned hearts.

Memories flood back as I recall so many instances of that message getting through. An Army officer, admittedly pagan, came to the New York Avenue Presbyterian Church in Washington one Sunday morning to hear Dr. Marshall out of deference to his host and hostess. He left saying, "If I heard that preacher often, I'd have to change my way of life—that's all."

A Dallas businessman who had not been inside a church for years finally yielded to his wife's pleading and came to hear Peter. At the close of the service his eyes were filled with tears. "That's my preacher," he said. "Why did I wait so long to come? I'll never miss him again." And he never did.

Such incidents did not surprise me. Peter's Sunday morning service at his previous pastorate, the Westminster Presbyterian in Atlanta, Georgia, had the same impact on me when I had first heard him as a college girl.

It was weeks later before I summoned up the courage to introduce myself to the young preacher—a meeting that was to change the direction of my life.

Tall, with broad shoulders, Peter Marshall's physique told of the years spent playing soccer and working in that steel mill. Sandy, curly hair—now a bit darker—and the Scottish accent spoke of his native land. In keeping with his British background he always wore a robe in the pulpit, though never a clerical collar.

For us college and university students who helped pack that Atlanta church, there was a differentness about this young preacher. Never before had we heard one who made God so real to us *now*. Because Peter loathed piosity and stuffiness or what he called "the ministerial tone," his preaching always "laid it on the line" in picturesque style. We were astonished at his idealism about honesty in all dealings, including sex. He was an unabashed romanticist about women and marriage, made no apology whatever in talking about purity for both sexes—chastity before marriage—and an end to adultery and divorce.

We kept coming back for more because the speaker's word pictures, his humor, and that down-to-earth quality riveted our attention. I wondered how a man coming out of the grimy atmosphere of the Glasgow area's industrialism had come by the poet's feel for descriptive words. And this was combined with such an irrepressible vitality.

The zest with which Peter preached was characteristic of the way he did everything from bowling to following the fortunes of his favorite baseball teams. He worked hard, and he relaxed hard. Young people loved to be with him, and somehow, through sharing with him on a fishing trip or during an evening of bowling, they got a clearer glimpse of their Lord.

Since part of God's plan for Peter was coming to this country, one whole side of his personality never would have been developed had he missed that Master Plan and stayed in Scotland. In him was a depth of feeling for his adopted country that few native-born Americans ever have. This sprang partly from Peter's overflowing gratitude for all this country had done for him as a naturalized citizen, and partly from his passionate conviction about America's God-appointed destiny.

All along, God must have meant for the nation's capital to have this message. That was why a year after Peter, then thirty-four, and I, at twenty-two, were married, my new husband accepted the pastorate of Washington's historic old New York Avenue Presbyterian Church. He said he was scared to death—and he was. Always Peter felt inadequate for the tasks to which God called him, but because he knew God had called him, he also knew he would get the help he needed.

Soon it was apparent that living at the heart of the nation's capital was adding a new dimension to Peter's preaching. Washington was becoming accustomed of a Sunday morning to the unprecedented sight of two long lines of people waiting on the sidewalk for admission to the New York Avenue church. There was a fresh, prophetic quality, a vision for America's greatness. Here was a voice to which Washington began to listen.

It was in the pulpit that the mantle of true greatness fell upon this preacher, though his art was an unlearned one. An almost perfect diction, all the tricks of great oratory, as well as the actor's skill, he employed unconsciously. Yet it was the content that really mattered.

No one was more surprised than Peter Marshall himself when he was offered the chaplainship of the United States Senate. He was in the yard pruning bushes when Senator Kenneth Wherry (Nebraska) telephoned. Upon being asked if he would consider taking this post, Peter was astonished and said immediately, "No, I couldn't." But when Senator Wherry insisted, he agreed to pray about it and let him know. "I wouldn't think of allowing my name even to be considered, unless God definitely gives me a green light," was Peter's quick response.

As it turned out, the senators, the visitors in the gallery, the page boys, indeed, the country as a whole, came to look forward to those terse, punchy prayers. Never will those who heard it forget the briefest of all, that of January 6, 1948: "Our Father," he prayed, "who art Lord of heaven and of all the earth, Thou knowest the difficulties these men have to face and the grave decisions they must make. Have mercy upon them. For Jesus' sake, Amen." As Peter turned to go, Senator Arthur Vandenberg leaned over, smiled broadly, and whispered, "Now I know just how a condemned man feels."

Here, too, Peter felt his inadequacy. Once he actually pleaded: "Our Father, let not my unworthiness stand between Thee and the members of this body as we join in prayer. Hear not the voice that speaks, but listen to the yearnings of the hearts now open before Thee—"

So much did Peter love to preach, so sure was he that this was the thing God had designed him to do, that it was hard for him to turn down engagements. Though he had a rugged constitution—for Scotland's rigorous climate does not pamper its people—his strength did not quite equal his enthusiasm. On the morning of March 31, 1946, he collapsed in the pulpit with an attack of coronary thrombosis. After a few months of convalescence, he launched into the most vigorous and productive period of his life. Then on January 25, 1949, at 8:15 in the morning, quietly he slipped through those phantom walls

that separate this life from the next. We had only five hours'
warning.

"When the clock strikes for me," he had said, "I shall go, not
one minute early, and not one minute late. Until then, there is
nothing to fear. I know that the promises of God are true, for
they have been fulfilled in my life time and time again. Jesus
still teaches and guides and protects and heals and comforts,
and still wins our complete trust and our love.

"The measure of a life, after all, is not its duration, but its
donation."

Those of us who stood helplessly by—often with uneasy
minds and wistful hearts—watching him pack his threescore
years and ten into a scanty forty-six, could never have imagined how God would extend Peter's "donation": Your ministry, Peter, goes on and on.

February 18, 1983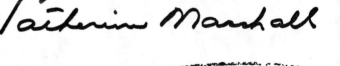

Book I

Mr. Jones, Meet the Master

Christianity began as good news . . . .
We have permitted it to be
diluted into good advice.

Peter Marshall was convinced that "no man can look at Jesus of Nazareth and remain the same." It followed that the purpose at the heart of his preaching was to make sure that we in his congregation really met the One called Peter's "Chief."

The public's reception of the first book of Peter Marshall's sermons, *Mr. Jones, Meet the Master* (edited and released in 1949, a little over nine months after his death), was a surprise to everyone. Although material intended for oral presentation can be dull and repetitious on the printed page, *Mr. Jones* proved the exception.

By the end of Publication Day, November 28, 1949, all 10,000 copies of the first printing were gone. Six weeks later *Mr. Jones* was mounting the *New York Times* best-seller list. In the years that followed book club, foreign and paperback editions increased sales to around 1,200,000 copies.

The unusual format undoubtedly helped. Trained to write his sermons out fully before delivering them from the pulpit, these sermons have been set up just as Peter's manuscripts were typed. This readable style that looks like blank verse makes even more effective the vividness of the material itself.

But the real success of the book lay in what the sermons were meaning to people. Their letters poured in. What they revealed was that the central purpose at the heart of Peter Marshall's ministry was living on in uninterrupted fashion: out of the pages of *Mr. Jones* had stepped a living Lord. "The Chief" had brought joy and excitement to everyday life.

Following are seven favorite sermons from this first collection, addressed to the man Peter Marshall liked to call "Mr. Jones"—businessmen, politicians, clerks, bus drivers, butchers, housewives, professional men, students, the lonely serviceman overseas or the girl in the hospital ward. Here, interpreted masterfully for "Everyman," is an introduction to the Master.

C.M.

Disciples in Clay

I wonder how you would like to be on an investigating committee. Apparently there are some people in Washington who enjoy that sort of thing.

Suppose you had been on such a committee nineteen hundred years ago, to inquire into the qualifications of those who sought to become disciples of Jesus. Suppose you had been one of a group with authority to examine the credentials of the men who presented themselves as candidates for discipleship. How would you have voted on them?

Let us imagine we were there on an examining board.

Here comes the first candidate.
He has just come up from the beach.
His fishing boat drawn up on the pebbled shore has worn seats, patched sails, and the high rudder that is characteristic of Galilean fishing craft.

As you can judge from his appearance, he has just entered middle age.
But he is already bald, and the fringes of hair that remain are already gray.
His hands are rough and calloused.
His fingers are strong.
He smells of fish!
He is an uncouth person—not at all refined, or cultured, or educated.
Blustering
  blundering
    clumsy
      impulsive
he does not strike us as being material for the ministry.
Then, too, his age is against him.

Maybe he is too old.
Why, he is forty if he is a day.
Does not the ministry demand young men?

Not so, when we need medical attention.
We do not specify that the attending physician be in his late
twenties. No, we don't want anyone practicing on us!
Or when we find ourselves in legal trouble, we do not insist
on retaining as our counsel the most recent graduate of the
law school.

On the contrary, we seek someone with experience—someone who knows the ropes well.
If he happens to know a judge or two, so much the better.

But considering a minister, a preacher, we cannot ignore his
age—and this man's age is against him.
His ideas will be very hard to change.
He will be stubborn
   set in his ways.

He is a rough man, and he has lived a rough life.
When provoked, he is liable to burst into profanity, and his
vocabulary is lurid.

Can you imagine this big fisherman as a disciple of Jesus?
He would not be your choice, would he?
No, we'd better send Simon back to his nets.

The next candidates are brothers; they come in together.
They, too, like Simon Peter, are fishermen.
They come from the same village, from the same colony of
rough, strong men who work with their hands for a living.

But you are not going to hold that against them, are you?
Let no social snobbishness sway your judgment.
Remember the Lord Himself was a carpenter.
There is no shame in manual labor, and would it not be to a
preacher's advantage to know what it is to do manual labor?
Would it not be excellent preparation for the ministry?
These two men are looking at you.
Their eyes are steady, accustomed to far distances.
They are good weather prophets.

A glance at the sky and a look at the lake, and they can tell you what is brewing.

They know the signs of the sudden squalls that whistle through the mountain passes and come screaming down to make the water dangerous.

They, too, have strong hands and nimble fingers.
They make quite a team, these brothers.
They operate a boat in partnership, and they are very successful.
In fact, it is a mystery to their competitors how they always manage to find the fish
   always catch more than the other boats
     and how they manage to get better prices for their catch.
This naturally does not increase their popularity among the fishermen.

But it is chiefly their attitude that irritates the others.
They are not modest men.
They are boastful, and through cupped hands they like to shout taunts to the other fishermen hauling in their nets. They have earned for themselves the nickname "the sons of thunder," because they are always rumbling about something.

The way they feel, they have little patience with people who cross them, and they would be inclined to call down fire from heaven to burn them up.
Get rid of objectors!
That's their motto.

They are ambitious men, and if the stories are true that are whispered about them, they have been brought up to believe that if you want anything in life—grab it.
Their mother had taught them that to get on in the world you have to push.

They would want to be in the chief places.
They think they belong in front.
If they became disciples of Jesus, they would naturally want to be His chief lieutenants—one on His right hand and the other on His left.
If we took time to hear all the testimony from people who

know them, our verdict would be unanimous that James and
John would simply not do.

So let us pass on to the next candidate.
There is a wild gleam in his eyes—and no wonder.
He is a leader of the Underground.
He seems to be of the fanatical type, impatient and nervous.
See—he cannot keep his hands still—
    his fingers clench and unclench.

They itch to reach up and haul down the hated pennants of
Rome that hang in desecration from the walls of old Jerusalem. His blood fairly boils when he is forced, by some clanking legionnaire, to make way on the pavement and step into
the gutter.
He dreams of the day when the Kingdom shall be restored to
Israel, and the promise of the sacred writings, that when the
Messiah comes He shall restore the Kingdom, is his meat and
drink.
His eyes dance at the thought of the Messiah, at the head
of a liberating army,
    driving the hated Romans into the sea.

Yes, from the hill country they would come, and from the
cellars of the Holy City they would rise up to bring back the
glories of David and of Solomon. He wants, more than life
itself, to be a part of that glorious campaign.

But this young man might be too dangerous.
He is highly inflammable material.
He is likely to become violent, and his impatience will burn
him up.
He is a great risk—a very great risk.
We could not take a chance on Judas.
    We dare not.

Notice how the ladies greet this next candidate.
He will have their vote right away.
We are all drawn to him, and the men, however grudgingly,
have to admit that he is handsome.
He walks with an easy grace.
There is nothing effeminate about him,

but he is gentle
   refined
every inch a gentleman.

Endowed with all the social graces, who could possibly say a word against him?
His eyes are like limpid pools.
His smile melts your heart.
But when he starts the day, it is not to take up the tools of his trade, for he has none.
It is not to yoke the oxen to work in the fields, for he never soils his hands.
It is to wander off to daydream.

He is a Ferdinand sort of man. He likes to smell the flowers.
He is an introvert—a dreamer.
But don't you know that the work of the Kingdom demands extroverts—men who are interested in other people?
Don't you realize that it is not castles in the sky we pray for—but the coming of the Kingdom of God upon this earth?
We have to pray for it—
   and work for it, too.

No, Nathaniel is a good man, everybody agrees, but he is simply not the type we need.

We are not doing very well in selecting disciples, are we?
But think of the material we have to choose from.

Well, what about this fellow?
He, too, is a fisherman.
Let's not hold that against him.
If you are not a tradesman, or a farmer cultivating a bit of land, dressing some fruit trees or tending grapes, if you have no sheep or goats, there isn't much else for you to do but fish. For people have to eat, and fish is the best money crop in this part of the country.

This man might have it in him to be a disciple.
He is not impulsive by any means.
He will not be swept off his feet.
He is very cautious, slow to convince.
He must have been born in some little Palestinian "Missouri."

You have to show him.
He demands proof for everything.
He'll take nothing on faith.

Now, this twist of mind and character will always slow up
the work of any group to which he might belong.
He will be like the rusty little tramp steamer in the convoy.
He'll slow down the others to his own wheezy seven or eight
knots.
In fact, he has only two speeds, dead slow and stop.

Can you imagine him as a member of the apostolic band?
Always advocating delay.
"This is not the time" will be his theme song.
"Let's wait and see" will be his advice.

But the Kingdom is a venture of faith—not of doubt.
It is a matter of perception—not of proof.
How could Thomas possibly fit into that picture?

Now, if we were Jews living at the time the disciples were
originally chosen, we would boo or hiss as this next candidate
enters, for he is a quisling.
He has sold out to the army of occupation and is collecting
taxes for the Roman government.

Think of how the collaborators were regarded in Norway and
in France, and you have some idea of the feeling that runs
against this man.
Tax collectors are seldom the most popular men in any community, and this fellow is a racketeer to boot.

He has devised his own particular racket and it is making him
many enemies and making him rich as well.

But that's not all.
He has a mind like an adding machine.
He has been counting money all his life.
Money and evidences of wealth alone impress him.

That's bad enough, but there's worse to come.
He is a genealogist.
He is one of those men whose passion is family trees.
He will bore you with long recitals of the best families—

where they came from
   whom they married
      how many children they had
         and whom they married and so on . . . and on.

Can you imagine a quisling as a friend of Jesus,
   a statistician walking with the carpenter from Nazareth,
   a man who had made a god of money?
No, Levi, or Matthew if you like, must be rejected.

What about this fellow Andrew?
Does anyone know about him?
I have heard it said that he has no personality—whatever
that means.
I know that he is Peter's brother, but I know of no good
reason why he should be chosen.

There are others still waiting—Bartholomew
     Thaddeus
   Philip and another James
  and a man called Simon from Canaan.
They are all interested in becoming disciples, but I know of
no particular reason why they should.
We would not vote for any of them.

Yet these are the very men whom Jesus chose to be His
disciples, that is, all except Nathaniel.
I simply included him because he is attractive and Jesus liked
him.

I feel sure you would not argue with me if I suggested that
these men had more influence on the course of human history
than any other dozen men who ever lived.

Each man was different.
As Dr. Buttrick has commented,
"Philip looks before he leaps;
Peter leaps before he looks."[1]
Thomas was a dogged unbeliever until the last minute.
Judas sought regeneration through revolution, instead of
revolution through regeneration.
James and John wanted to get rid of people who differed with

them, instead of getting rid of the differences, so that they could get the people.

Had you and I been members of any investigating committee we would have rejected every one of them.
Yet Jesus chose them.
Why?

Mark tells us in his Gospel that Jesus chose them *"that they should be with him* and that he might send them forth to preach, And to have power to heal sicknesses, and to cast out devils.*

Well, they were with Him for three years, in intimacy of fellowship.
They walked with Him, they lived with Him.
They heard His incomparable parables.
They listened to every sermon He ever preached.

They saw with their own eyes each one of His wonderful miracles.
They saw the blind receive their sight, the lame throw away their crutches.
They saw withered limbs become straight and strong.
They even saw the dead raised to newness of life.

All these things they saw and heard.
Yet these things did not change these men.
For during the last week of Jesus' earthly ministry, they were quarreling among themselves.
James and John wanted the chief places in the cabinet of the Kingdom.
They were jealous of each other.

They were not very brave.
When Jesus was arrested they all ran away.
After He died, they scattered and went underground.
They met behind closed doors.
No, they were not very brave.

They did not have much faith.
Thomas refused to believe that the Master had risen from the dead until he had proof.
He even stipulated what that proof had to be.

Of course these three years did something to them and in them.
The fuel had been laid on the fire, but it was not lit.
The seed had been sown, but it had not germinated.

All the possibilities of change in them had been created, but the changes had not yet happened.

What did change them?
Not the crucifixion
    not the resurrection
        but the coming of the Holy Spirit at Pentecost.

Not until these men were filled with the Holy Ghost were they changed.
Not until the Spirit had come upon them in power were they changed,
    so that cowardice gave place to courage
        unbelief became a flaming faith and conviction that
        nothing on earth could shake
            jealousy was swallowed up in brotherly love
                self-interest was killed and became a ministry to others
                    fear was banished, and they were afraid of no man
                    . . . no threat, no danger.

And therein lies our hope.
We have not seen Jesus as they did.
We never heard the sound of His voice or saw the sunlight dance on His hair or traced His footprints in the sands of Palestine.

But we have the same opportunity to be changed, because the same Holy Spirit is available to us today.
He has been sent into the world to lead us into all truth,
    to convict us of sin,
        to be our Helper, our Guide.

This is a day of little faith—of few convictions—a day when men seem to have no great causes and no great passions.
So in frustration, in disappointment they are inclined to say, "You can't change human nature."
It is true that we cannot change human nature.

But God can.

It is the modern heresy to think that human nature cannot
be changed.
Human nature must be changed if we are ever to have an end
to war,
or to correct the wrong situations that make our lives uneasy
and our hearts sore.

Now, Christianity, the power of Jesus Christ,
    the Holy Spirit of God,
is the only force that can change people for good.
It is the only power in the world that can change the gears
in a man's life from self-will to God's will.
It is the only power that can give a man the right motives—
to do what God wants him to do.

Nothing else can bring him to seek first the Kingdom of God
and His righteousness, and to want most of all *to be a part of
the answer to the world's ills, and not part of the problem.*[2]

But how?

All that is needed is your own sincere desire,
    your willingness to confess your mistakes
        and your stubborn selfishness
and to face up to your sins.

When they are acknowledged and you begin to see yourself as
God sees you,
and when you ask His forgiveness, the miracle has begun.

For forgiveness can be yours—now—right away—and you
begin to be a new person from this moment.

When you yourself have begun to be a new person, then there
is hope for your own problem, whatever it is—hope for a
solution to the strained relations in your office . . .
hope for a better understanding and a discovery of a new love
for your husband or wife, a new spirit in your home and a
happiness you had thought was gone forever . . .
hope for a new meaning to your life and a new reason for
living hope . . . hope . . . hope.
Don't give up.

There's still hope.

God hasn't given up yet on His world, which is one world, and could be one world of security, peace and brotherhood instead of two worlds of suspicion and fear.
God hasn't given up on this country, which is His latest experiment in human freedom and opportunity.

God hasn't given up on you.
He can still do great things for you, in you, and through you.

God is ready and waiting and able.
What about you, and me?

We are, after all, like lumps of clay.
There are brittle pieces, hard pieces.
We have little shape or beauty.
But we need not despair.
If we are clay, let us remember there is a Potter, and His wheel.

The old gospel song has it right:
  "Have Thine own way, Lord,
  Have Thine own way.
  Thou art the Potter, I am the clay;
  Mold me and make me, after Thy will,
  While I am waiting, yielded and still."[3]

That's it.
We have only to be yielded, that is, willing, surrendered, and He will do the rest.
He will make us according to the pattern for which, in His love,
He designed us.
And it will be good—for our own good—and for His glory.

Do not despair.
If you want to be different, you may.
You, too, can be changed for the better. Therein lies our hope—and the hope of the world.

We are disciples in clay.

And there is still the skill of the Potter.

L ORD JESUS, we come to Thee now as little children. Dress us again in clean pinafores; make us tidy once more with the tidiness of true remorse and confession. Oh, wash our hearts, that they may be clean again. Make us to know the strengthening joys of the Spirit, and the newness of life which only Thou can give. Amen.

The Saint of the Rank and File

I n any list of the apostles, most of us would begin by naming the triumvirate—
Peter
   James
      and John, and then we go like this:
Peter . . . James . . . and John . . . and Matthew . . .
and Judas of course . . . and . . . and Philip . . . and, oh,
yes, Thomas . . .
let's see . . . and . . . and . . . who were the rest anyway?

Most of us know nothing much about Andrew—except that
he was Peter's brother, and one of the apostles.[4]

But we ought to know Andrew better than that, because we
see him every day.
He is the man who sits beside you on the bus.
He may be the fellow who blows the mailman's whistle down
the street . . .
or drives the streetcar . . .
   or waits on you in the store . . .
or works at the next desk in your office . . .
   or sells you your ticket at the railroad station,
or even carries your bags.

Andrew is all around you.
You meet him every day, and he holds the key to many situa-
tions.
Andrew appears on the New Testament scene but seldom.
Perhaps we have not grasped all the significance of the
appearances he does make.

But first, let us begin at the beginning.

Andrew's boyhood home was Bethsaida of Galilee.

It lay about seventy miles north of Jerusalem on the Sea of Galilee. It was there that Jesus found five of His twelve disciples—John and James, Philip, Peter and Andrew.

In Bethsaida we inquire for the house of Jonas, where live the two brothers Peter and Andrew, who with their father operate a fishing boat on the Sea of Galilee.
We find that Andrew is not at home, but they point out to us the house of Zebedee, where we may find him.

As we approach, we see two young men in earnest conversation with an old man who must be Zebedee, the father of James and John. The younger men are talking about a journey they hope to make down the Jordan to a ford, where they have heard a daring young preacher was drawing great crowds with a stirring message about the coming Kingdom of God.

The travelers are full of it.
The camel-drivers, as they swing north toward the ridges of Lebanon and on into Asia, can talk of nothing else, and these two young Galileans are anxious to see for themselves this striking young prophet.

"Yes, John," Zebedee is saying, "Andrew is just the companion. You want to take him with you rather than Simon. If Simon went along, he would do all the talking. He would even do your thinking for you.
    Why don't you two go by yourselves?
And if Simon should insist on going with you—you and Andrew stay together. Make up your own minds.
    And may the peace and blessing of God go with you."

We remember what happened when they arrived at the place. They heard the message of John the Baptist—a strange man who with piercing,
    glowing eyes and eloquent tongue stirred
them as they had never been stirred before.

His prophecy and the fire in his eyes as he spoke won the hearts of Andrew and John and they joined themselves to John the Baptist.

In a very short time their attention was shifted from him to Another, who, when He came, was announced by John as "the Lamb of God which taketh away the sin of the world."

Later, they met Jesus and spent some time in personal conversation with Him, and pledged themselves to become His disciples. And the very first thing that Andrew did after he found Jesus was to search out his own brother, Simon, and introduce him to Christ.

Andrew went with Jesus when He came to Galilee and was present when Jesus worked His first miracle.
Andrew saw Him at the marriage of Cana,
    saw Jesus with laughter in His eyes and smiles
tugging at the corners of His mouth.
Andrew was with Him in Judea when He baptized there.

Andrew probably was in the garden among the olive trees when Nicodemus came to sit talking with Jesus about spiritual things, until the dawn came up behind the hills.

Andrew had been with Jesus for a time as His public ministry opened, and then apparently he went back to Bethsaida.

Somehow, for Andrew, things did not seem the same.
He worked abstractedly;
    he daydreamed a lot.
This was particularly exasperating to Peter and to their partners,
    for Andrew seemed to be so preoccupied
        and clumsy
            and absentminded.
They wondered if Andrew was in love.

Ah, maybe that was it!
Little did they know how true it was—for indeed he was in love. He had fallen completely in love with Jesus of Nazareth.
He was in love with a Voice.
    He was in love with a vision
        in love with a Face
            in love with a faith
and every day and every night he dreamed and wondered in his

heart about the things that Christ had said . . .
      "this Kingdom of God on earth . . ."

The waves lapping against the boat seemed to be saying over
and over the things he had heard Him say.
      His voice was in the wind.
      His face was in the sunlight dancing on the waves.

So Andrew dreamed and waited.
Then came the never-to-be-forgotten day—that day of the
second call—
      when, as Simon and Andrew bent over their nets
spread across their knees, His shadow fell upon them and
they both looked up.

And Andrew's heart beat faster, for it was *He*—the Face, the
Voice . . .
Again He talked of that "Kingdom of God" . . .

He made a gesture with His hand—a beckoning sort of gesture that brought them scrambling to their feet, and then
He said:
      "Come . . . come with me . . .
      and I will make you to become fishers of men."

They dropped their nets and their lines.
They turned their backs on the little village in which they were
born and went away following Him who spoke about the
Kingdom of God.

It was to be three years until they came back to their boats
again.
Thus Andrew became one of the twelve and was consecrated
as an apostle.

There is something significant in the fact that Andrew was
the first of the apostles to be called.
The choice was important, for it was the example of Andrew,
      the lead he gave
            and the influence he brought to bear upon the others
that to a large extent decided them.

Christ saw right away that the soul's unrest,
      the straining after higher things,

and the deeper knowledge of God which made Andrew walk from Bethsaida to Bethany indicated a promise of large spiritual growth and a fertile field in which the seed could be cast.

Andrew has usually been referred to as Simon Peter's brother.
He himself was not a leader of men . . .
He was not aggressive like Simon.
We find him usually playing second fiddle to his famous brother, and we know perfectly well that it takes a lot of grace to play second fiddle.

It is not easy to live out your life day after day
    and week after week
  and year after year in a subordinate
position while somebody else gets the notice
        the publicity
      the attention
    the credit
   the praise
  the spotlight
and perhaps the reward.

It takes a lot of grace to accept a role like that, and yet Andrew seems never to have complained.

Being the brother of Simon must have been hard all along. We can imagine the children at play—it would be Simon who would choose sides . . .
   Simon who would nominate the game to be played . . .
   Simon who always spoke for them both . . . .

And if they were walking along the road that wound round the head of the lake and some traveler inquired the way— it was always Simon who made reply, although Andrew knew it just as well as Simon.

In school, no doubt, they sat together, and again, no doubt, it would be Simon whose hand would go up in eagerness to give the answer.

Andrew had always had to play second fiddle, and yet he seemed to have done so with the best of grace.

When we look into the lives of these two brothers, it must be
admitted that Andrew was not the great preacher Peter was.
He was not the great missionary leader who helped
    establish churches that were to spring up
  like flowers in the wilderness,
but it must never be forgotten *that it was Andrew who brought
Peter to Christ.*

As Dr. McKay has said,
*"There would have been no eloquent Peter at Pentecost had
there been no humble Andrew to bring him to Jesus."*[5]

There are two pictures of Andrew in the New Testament that
we might examine, for they show us the man better than any
analysis we might make.

The first scene is late afternoon. The shadows of the sun have
lengthened, and the long hot day is drawing to a close.
The birds are winging their way homeward.
The crowd that has followed Jesus all day long, listening to
His marvelous message, has forgotten time altogether.

But now they suddenly realize that soon night will fall, and
they are hungry.
Children begin to whimper, tired and weary . . .
So Jesus asked His disciples how they could get enough bread
to feed this crowd of people.

Then we read that it was Andrew who said:
    "There is a boy here who has five barley loaves and a
    couple of fish, but what is that among so many people?"
    (John 6:9, Goodspeed).

Now, have you ever wondered how Andrew knew about the
lunch the boy was carrying?
I have, and I suggest to you that Andrew knew because he
had made friends with the boy.
He had talked with him; perhaps the boy had been at his
side all day.
Maybe the boy's mother had asked Andrew to keep an eye
on him.

What would they talk about?

Well, Andrew was a fisherman.
   There was much that would be of interest to the boy . . .
      how to tie certain knots
      how to fasten a fishhook on a line
    all the tell-tales that indicate where the fish are
   the part the weather plays in fishing.
There are many things that would be of interest to the boy.

I suppose it would be perfectly natural for the lad to share
his lunch with Andrew—this man who had been so kind to
him—so friendly.
But they decided that they would wait a bit and see what the
Master intended to do.

At any rate, I believe Andrew was essentially interested in
people. I have heard it said many times that a good index to
character is a man's ability to make friends
         with children
       and with dogs.
   I believe it to be true.
The man who can interest a boy and make friends with a boy
and who can win the confidence of a dog must be all right.
Children and dogs, usually, are good judges of character and
of human nature.

The other glimpse we have of Andrew is when the Greeks
come and ask that they might see Jesus.
We read that they inquired of Philip, and he turned for advice
to Andrew, and it was Andrew who introduced them to Jesus.

Have you ever wondered why Philip did not go himself?
I suggest to you that Andrew had by this time a knack of
introducing people to Jesus, and had done it so often that they
all turned to him.

Andrew first comes to our attention introducing his own
brother Simon to the Lord.
Here now, he is introducing Greeks.
He really might be called Andrew the Introducer.
Andrew is not one of the greatest of the disciples, but he is
typical of those men of broad sympathy and sound common
sense, without whom the success of any great movement
cannot be assured.

It is all very well to be impressed with the contributions to human happiness that are made by the world's leaders—the great men and women—the five-talent people
>   who do things
>   do them well
> and who usually get the notice
>   the publicity
>   the praise
> and the rewards.

But what we are all inclined to forget is the fact that behind them are unnumbered hosts of ordinary men and women whose names are never printed
>   whose faces are never captured by the newsreel cameras
>   but whose quiet unassuming labor makes the work of the leaders possible.

The vast majority of people fall into the two-talent class— the useful hosts of mediocrity
>   the average men and women
>   who are always taken for granted
>   but without whom nothing could ever be accomplished.
They are willing to play second fiddle.
They know that they will not be singled out for honors or medals.

They have a job to do, and they are willing to do it without complaint,
and often with bravery and consecration of the highest order.

They are willing—not only to lose their identities in the job to be done, but even to lose their lives for the sake of others. They have discovered the truth of the paradox of Christianity that only by losing one's life can one find it.

The Battle of Britain in World War II, which lasted from August 8 to October 31, 1940, cost the Germans 2,375 planes
>   destroyed in daylight alone,
> and many more at night.
It cost the British 375 pilots killed and 358 wounded.

A handful of RAF fliers had saved Britain,

and perhaps the world,
    from destruction.
You will remember what Winston Churchill said of his people:
    "Never in the field of human conflict was so much owed by
    so many to so few!"
That victory was achieved, you see,
    not by the top-ranking generals
        the brass hats
            the big shots
but by young men—a team—playing and fighting—and
dying together.

Another example was afforded in the famous retreat to
Dunkirk after the collapse of the Maginot Line and the
surrender of Belgium.
Covering the retreat was the 51st Division of the British Army,
Scottish troops of regiments with famous names. They stood
at St. Valerie to make the evacuation possible.

They were a roadblock, whose only job was to hold back the
Panzer divisions long enough to permit the motley fleet of
small boats, manned by the nameless volunteers, to take off as
many British and French soldiers as they could.

Well, the 51st did their job well. They were lost . . . expend-
able . . .
    but they did their job and made Dunkirk possible.

To fellow members of St. Andrew's Societies across this country I would say this: "Remember the name you bear."
If we are St. Andrew's men, we must exemplify the characteristics of our patron saint.

How could I sum them up?
    A self-effacing ministry to those in need.
A willingness to play second fiddle, if need be,
    in order that the job can be done.

There are times when this is hard for the Scot,
    for he is not only independent
he has a strong confidence in his own ability.
This is often mistaken for conceit and boastfulness.
It does not grow out of his egotism at all,

for the Scot is traditionally a modest man—reticent and shy.
He does not wear his heart on his sleeve.

He is an enigma to the Englishman—
    for whereas the Sassenach is emotional at times
        the Scot is phlegmatic.
But beware of the strong currents that run deep in the Scottish
heart.

General Montgomery has said that in the Eighth Army the
troops most easily raised to a high pitch of enthusiasm and
high morale for the fight were the troops of the Highland
Division.

These are the traits of character most sorely needed in our
world today—a willingness to play second fiddle
    or, if you prefer,
        humility,
and that broad sympathy and sound common sense without
which the success of any great movement cannot be mea-
sured.

You see, it is the Andrews that are the glory of any democracy
. . . the people who do the mundane things of our workaday
life.
For example, think of the garbage collectors.
Do you realize how important they are?
Theirs is not a pleasant job, but there are few jobs more
important to the health and well-being of all of us.

    "We have the nicest garbage man,
      He empties out our garbage can;
    He's just as nice as he can be,
      He always stops and talks with me.
    My mother doesn't like his smell,
      But then, she doesn't know him well."

You see, it is the Andrews after all who carry on the work of
the nation and of the church.
For after all the five-talent men and women have flashed like
meteors through the skies
    leaving behind a trail of glory
after their great gifts for organization

after all their visions and their plans
   they depend upon Andrew to do the job.

So, the success of the whole business largely depends upon Andrew,
for Andrew was interested in people
   and Andrew brought them to Christ.
Only as the church today is interested in people and will bring them to Christ can the work go forward.

The work that needs to be done today is the work that Andrew is best able to do.
It is the work of the ordinary men and women in the church, and Andrew is their patron saint.

It is not without significance that Andrew was chosen to be the patron saint of Scotland, and St. Andrew's cross, a diagonal white cross on a blue ground, is the foundation on which St. George's cross of England and St. Patrick's cross of Ireland were laid to make the Union Jack.
Andrew was at the bottom.

It is always so—in everything that is worthwhile—
   everything that is good and true.
It is supported by Andrew—the two-talent man.

Each time Andrew appears on the New Testament scene he is introducing someone to Jesus.
"Only two talents?"
Aye, but the two talents are surrendered to Christ.

Andrew, we too would meet the Master!

L ORD JESUS, bless all who serve us, who have dedicated their lives to the ministry of others—all the teachers of our schools who labor so patiently with so little appreciation; all who wait upon the public, the clerks in the stores who have to accept criticism, complaints, bad manners, selfishness at the hands of a thoughtless public. Bless the mailman, the drivers of trucks, subways and buses who must listen to people who lose their tempers.

Bless every humble soul who, in these days of stress and strain, preaches sermons without words.

In the name of Him who called us to be the servants of all, Amen.

By Invitation of Jesus

Then saith he also to him that bade him, When thou makest a dinner or a supper, call not thy friends, nor thy brethren, neither thy kinsmen, nor thy rich neighbours; lest they also bid thee again, and a recompense be made thee.
But when thou makest a feast, call the poor, the maimed, the lame, the blind:
And thou shalt be blessed; for they cannot recompense thee: for thou shalt be recompensed at the resurrection of the just (Luke 14:12-14).

S uppose someone in Washington living far out on Massachusetts Avenue
or in Spring Valley
happened one day to open a Bible and, by that mysterious process known only to angels, chanced to read these verses in the Gospel of Luke.

Suppose the reader concluded that these words, probably spoken in Aramaic so long ago beneath a Syrian sky, were just as applicable in the twentieth-century society.

Suppose that person believed that the blessings Jesus mentioned were worth having and decided to claim them.
Suppose he had the courage and the love that would be required to take Jesus at His word. What do you think would happen?

One bitterly cold night, when Washington was covered with a blanket of snow and ice, a man sat in his home on Massachusetts Avenue.
The house was very comfortable . . .
A crackling log fire in the fireplace threw dancing shadows on the paneled walls.

The wind outside was moaning softly like someone in pain, and the reading lamp cast a soft warm glow on the Book this man was reading.

He was alone, for the children had gone to the Shoreham for supper and dancing, and his wife had retired early after a strenuous afternoon's bridge game.

He read the passage of Luke which is our text, and then could read no more.

Somehow he could not get away from those simple words. He had read the Bible often, for he was a good man, but never before did the words seem printed in flame.

He closed the Bible, and sat musing, conscious for the first time in his life of the challenge of Christ.

He felt as though Someone were standing behind him; he knew he was no longer alone.

What strange fancy was this?
Why was it that he kept hearing—in a whisper—the words he had just read?

"I must be sleepy and dreamy," he thought to himself. "It is time I went to bed."
But it was long ere he fell asleep, for still the voice whispered, and still he was conscious of a Presence in the room.

He could not shake it off.
Never before had he been so challenged.
He thought of the dinners and parties that they had given in this beautiful home.

He thought of those whom he usually invited.
Most of them were listed in "Who's Who in Washington"; and there were those whose names were household names
in business
   finance
      clubs
         and in government circles.
There were men with the power to grant political and social favors.

But *they* were not poor
   or maimed
      or lame
         or blind.

What had put this absurd thought into his head anyhow?
He tried to sleep, but somehow he could not close the door of
his mind to the procession that shuffled and tapped its way
down the corridors of his soul.

There were beggars with trembling lips.
There were sightless eyes that stared straight in front and
faces blue with cold.
There were sticks tapping on the pavement.
There were crutches that creaked with the weight of a twisted
body.

As he watched them pass, he felt his own heart touched.
He whispered a prayer that if the Lord would give him courage, he would take Him at His word and do what He wanted
him to do.
Only then did he find peace and fall asleep.

When the morning came, his determination gave him new
strength and zest for the day.
He must begin his preparations
    and he was impatient to go downtown.

His first call was on the engraver who knew him well.
At the counter he drafted the card he wished engraved,
    chuckling now and then as he wrote, his eyes shining.
The clerk who read the card looked somewhat puzzled but
made no comment, although he stood watching the retreating
form swing down the street.

The card read:

JESUS OF NAZARETH
Requests the honor of your presence
at a banquet honoring
The Sons of Want
on Friday evening, in a home on Massachusetts Avenue
Cars will await you at the Central Union Mission
at six o'clock
"COME UNTO ME, ALL YE THAT LABOR AND ARE HEAVY LADEN,
AND I WILL GIVE YOU REST."

In the engraving room, they did not know what to make of it; but the conclusion they reached was that someone had more money than sense, but that it was none of their business.

A few days later, with the cards of invitation in his hand, he walked downtown and gave them out, and within an hour there were several people wondering what could be the meaning of the card that a kindly
    happy
  well-dressed man
had placed in their hands.

There was the old man seated on a box trying to sell pencils; and another on the corner with a racking cough and a bundle of papers under his arms.
There was a blind man saying over and over to himself, "Jesus of Nazareth requests the honor of your presence."

A fellow who was fingering a gun in his pocket and bitterly thinking of suicide wondered whether he should wait until night.

Because he had a sense of humor, this good man called the newspapers and was connected with the writers of the society column. To them he announced the banquet that was to be given in his home that night, and asked if perhaps they would like to make mention of it or have some pictures made.

Because his name was an impressive one,
  because he was rich and influential in Washington business
  and politics,
he met with an enthusiastic response.

When he was asked the names of his guests, he simply said:
  "I do not know their names; I have not asked them."
Somewhat puzzled, the editor of the society column laughed, thinking that he was joking,
but she was even more puzzled when this man laughed and said: "If you care to come out tonight, I promise you a unique experience."

At six o'clock, a strange group of men stood waiting in the vestibule of the Central Union Mission, talking softly together.

"What is the catch in this, anyhow?" asked one cynical fellow.
"What's the game?"
  "Who's throwing this feed?
  Anybody know the bird what gave out the tickets?"

"Well, what difference does it make?
  I'd stand almost anything for a feed."

And the blind man, with the little boy at his side, ventured to
remark: "Maybe it's part of the government relief program."
And the cynic was saying, "Aw, somebody's kiddin' us, as if
we weren't wretched enough already."

Just then someone came over and announced that the cars
were at the door; without a word, they went outside.

Perhaps there was something incongruous about it all, seeing
these men, clutching their thin coats tightly around their thin
bodies,
  huddling together, their faces pinched and wan
    blue with cold and unshaven
their toes sticking out of their shoes, climbing into two shiny
limousines.
It was touching to see the lame get in, dragging one foot.
Swinging up with a twitch of pain,
  and to see the blind man fumbling for the strap.

At last they were all inside, and the cars glided off with the
strangest and most puzzled load of passengers they had ever
carried.

When they dismounted, they stood gazing at the house, its
broad steps and lamps
  its thick-piled carpets.
They entered slowly, trying to take it all in.
They were met by the host, a little nervous, but smiling.

He was a quiet man, and they liked him—these guests of his
whose names he did not know.
He did not say much; only, "I am so glad you came."

By and by, they were seated at the table.
They had looked at the tapestries that hung on the walls.

They had seen the illuminated pictures in their massive
frames, and the giant crystal chandelier
     the concert grand piano that stood across the hall,
          the spotless linen, and the gleaming silver on the table.

They were silent now; even the cynic had nothing to say.
It seemed as if the banquet would be held in frozen silence.

The host rose in his place, and in a voice that trembled slightly
said: "My friends, let us ask the blessing."

     "If this is pleasing to Thee, O Lord, bless us as we sit around
     this table, and bless the food that we are about to receive.

     "Bless these men. You know who they are, and what they
     need.
     And help us to do what You want us to do.
     Accept our thanks, in Jesus' name. Amen."

The blind man was smiling now.
He turned to the man seated next to him and asked him about
the host.
     "What does he look like?"

And so the ice was broken; conversation began to stir around
the table, and soon the first course was laid.

"My friends, I hope you will enjoy the dinner.
I would suggest that we waste no time, for I have no doubt that
you are hungry. Go right ahead."

It was a strange party, rather fantastic in a way, thought the
host, as he surveyed his guests.

There they were—men who otherwise might be still loitering
on the back streets of Washington
     crouched in doorways
          or huddled over some watchman's fire.

What an amazing thing that he didn't even know the name of
a single man!
His guests had no credentials
     no social recommendations
          no particular graces—so far as he could see.

But, my, they were hungry!

It was funny, as he sat there talking, how the stories in the Gospels kept coming back to him, and he could almost imagine that the house was one in Jerusalem.

It seemed to him that these men would be the very ones that Jesus would have gathered around Him—the legion of the world's wounded,
    the fraternity of the friendless
        peices of broken human earthenware.
He remembered what the family had said . . .
How they had insisted on demanding, "Why? Why are you doing such a thing?"
Well, why was it, anyway?
    Wasn't it plain?

His reason was the same old glorious reason that Jesus had for every miracle
    for every gesture of love
        for every touch of healing.
It was simply because he was sorry for these people, and because he wanted to do this one thing on an impulse of love.

Yet there was not a trace of condescension in his attitude.
He was treating them as brothers, talking to them as though they had a right to be sitting where they were.

It was a grand feeling—a great adventure.
Never before in his life had he felt this thrill.
These men could not pay him back!
    What had they to give him?

He watched each plate and directed the servants with a nod or a glance.
He encouraged them to eat;
    he laughed at their thinly disguised reluctance,
    until they laughed too.
As he sat there, it suddenly occurred to him how different was the conversation!

There were no off-color stories, no whisperings of scandal, no one saying, "Well, I have it on good authority."

They were talking about their friends in misfortune, wishing
they were here too . . .
>   wondering whether Charlie had managed to get a bed in
>   the charity ward
>   whether Dick had stuck it out when he wanted to end it all,
>   whether the little woman with the baby had got a job.
Wasn't the steak delicious!
And they marveled that they still remembered how different
foods tasted.
They wondered, most of all, who this man was, and why he
had invited them all here.

When the meal was over, there was music.
Someone came in and sat down at the piano.

He began to play softly, familiar melodies, old songs;
and then in a soft but understanding voice, he began to sing.
They listened to "Love's Old Sweet Song"
>   "Silver Threads Among the Gold"
>   and then a march by Sousa
>   and then "Traumerei"
>   and then "The Sidewalks of New York."

Someone else joined in—a cracked, wheezing voice, but it
started the others.
Men who had not sung for months
>   men who had no reason to sing
there they were, joining in.

Now some old favorites: "Daisy"
>   "A Bicycle Built for Two"
>   "Swanee River."
Soon they began to request this and that, and before they
knew it, they were singing hymns:
>   "What a Friend We Have in Jesus"
>   "The Church in the Wildwood"
>   "When I Survey the Wondrous Cross."

The pianist stopped, and the guests grouped themselves in
soft, comfortable chairs around the log fire; some of them
smoked.

The host moved among them, smiling . . . his eyes shining.
Then when he had settled himself again, and his guests were
comfortable, he said:

"I know you men are wondering what all this means.
I can tell you very simply.
But, first, let me read you something."

He read from the Gospels stories of One who moved among
the sick
   the outcasts
      the despised and the friendless
how He healed this one
   cured that one
      spoke kindly words of infinite meaning to another,
         how He visited the ostracized
and what He promised to all who believed in Him.

"Now I haven't done much tonight for you, but it has made
me very happy to have you here in my home.
I hope you have enjoyed it half as much as I have.
If I have given you one evening of happiness, I shall be forever
glad to remember it, and you are under no obligation to me.
This is not my party. It is His!
I have merely lent Him this house.
He was your *Host.* He is your *Friend.*
And He has given me the honor of speaking for Him.

"He wants you all to have a good time.
He is sad when you are.
   He hurts when you do.
   He weeps when you weep.
He wants to help you, if you will let Him.

'I'm going to give each of you His Book of Instructions.
I have marked certain passages in it that you will find helpful
when you are sick and in pain
   when you are lonely and discouraged
      when you are blue and bitter and hopeless
         and when you lose a loved one.
He will speak a message of hope and courage and faith.

"Then I shall see each one of you tomorrow when I saw you
today, and we'll have a talk together to see just how I can help
you most.

"I have made arrangements for each one of you to get back
to your homes, and those who have nowhere to go, I invite
to spend the night here."

They shuffled out into the night, a different group from what they had been.

There was a new light in their eyes
  a smile where there had not been even interest before.

The blind man was smiling still, and as he stood on the doorstep, waiting, he turned to where his host stood.
  "God bless you, my friend, whoever you are."

A little wizened fellow who had not spoken all night paused to say,
  "I'm going to try again, Mister; there's somethin' worth livin' for."

The cynic turned back, "Mister, you're the first man who ever gave me anything. And you've given me hope."

"That is because I was doing it for Him," said the host and he stood and waved goodnight as the cars purred off into the darkness.

When they had gone, he sat again by the fire and looked at the dying embers, until the feeling became overwhelming again that there was Someone in the room.

He could never tell anyone how he knew this, but he knew that He was smiling and that He approved.
And that night, on Massachusetts Avenue, a rich man smiled in his sleep.

And One who stood in the shadows smiled too,
because some of the least of these had been treated like brothers for His sake.

Of course, that never happened.
  It is only a piece of imagination.
But why shouldn't it happen, on Massachusetts Avenue in Washington?
          on Park Avenue in New York?
        in Druid Hills in Atlanta?
      on the Gold Coast in Chicago?
    in Beverly Hills in Los Angeles?
I wonder what would happen if we all agreed to read one of the Gospels, until we came to a place that told us to do some-

thing, *then went out to do it,* and only after we had done it
. . . began reading again?

Why don't we do what Jesus says?
How exciting life would become were we to begin living
according to His way of life!

Friends would say we had lost our minds—perhaps.
Acquaintances would say we were "peculiar."
Those who dislike us would say we were crazy.

But Someone Else, who had these same things said about
Him, would smile, and the joy and peace in our own hearts
would tell us who was right.

There are aspects of the gospel that are puzzling and difficult
to understand.
But our problems are not centered around the things we don't
understand, but rather in the things we do understand,
    the things we could not possibly misunderstand.

This, after all, is but an illustration of the fact that our problem
is not so much that we don't know what we should do.

We know perfectly well . . . but *we don't want to do it.*

F ORGIVE US, LORD JESUS, for doing the things that make us
uncomfortable and guilty when we pray.

We say that we believe in God, yet we doubt God's promises.

We say that in God we trust, yet we worry and try to manage our own affairs.

We say that we love Thee, O Lord, and yet do not obey Thee.

We believe that Thou hast the answers to all our problems, and yet we do not consult Thee.

Forgive us, Lord, for our lack of faith and the willful pride that ignores the way, the truth, and the life.

Wilt Thou reach down and change the gears within us that we may go forward with Thee.

In Thy name we pray, Amen.

Mr. Jones, Meet the Master

A minister was recently asked to make a patriotic address at a dinner attended by many men prominent in government and business,
and by high-ranking military officials.

It was a swank affair, and cocktails and champagne were flowing freely.
Mr. Jones—immediately to the minister's left—was a big name in steel.
He was—quite obviously—greatly enjoying the champagne.

"Best champagne I've had in many a day," he said. "Wonder where they rounded it up."

And then, suddenly noticing the still untouched glass before the minister's place—
"Say, you haven't touched yours . . . why not?
Guess I'm rude to mention it, but surely you haven't any scruples against champagne?"

The minister smiled, "No, you're not rude to ask, but it might take me a couple of minutes to answer you fully.
Are you asking out of curiosity, or just to make conversation
   . . . or because you really want to know?"

Mr. Jones appeared somewhat startled by the minister's candor.
"Say, now you do have my curiosity aroused.
I'm asking because I'd really like to know.
Everybody I know drinks.
What objection could there possibly be to a little champagne?"

The minister finished spreading a bit of butter on his roll before answering.

"Weekdays," he said, "I have a steady stream of people who need help coming to my study in the church.
Their lives are all messed up, and I guess you'd be surprised to know how often liquor is involved in the mess.

"They're from every walk of life
       rich and poor
    young and old
  men and women.
They look at me across my desk, and calmly . . . usually these days, without any sense of guilt or conviction of sin at all . . . tell me things awful enough to rock a man back on his heels.

"I hear the most fashionably dressed young women, and well-dressed men, tell stories of sordidness
       of moral filth
    of promiscuity
  even violence
which not even furs
  Cartier jewels
    or Prince Matchabelli perfume
could gloss over or make lovely.

"I hear these stories, until I have come to the place where, watching the faces of passers-by, as I walk along the street, I wonder if anywhere in this country there is any real decency
    and honesty
       and purity walking around on two legs.

"I hear these stories, and I don't have to delve very deep into any one of them to find that liquor in some form—sometimes a very fashionable form—has aided and abetted this moral chaos.
I believe it's one of the most potent weapons the devil has in America today."

He paused . . . "Are you quite sure you want to hear all of this?"

Mr. Jones nodded, "Of course I do . . . if for no other reason than that I haven't heard anybody talk like this since I was a boy.

But I fail to see what all this has to do with not drinking that glass of champagne."
The minister stirred his coffee slowly and thoughtfully . . .
"I was coming to that.
That's what I meant, when I said I couldn't answer your question very briefly.

"Well, to continue . . . It seems to me that behind every sin
    every vice
        every mess
is a lack of self-discipline . . . of God's discipline.

"I heard somebody say the other day that the future of our world is going to be in the hands of disciplined people. That's true.
The German people were disciplined, disciplined by their Nazi overlords, and they almost succeeded in getting the world in their hands.

"In a democracy, citizens have to be self-disciplined, or the country goes down, defeated from within by moral rot. That was why France fell, you know.

"I'm beginning to see that if I, and others like me, are to help people . . . really help, we, too, are going to have to be disciplined in small ways as well as big.

"There's going to have to be a total lack of compromise. I think liquor is one of our greatest problems.
It is a problem that has every thoughtful American worried.
Mind you, the anxiety is being felt by others than those who have always been concerned about our growing addiction to alcoholic beverages.
It is not the 'blue-noses' this time.

"It is the doctors, the sociologists, the educators, the law-enforcement people, the employers who see its effects in absenteeism,
    people like them who are really worried.

"And I predict that the United States, in the next ten years, will have to do something about the problem, unless we are to face a moral collapse with health and economic implications.

"Incidentally, don't you think it funny that here in Washington—the one place in the country where we need clear heads, steady nerves, and sound judgment for great decisions—more hard liquor is consumed than in any other city in the land?

"I can't say that it would be any sin for me to drink that glass of champagne.
No, but I know I shall not be able to speak with authority on that whole question, unless I myself have absolutely refused to compromise.
That's the reason why I won't touch it."

"I see your point all right," said the steel magnate, "but it seems like a high price to pay just for handing out a little advice across your desk."

"A high price? . . . Perhaps.
I supposed it really boils down to the question of how much we care about other people and about the future of our country."

"Of course I must admit," Mr. Jones replied, "that I've never been much for religion, never could see how it could affect my life one way or the other.
Preachers' talk usually sounds like theological gibberish to me."
He paused . . . "Say, though, if you really think things in this country are that bad, what's the answer?
What can we do about it?"

"There's only one answer that I know of—God . . .
People like you and me becoming personally acquainted with Him.
When a man cultivates a personal friendship with the Chief, there's no life too much of a mess for Him to straighten out—and keep straightened out—
    no problem He can't handle."

"I'm a hard-boiled sinner, parson, but somehow I'd like to hear more.
How about having lunch with me sometime—say Tuesday?"

The minister pulled his little engagement calendar out of his breast pocket . . . "Tuesday? . . . Tuesday it is."

So began a series of events that led a big businessman to Christ—that utterly and completely changed his life.

Our country is full of Joneses,
and they all have problems of one kind or another.
"All God's chillun got trouble these days."

The Church has always contended that God can solve these problems through the individual's personal fellowship with a living Lord.

Let's put the question bluntly, as bluntly as Mr. Jones would put it.
Can you and I really have communion with Christ as we would with earthly friends?
Can we know personally that same Jesus whose words are recorded in the New Testament,
who walked the dusty trails of Galilee two thousand years ago?

I don't mean can we treasure His words
     or try to follow His example
   or imagine Him.
I mean is He really alive?
Can we actually meet Him,
   commune with Him,
     ask His help for our everyday affairs?

The Gospel writers say "yes."
A host of men and women down the ages say "yes."
The Church says "yes."

I realize that to the man in the street it is quite puzzling to speak about the "Chief" guiding one's life, arranging the details of everyday existence.
To say that John Smith, working in a government office, can directly, and in full possession of his faculties, get into communication with God sounds almost fantastic.

But that is precisely what I do mean—that the housewife standing in her kitchen over a pile of dishes . . .

and the student reading in the library until midnight . . .
    and the streetcar motorman ringing his bell through the
    city traffic . . .
        that the lonely one in the hospital ward . . .
can be in direct communion with God.
That is exactly what this imaginative faith involves.

Since this is true, do we realize what a tremendous, breath-
catching fact it is?
Do you realize how significant it is for *you*?

It means that no single event of your life will ever have to be
faced alone—
    neither sorrow nor bereavement
      pain nor loneliness
        joy nor laughter
          pleasure nor fun.
It means that you need never make any decision without His
help and His guidance.
It means the sanctifying of every part of your life.

The Church, you see, rests its unshakable conviction that
fellowship of that kind with a living Lord is possible, squarely
on the fact of the Resurrection.

The Gospel writers say that at the beginning of Christ's ministry,
He chose twelve men . . . "That they might be with him."

They were very ordinary men.
By our standards of judgment, not a single one of them would
have been considered disciple material.
Tax collectors
  fishermen
    peasants
    simple folk, unlettered
for the most part with no special qualifications.

But as Christ chose them He was seeing, not so much what
they were, as what they were to become.
The clue to their selection was that they were to be with Him.
That was the beginning of their development and their trans-
formation.

He created a fellowship which was a deep content for Him, but for them was all in all.

It was a new thing in human experience.
For three years they saw with their eyes and heard with their ears.

They heard the music of His voice.
   They watched His slow smile.
      They saw the sunlight dancing on His hair.
        They saw Him perform miracles.
         They heard Him tell unforgettable parables.

He told them that when they had seen Him they had seen the Father.

And then came ebbing popularity and the shadow of the Cross.
Was their fellowship to end with His death?
Their testimony is that it did not—that the fellowship not only survived death, but was consummated after it through His Resurrection.

It is an astounding claim to make.
They claim that in the days between the Resurrection and the ascension Jesus established this friendship so that it would be available to men in all ages.

Have you ever wondered about the Resurrection appearances?
Have you ever wondered why, when Jesus met Mary in the garden, He would not let her touch Him?

It was because He wanted to take her beyond the evidence of sight and touch.
He wanted her to learn that she could realize His presence without the need of eyes and hands.
He was busy bridging the gap, planting the friendship in the unseen.

So in the other post-Resurrection appearances . . .

Two men are on their way to Emmaus.
Suddenly they find a Companion by their side.

He walks with them
  teaching them
    appealing to their understanding
and finally sits down to break bread with them.

Then they recognize Him, and He is gone.

The twelve are gathered in the Upper Room.
Suddenly they are aware of His presence.
There is a word of peace, then He is gone.

They began to expect Him around every corner.
What do these strange appearings and disappearings mean?
They are His perfect way of showing them that He will never
be far away.
He is making them aware of the truth of the promise that He
left:
  "Lo, I am with you always, even unto the end of the world."

So convinced did they become of His presence that they found
themselves expecting to meet Him as they turned a corner,
and would look back over their shoulders, not to be surprised
were He to catch up with them as they walked.

If this fellowship with the risen Lord, which the apostles
experienced, is also available to us, how may we go about
finding it?

Now let us be honest—do we really want to find Him?

There is a glorious promise given in the days of old that has not
yet faded from the written record:
  "If with all your hearts ye truly seek me,
  ye shall ever surely find me."

Ah, there perhaps is our first clue—"If with all your heart" . . .

Ask yourself, am I after all seeking God with my whole heart?
Or must I say in all honesty, "I want God, and yet I don't want
Him.
I want to find Him, and yet I don't, for I would be afraid to . . .
Or, I would not want Him to find me just yet . . .
Am I really seeking God with my whole heart?"

Then there is another side to the picture. I wonder if we are brave enough to face it.

Perhaps there are times, when some of us "want God as we want a hot water bottle at night"[6]—to help us over some temporary discomfort.
Or we look for God to help us when we stand in the roadway looking for a passing motorist to push us to the next gas station.

But we can't treat God that way!
We simply can't think of God as a kind of luncheon club president,
or as a telephone operator who will always answer whenever we lift the receiver!

Nor must we think of Him as a department store shipping clerk, who nightly arranges the orders and sends them sliding down the chutes while we sleep, to greet us in the morning.
We are guilty of the most terrible presumptions!

In the old days, if you touched the Ark of the Covenant—you were a dead man.
If you went near the mountain in which God dwelt while giving His revelations it was to court instant death.

And when God was pleased to reveal Himself even partly to mortal men they were blinded and bedazzled, stricken to the ground.
Always they covered their faces and cried out at the awful majesty of God.

Yet here we are, glibly saying that we want to find Him and come into His presence.

Suppose God were to reveal Himself to us—here—now!

We say we want to find God—well—suppose we did!
We say we long to be assured that the Lord is with us—
Well, suppose suddenly you reached out your hand and felt Him!
Suppose suddenly you lifted up your eyes and saw Him looking down at you.
What would you do?

Do we really want to find Him?
Are there not some things we love better than Him—the neat compromises we have made, whereby our religion will not interfere with our business . . .
the secret sins which we indulge and have managed to keep hidden—
do we love them more than we love Him?

There are a lot of us who have known moments of a terrible conflict.
We want Him, and we don't want Him.
We want His way, and we want our way.
We pray, "Thy will be done," but we mean our will.
We want to be clean inside, and still do things that make us unclean.

We want to see the Kingdom come, but meanwhile we vote against the Kingdom.
We want to be Christians, but we don't want our friends to think we are strange.
We are against strong drink, but we must be sociable.
We long for purity, but we covet popularity.

Most of us are too familiar with this conflict.
We want to play on both sides.
We want to be friends with everybody.
But He said long ago, "Ye cannot serve God and mammon."

Yet many of us have settled down to a compromise.
We are willing to serve in His church, but we compromise on the number of services we shall attend, for we must also serve the world.

We will support the church financially, but not as much as we might, for we must also support the things that are not of the church.

We will argue for the intellectual and doctrinal positions of the church, and then, with a shrug of our shoulders, express the right to live as we please.

Then we wonder why we cannot have a real
    thrilling

satisfying communion with God.

It is still true—for you and me today:
"If with all your hearts ye truly seek me, ye shall ever
surely find me."

God is not hiding—but we are!
God is not pretending—look at the Cross!
But we are pretending. Look into your own heart and see.

It is possible for you and for me to live in this world as sure that
the Lord is with us as we can be sure of anything—
to have no fear at all
to be able to anticipate tomorrow with a thrill of delight
to have no fear of anything—neither of sickness
nor unemployment
nor loneliness
nor death
Nor anything at all.

It is possible for us to be as sure as Paul was.

But there is a price to be paid. We must be ready to give up
some things, and that is always hard to do.
It may require some spiritual surgery, and that's not pleasant.

And your heart might ask: "Is it worth all that?"
Yes, it is worth any price.
Indeed, it is the Pearl of Great Price.

I read a story of a woman who was trying to find God.
She had a certain dream which she dreamed more than once,
namely, that she was standing in front of a thick, plate-glass
window.

As she looked at it, she seemed to see God on the other side.

She hammered on the window, trying to attract His attention,
but without success.
She grew more and more desperate, and began to call to Him
and found herself shrieking at the top of her voice.

And then a quiet, calm voice at her side said:
"Why are you making so much noise?
There is nothing between us."[7]

Perhaps that illustrates our difficulty, does it not?
We have been thinking all along that God was somewhere far
away, unapproachable . . .
someplace that was difficult of access . . .
and we have been groping around for a long time, and all the
while He is standing beside us.

I know that He is here at this moment—
interested in each one of us.

Mr. Jones *can* meet the Master, and you can too.
And I know that no matter where you go, you will not leave
Him behind, for He will go with you.

He will be near as you push through the crowds downtown.
He will be at your side.
As you sit in your room alone He will be there.

Won't you think now of His presence and test it by an act of
faith, so that you too will know that He is near?

You have time!
Won't you close your eyes now, and with all the faith you
have, even though it be very little, tell Him that you believe?
Tell Him that you want Him to guide your life and to keep it.

For if you let Him take control of your life completely,
if you are willing to bow to His will for you,
then you will enter into that transforming fellowship
   which brings with it that glorious exhilaration, that inde-
   scribable peace, and escape from all bondage promised in
   the New Testament.

Then you will never doubt again that fellowship with this
living Lord is possible, but you will discover that it is the most
glorious fact in our whole world.[8]

WE PRAY, O GOD, that Thou wilt fill this sacred minute with meaning, and make it an oasis for the refreshment of our souls, a window cleaning for our vision, and a recharging of the batteries of our spirits. Let us have less talking and more thinking, less work and more worship, less pressure and more praying. For if we are too busy to pray, we are far busier than we have any right to be.

Speak to us, O Lord, and make us listen to Thy broadcasting station that never goes off the air. Through Thy Holy Spirit, who is waiting to lead us into all truth, Amen.

Keepers of the Springs

O nce upon a time, a certain town grew up at the foot of a
mountain range. It was sheltered in the lee of the pro-
tecting heights, so that the wind that shuddered at the doors
and flung handfuls of sleet against the window panes was a
wind whose fury was spent.

High up in the hills, a strange and quiet forest dweller took it
upon himself to be the Keeper of the Springs.

He patrolled the hills and wherever he found a spring, he
cleaned its brown pool of silt and fallen leaves, of mud and
mold
    and took away from the spring all foreign matter, so that the
water which bubbled up through the sand ran down clean and
cold and pure.

It leaped sparkling over rocks and dropped joyously in crystal
cascades until, swollen by other streams, it became a river of
life to the busy town.

Millwheels were whirled by its rush.
    Gardens were refreshed by its waters.
        Fountains threw it like diamonds into the air.
        Swans sailed on its limpid surface
and children laughed as they played on its banks in the sunshine.

But the City Council was a group of hard-headed, hard-boiled
businessmen. They scanned the civic budget and found in it
the salary of a Keeper of the Springs.

Said the Keeper of the Purse: "Why should we pay this ro-
mance ranger? We never see him; he is not necessary to our
town's work life. If we build a reservoir just above the town,
we can dispense with his services and save his salary."

Therefore, the City Council voted to dispense with the un-necessary cost of a Keeper of the Springs, and to build a cement reservoir.

So the Keeper of the Springs no longer visited the brown pools but watched from the heights while they built the reservoir.

When it was finished, it soon filled up with water, to be sure, but the water did not seem to be the same.
It did not seem to be as clean, and a green scum soon befouled its stagnant surface.

There were constant troubles with the delicate machinery of the mills, for it was often clogged with slime, and the swans found another home above the town.

At last, an epidemic raged, and the clammy, yellow fingers of sickness reached into every home in every street and lane.

The City Council met again. Sorrowfully, it faced the city's plight, and frankly it acknowledged the mistake of the dismissal of the Keeper of the Springs.

They sought him out of his hermit hut high in the hills, and begged him to return to his former joyous labor.
Gladly he agreed, and began once more to make his rounds.

It was not long until pure water came lilting down under tunnels of ferns and mosses and to sparkle in the cleansed reservoir.

Millwheels turned again as of old.
Stenches disappeared.
Sickness waned
and convalescent children playing in the sun laughed again because the swans had come back.

Do not think me fanciful
too imaginative
or too extravagant in my language
when I say that I think of women, and particularly of our mothers, as Keepers of the Springs. The phrase, while poetic, is true and descriptive.
We feel its warmth . . .

its softening influence . . .
and however forgetful we have been . . .

however much we have taken for granted life's precious gifts we are conscious of wistful memories that surge out of the past—
　the sweet
　　tender
　　　poignant fragrances of love.

Nothing that has been said
　nothing that could be said
　　or that ever will be said,
would be eloquent enough, expressive enough, or adequate to make articulate that peculiar emotion we feel to our mothers.

So I shall make my tribute a plea for Keepers of the Springs, who will be faithful to their tasks.

There never has been a time when there was a greater need for Keepers of the Springs,
or when there were more polluted springs to be cleansed. If the home fails, the country is doomed. The breakdown of home life and influence will mark the breakdown of the nation.

If the Keepers of the Springs desert their posts or are unfaithful to their responsibilities the future outlook of this country is black indeed.

This generation needs Keepers of the Springs who will be courageous enough to cleanse the springs that have been polluted.

It is not an easy task—nor is it a popular one, but it must be done for the sake of the children, and the young women of today must do it.

The emancipation of womanhood began with Christianity, and it ends with Christianity.
It had its beginning one night nineteen hundred years ago when there came to a woman named Mary a vision and a message from heaven.

She saw the rifted clouds of glory
and the hidden battlements of heaven.
She heard an angelic annunciation of the almost incredible
news that she of all the women on earth . . .
of all the Marys in history . . .
was to be the only one who should ever wear entwined the red
rose of maternity and the white rose of virginity.

It was told her—and all Keepers of the Springs know how
such messages come—that she should be the mother of the
Savior of the world.

It was nineteen hundred years ago "when Jesus Himself a
baby deigned to be and bathed in baby tears His deity" . . .
and on that night, when that tiny Child lay in the straw of
Bethlehem, began the emancipation of womanhood.

When He grew up and began to teach the way of life, He
ushered woman into a new place in human relations. He
accorded her a new dignity and crowned her with a new glory,
so that wherever the Christian evangel has gone for nineteen
centuries, the daughters of Mary have been
respected
revered
remembered
and loved,
for men have recognized that womanhood is a sacred and a
noble thing, that women are of finer clay . . .
are more in touch with the angels of God and have the noblest
function that life affords.
Wherever Christianity has spread, for nineteen hundred
years men have bowed and adored.

It remained for the twentieth century,
in the name of progress
in the name of tolerance
in the name of broadmindedness
in the name of freedom
to pull her down from her throne and try to make her like a
man.

She wanted equality. For nineteen hundred years she had not
been equal—she had been superior.

But now, they said, she wanted equality, and in order to obtain it, she had to step down.

And so it is, that in the name of broadminded tolerance a man's vices have now become a woman's.
Twentieth-century tolerance has won for woman
　　the right to become intoxicated
　　　　the right to have an alcoholic breath
　　　　　　the right to smoke
　　　　　　　to work like a man
　　　　　　　　to act like a man—
for is she not man's equal?

Today they call it "progress" . . .
but tomorrow—oh, you Keepers of the Springs, they must be made to see that it is not progress.

No nation has ever made any progress in a downward direction.
No people ever became great by lowering their standards.
No people ever became good by adopting a looser morality.

It is not progress when the moral tone is lower than it was.
It is not progress when purity is not as sweet.
It is not progress when womanhood has lost its fragrance.
Whatever else it is, it is not progress!

We need Keepers of the Springs who will realize that what is socially correct may not be morally right.

Our country needs today women who will lead us back to an old-fashioned morality
　　to old-fashioned decency
　　　to old-fashioned purity and sweetness
for the sake of the next generation, if for no other reason.

This generation has seen an entirely new type of womanhood emerge from the bewildering confusion of our time.
We have in the United States today a higher standard of living than in any other country, or at any other time in the world's history.

We have more automobiles, more picture shows,
　　more telephones, more money

more swing bands, more radios,
more television sets, more nightclubs,
more crime, and more divorce
than any other nation in the world.

Modern mothers want their children to enjoy the advantages of this new day.
They want them, if possible, to have a college diploma to hang on their bedroom wall,
and what many of them regard as equally important—a bid to a fraternity or a sorority.

They are desperately anxious that their daughters will be popular, although the price of this popularity may not be considered until it is too late.

In short, they want their children to succeed, but the usual definition of success, in keeping with the trend of our day, is largely materialistic.

The result of all this is that the modern child is brought up in a decent
cultured
comfortable
but thoroughly irreligious home.

All around us, living in the very shadow of our large churches and beautiful cathedrals, children are growing up without a particle of religious training or influence.

The parents of such children have usually completely given up the search for religious moorings.
At first, they probably had some sort of vague idealism as to what their children should be taught.

They recall something of the religious instruction received when they were children, and they feel that something like that ought to be passed on to the children of today, but they can't do it,
because the simple truth is that they have nothing to give.
Our modern broadmindedness has taken religious education out of the day schools.

Our modern way of living and our modern irreligion have
taken it out of the homes.

There remains only one place where it may be obtained,
    and that is in the Sunday school,
but it is no longer fashionable to attend Sunday school.

The result is that there is very little religious education, and
parents who lack it themselves are not able to give it to their
children—so it is a case of "the blind leading the blind," and
both children and parents will almost invariably end up in the
ditch of uncertainty and irreligion.

As you think of your own mother, remembering her with love
and gratitude—in wishful yearning
    or lonely longing . . .
I am quite sure that the memories that warm and soften your
heart are not at all like the memories the children of today will
have . . . .

For you are, no doubt, remembering the smell of the starch in
your mother's apron
    or the smell of a newly ironed blouse
        the smell of newly baked bread
            the fragrance of the violets she had pinned on her
            breast.

It would be such a pity if all that one could remember would
be the aroma of toasted tobacco
    or nicotine
and the offensive odor of beer on the breath!

The challenge of twentieth-century motherhood is as old as
motherhood itself.
Although the average American mother has advantages that
pioneer women never knew—material advantages
        education
        culture
advances made by science and medicine
although the modern mother knows a great deal more about
sterilization, diets, health, calories, germs, drugs, medicines,
and vitamins, than her mother did, there is one subject about
which she does not know as much—

and that is God.

The modern challenge to motherhood is the eternal challenge
—that of being godly women.
The very phrase sounds strange in our ears. We never hear it
now.

We hear about every other kind of women—
   beautiful women,
    smart women,
     sophisticated women,
      career women,
       talented women,
        divorced women,
but so seldom do we hear of a godly woman—or of a godly
man either, for that matter.

I believe women come nearer fulfilling their God-given function in the home than anywhere else.

It is a much nobler thing to be a good wife than to be Miss
America.

It is a greater achievement to establish a Christian home than it
is to produce a second-rate novel filled with filth.

It is a far, far better thing in the realm of morals to be old-
fashioned than to be ultramodern.

The world has enough women who know how to hold their
cocktails
   who have lost all their illusions
    and their faith.
The world has enough women who know how to be smart.
   It needs women who are willing to be simple.
The world has enough women who know how to be brilliant.
   It needs some who will be brave.
The world has enough women who are popular.
   It needs more who are pure.
We need women, and men too, who would rather be morally
right than socially correct.

Let us not fool ourselves—without Christianity
   without Christian education

   without the principles of Christ
inculcated into young life, we are simply rearing pagans.

Physically, they will be perfect.
Intellectually, they will be brilliant.
But spiritually, they will be pagan.
Let us not fool ourselves.

The school is making no attempt to teach the principles of
Christ.
The Church alone cannot do it.

They can never be taught to a child unless the mother herself
knows them and practices them every day.

If you have no prayer life yourself it is rather a useless gesture
to make your child say his prayers every night.

If you never enter a church it is rather futile to send your child
to Sunday school.

If you make a practice of telling social lies it will be difficult to
teach your child to be truthful.
If you say cutting things about your neighbors and about
fellow members in the church it will be hard for your child to
learn the meaning of kindness.

The twentieth-century challenge to motherhood—when it is
all boiled down—is that mothers will have an experience of
God . . . a reality which they can pass on to their children. For
the newest of the sciences is beginning to realize, after a study
of the teachings of Christ from the standpoint of psychology,
that only as human beings discover and follow these inexora-
ble spiritual laws will they find the happiness and content-
ment which we all seek.

A minister tells of going to a hospital to visit a mother whose
first child had been born.
She was distinctly a modern girl.
Her home was about average for young married people.

"When I came into the room she was propped up in bed
writing.
'Come in,' she said, smiling. 'I'm in the midst of housecleaning and I want your help.'

"I had never heard of a woman housecleaning while in a hospital bed. Her smile was contagious—she seemed to have found a new and jolly idea.

" 'I've had a wonderful chance to think here,' she began, 'and it may help me to get things straightened out in my mind if I can talk to you.'
She put down her pencil and pad, and folded her hands. Then she took a long breath and started:
'Ever since I was a little girl, I hated any sort of restraint. I always wanted to be free. When I finished high school, I took a business course and got a job—not because I needed the money—but because I wanted to be on my own.

" 'Before Joe and I were married, we used to say that we would not be slaves to each other. And after we married our apartment became headquarters for a crowd just like us. We weren't really bad—but we did just what we pleased.'

"She stopped for a minute and smiled ruefully.
'God didn't mean much to us—we ignored Him. None of us wanted children—or we thought we didn't. And when I knew I was going to have a baby I was afraid.'

"She stopped again and looked puzzled. 'Isn't it funny, the things you used to think?'
She had almost forgotten I was there—she was speaking to the old girl she had been before her great adventure.

"Then remembering me suddenly—she went on: 'Where was I? Oh, yes, well, things are different now. I'm not free any more and I don't want to be. And the first thing I must do is to clean house.'

"Here she picked up the sheet of paper lying on the counterpane. 'That's my housecleaning list. You see, when I take Betty home from the hospital with me—our apartment will be her home—not just mine and Joe's.

" 'And it isn't fit for her now. Certain things will have to go— for Betty's sake. And I've got to houseclean my heart and mind. I'm not just myself—I'm Betty's mother.
And that means I need God. I can't do my job without Him.

Won't you pray for Betty and me and Joe,
    and for our new home?'

"And I saw in her all the mothers of today—mothers in tiny
apartments and on lonely farms . . .
Mothers in great houses and in suburban cottages, who are
meeting the age-old challenge—'that of bringing their children to the love and knowledge of God.'

"And I seemed to see our Savior—with His arms full of children of far-away Judea—saying to that mother and to all
mothers—the old invitation so much needed in these times:
    'Suffer the little children to come
    unto me and forbid them not, for of
    such is the kingdom of God.' "

I believe that this generation of young people has courage
enough to face the challenging future.

I believe that their idealism is not dead. I believe that they have
the same bravery and the same devotion to the things worthwhile that their grandmothers had.

I have every confidence that they are anxious to preserve the
best of our heritage, and God knows if we lose it here in this
country it is forever gone.

I believe that the women of today will not be unmindful of
their responsibilities; that is why I have dared to speak so
honestly.

Keepers of the Springs, we salute you!

O UR FATHER, remove from us the sophistication of our age
    and the skepticism that has come, like frost, to blight our
faith and to make it weak. We pray for a return of that simple
faith, that old-fashioned trust in God, that made strong and
great the homes of our ancestors who built this good land and
who in building left us our heritage.
    In the strong name of Jesus, our Lord, we make this prayer,
Amen.

The Problem of Falling Rocks

D riving along the highways that run through the mountains, you may have noticed the frequency of signs that read:

"Beware of falling rocks."

I have seen them many times and have often wondered why they did not say, "Beware of fallen rocks," for I do not know what one could do about rocks that were in the act of falling as one drove along.

Now this is a hazard of driving along these highways that no precautions can avoid.
Your rate of speed has nothing to do with it . . .
    nor the way you handle your car
        nor the condition of your tires.
It makes no difference whether you are a good driver or a bad driver, the hazard is there and there is nothing you can do about it.

It is typical of those troubles in life which no caution can avoid, and which have nothing to do with one's conduct, be it good or bad.
The insurance people call them "Acts of God."
When they come
    they come
        and that's that.

This is not fatalism, but a recognition that God has set up in this world He has made certain natural laws that govern inanimate things.

The question I ask you to consider is, What should be our attitude toward these troubles that we can do nothing to prevent? The commonest attitude is one of worry, for this is the most common and widespread of the transgressions that mark our inconsistency as Christians.

I suppose the cartoon character "The Timid Soul," meeting one of these signs along the highway, would peer anxiously above his shoulders, and seeing the overhanging boulders would turn his car around and drive back.

But suppose he decided to drive on and risk it.
He might drive very carefully and worry all the time, lest one of these huge rocks break loose and come crashing down upon him and his new car.
But what good would his worrying do him?
It wouldn't hold the rock up there; neither would it jar it loose.

The worrying of the driver has no effect upon the rock, but it has a tremendous effect on the driver.

People have never fully realized just how destructive a thing worry is.
It truly plays havoc with one's life.
  It ruins digestion.
    It causes stomach ulcers.
      It interferes with sound sleep and forces us to face another day unrested and irritable.
It shortens our tempers and makes us snap at the members of our family.

Anxiety and tension, which are twins, bring on heart disease
  high blood pressure
    and nervous disorders.

Ask any doctor, and he will tell you that the patient who is apprehensive retards his own recuperation.

Hard work, even overwork, never killed anybody.
It is not the amount of work we do, or have to do, that harms us. It is the strain or tension caused by our anxiety over the work that counts.

We would live longer, and do more and better work, if we could bring ourselves to the philosophy of an old Negro I read about, who said:

"When I works, I works hard;
When I sets, I sets loose;
When I worries, I goes to sleep."

Would that sleep would overtake us when we begin to worry.
We would be healthier.
 We would live longer.
 Our dispositions would be sweeter.
We would be nicer to know and easier to live with.

Jesus had a lot to say about this very thing.
In the sixth chapter of Matthew's Gospel you will find quite a
full quotation on this theme in the Sermon on the Mount.
Jesus said: . . . "take no thought for the morrow"—that is, no
anxious, troubled thought—
Or we might well say, "Don't worry about tomorrow"—for
that is precisely the meaning of His words.

"Which of you, by taking thought, can add one cubit unto his
stature?"
You can't suddenly make yourself a foot taller than you are.
That is one of the things of life you have to accept.
Fretting about your lack of inches will not increase them.

If you borrow trouble from tomorrow, anticipate the difficulties that you see, or think you see ahead, are you the better
able to cope with them?

Can you, by worrying, keep something unpleasant from happening?
 Do you soften the blow
  ease the burden
   or lessen the pain?
Of course not, but you stand a good chance of reducing your
ability to take it.

I want to make a distinction between thoughtful consideration
on the one hand, and the useless fretting on the other
 that destroys peace of mind
  takes away appetite
   and leaves a person sleepless and miserable.

It is this latter useless fretting that I have in mind.

The futility of it was illustrated perfectly in the case of our little boy.
The year he was in kindergarten he enjoyed it very much, for it was nearly all play.

Then when he moved up into the first grade,
he was shocked to discover that he had to learn things—
   In short, he had to think
     and had less time to play.

He was very unhappy about it,
and as he wrestled with the problem of learning the letters of the alphabet
   how to read them
     and how to write them
his mind was troubled.

Many a time, in the midst of his play,
his lower lip would tremble,
and he would burst into tears, crying as if his heart would break.

Having been told that he had twelve years of study before him, and then possibly four years of college after that, he was most miserable.
He would confess between his sobs that he was worrying about going to college, and what he would do when he got there.

Now that seems to us ridiculous—
but not any more so than some of the things we grown-ups worry about.
Of course, if you are *not* a Christian you have plenty to worry about.

But if you are a Christian
   if you are a child of God
then your worrying is not only futile,
   it is sinful.

For worry, to the Christian, is really a sin.

When Christ turns the searchlight of His penetrating insight and decisive intellect upon worry,

He defines it in a very simple way.
He sees it as nothing more or less than lack of trust in God.

With regard to the rocks that may fall upon us, and in these
days of the atom bomb they are heavy and sinister, the only
happy way to deal with them is the way of faith—
faith in the purposes of God.
  faith in the presence of God
    faith in the promises of God
      faith in the power of God to deliver us in any trouble.

Only when we have faith can we be free from fear.
If you are afraid, then we must suspect that you have no faith
in God.

A good deal of the strain and tension of modern life is due to
our unwillingness to accept situations that are beyond our
control. Christians must be realists as well as idealists, and
Christ was both.
There was never clearer realism than is to be found in the
teachings of Jesus.

When we resist things we cannot change, then we have strain
inside—inner tension—and that is what causes the trouble.

We plan a vacation trip and then somebody gets sick, and we
have to postpone it . . .
but inside we are filled with self-pity and resentment.
The train is late, and we miss our connection, and we sit and
fume trying to push the train along the track,
  and by glaring at our watch try to stop the hands.

The maid does not show up some morning, and the household schedule is thrown out of gear.
Frustration and resentment send us banging and slamming
through the house.

You have a lot to do in the office, but you discover that your
secretary is sick and not able to work,
  and you fume, and your blood pressure mounts,
    and you glare at the gremlin that sits on your desk and
    grins at your annoyance.

Common sense tells you that the best thing to do is accept what you cannot help and make such adjustments as are necessary.
An uncompromising attitude changes nothing but yourself, and the change is never for the better.

We have to learn to cooperate with the inevitable.
We'd better.
Man proposes, but God disposes.
There are so many things in life beyond our control that he is wise who recognizes the fact and who says:
   "God willing, I will do this or that . . . ."
This is not mock piety, but clear recognition of life's contingencies, and our helplessness in certain situations.

The rocks will fall.
We don't know when, and we cannot find out for sure.

Worrying about it, fearing it, does not help.
Life must go on, and so must we.
But we can go on without strain.

We all have had the experience of how in our lives there are stretches of uneventful days, and then, generally without warning, some crisis is sprung upon us.

You may at any moment be plunged into some great calamity that brings your dreams crashing around you . . .
   takes the song out of your life
      and makes your heart so sore that you wonder why it doesn't break.

It would not be so bad if troubles sent us warning.
If we received night letters telling of approaching difficulties, at least we might be prepared—although with most of them there would be little we could do.

At least the shock would not be so great.
But troubles do not do that.
They do not come marching down the road—out in the open.
No, they wait in ambush, and they spring out at us when we least expect them.

Most of us live sunny lives of ease and comfort and hear only rumors of pain and distress.

Tales of human terror are blown to us very faintly from another world that seems unreal
  distant
    having nothing to do with us.

As long as the sun shines for us we find life a happy thing. But
when the sun is hidden, and the dark clouds gather, we have
no right to whine or cry out as if we were being ill-treated to
some injustice that was invented solely for our distress.

We know already that at this very moment a great many
people are in real trouble.
We know it in our minds, but not in our hearts.

Shakespeare said that it is not difficult to bear other people's
toothache.
The surprising thing is that each of us considers his own
trouble to be important and worthy of sympathy, until he
learns of the troubles of others.
Then he realizes that perhaps he is not so bad off after all.

Troubles are cannibals in the sense that the big troubles eat up
the little ones.
Every pastor knows full well that in his congregation there are
people who keep going with real trouble, so that he can be
forgiven if sometimes he seems lacking in sympathy with the
people who are merely petulant.

I never feel so unworthy and so indicted in my own grum-
blings, as when I learn of the troubles of others.

Suppose you were bereaved suddenly,
and so many expressions of love and gratitude were left un-
said.
Suppose you were left alone now,
and then you thought of so much that love could have said,
and gratitude could have done.
Just suppose that happened to you!

One of the things Christ definitely promised us was trouble.
  "In the world ye shall have tribulation," He said.
But we must never forget that He added:
  "But be of good cheer" . . . or, in other words,

"Cheer up . . . I have overcome the world."

Now, when trouble comes, when the rocks do fall, it will not help to reject faith altogether, and fling away in revolt from all that you once believed.

For in God's name where will you go?
   To what else will you cling?
What would you substitute for Christian faith?

Just because you may not understand what has happened to
   you or why it should have come
is no reason why you should throw it all away.

If Christ is right, then there is a loving purpose in it all . . .
even though our tear-filled eyes cannot see it.

If Christ has not lied to us, then there is a reason behind even
the darkest providence.
There must be a reason, for God rules;
and the reason must be good, for God is good.

It must be the underside of love, for God is a God of love.
When you are in the sunshine you may believe it.
But when you are in the shadow you must believe it, for you
have nothing else.

The promises of the Scriptures are not mere pious hopes or
sanctified guesses.
They are more than sentimental words to be printed on deco-
rated cards for Sunday school children.
They are eternal verities.
   They are true.
      There is no perhaps about them.

How does the prophet know that God will neither leave us nor
forsake us?
How does the psalmist know that the brokenhearted and the
afflicted will be comforted?

Because they themselves had dark days and lonely nights.
That's why!
Because they themselves had gone through it.

These Scripture truths are fragrant flowers that their own
fingers plucked from the gardens of human experience.

Sometimes the thorns pricked them, but they held onto the flowers.

"I will not leave you comfortless," Christ says.
And only those whose hearts have been left desolate . . .
    only those who have needed comforting . . .
        needed it desperately . . .
know how true that promise is.

Christ does not leave us comfortless, but we have to be in dire need of comfort to know the truth of His promise.

It is in times of calamity . . .
    in days and nights of sorrow and trouble
        that the presence
            the sufficiency
                and the sympathy of God grow very sure and very wonderful.

Then we find out that the grace of God is sufficient for all our needs
    for every problem
        and for every difficulty
for every broken heart, and for every human sorrow.

It is in times of bereavement that one begins to understand the meaning of immortality.
You think today, as the sun streams in golden shafts through the window and the birds sing of spring, you think that you believe it.

But wait until you stand at the edge of an open grave . . . Then you will know what it means to believe it.

You will not then be interested in chattering about immortality . . .
    or gossiping about the theories of the hereafter . . .
You will know . . .
deep down in your own heart, you will know.

We have such pagan ideas about death—most of us—not at all Christian or in keeping with the revelation we have in the Scriptures.

We are wrong who haunt the cemetery as if to feel the presence of loved ones who are not there, if Christ has told us the truth!
We have our eyes wrongly focused.
We do not understand.

Our tears are selfish, for we are self-centered—self-absorbed.
We keep thinking of what it means to us.
We reflect how much we miss the departed,
and we weep because we begrudge their going.
We wish they had stayed on with us awhile . . .
We wish things had gone on as they were.
We resent the change, somehow, never thinking what it must mean to them that are gone.

In the New Testament we hear little of the families with that aching gap,
very few pictures of mourners huddled together sitting silently in their homes . . . weeping . . .
No, but you do hear a great deal about the Father's house of many mansions . . . and the angels.

Let us therefore act like believers,
live like Christians so that we can die like Christians . . .
with songs and rejoicing.
That is the true Christian attitude.

Those we love are with the Lord, we believe,
and the Lord has promised to be with us,
never to leave us nor forsake us:
"Behold I am with you always."

Well, if they are with Him,
and He is with us . . .
they cannot be far away.

It is not true to sing—or even think—of heaven as being far away.
It is no distant land
no alien shore
but near us—very close.

It gets nearer as we grow older.

As more and more of our friends and loved ones go home, our thoughts and expectations turn ahead to the time when we shall all meet again in the new life . . .

in the other room
never again to part.

But meanwhile, between now and the time when the bell shall toll for us, we still have a pilgrim way to travel.
It may be smooth or rough, we cannot tell.
Troubles may come—troubles will come.

How shall we deal with them when they do come?

It is a truism that "all God's chillun got trouble," and the only thing, after all, that sets God's children apart from other people is what they do with trouble.

I think the Christian treatment of trouble is splendidly illustrated by the oyster, into whose shell one day there comes a tiny grain of sand.

By some strange circumstance, this tiny piece of quartz has entered into the shell of the oyster and there like an alien thing
an intruder
a cruel, unfeeling catastrophe
imposes pain
distress
and presents a very real problem.
What shall the oyster do?

Well, there are several courses open.
The oyster could, as so many men and women have done in times of adversity and trouble, openly rebel against the sovereign providence of God.

The oyster, metaphorically speaking, could shake a fist in God's face and complain bitterly:
"Why should this have to happen to me?
Why should I suffer so?
What have I done to deserve this?

"With all the billions of oyster shells up and down the seaboard, why in the name of higher mathematics did this grain of sand have to come into my shell?"

The oyster could conclude:
"There is no justice.
All this talk of a God of love and mercy is not true.
Now, since this calamity has overtaken me, I'll throw away
all the faith I ever had. It doesn't do any good anyway."

Yes, the oyster could say that.
So many men and women have in times of trouble.
But the oyster doesn't!

Or the oyster could say—again like some men and women
when adversity strikes . . .
"It can't be true!
It isn't true.
I must not permit myself to believe it."

The oyster could say—as some of our very best people today
are trying to say in the face of cruel circumstance:
"There is no such thing as pain. This grain of sand doesn't
make me uncomfortable, and I'm not going to allow my
mind to think of unreality.

"There is no such thing as pain. It is an error of the mind,
and I must, therefore, project my thoughts on positive
planes of beauty
truth
goodness
and if I fill my mind with such thoughts, then I shall know
that pain is unreal."

But the oyster doesn't do that.

There is another attitude the oyster could adopt—a very com-
mendable one—one that calls for a lot of fortitude and courage
and determination.

The oyster could say:
"Now that this hard calamity has overtaken me
this thing that hurts and cuts and stabs
this enemy that bruises and bleeds
now that this has come upon me, I must endure to the end.
"I must show them all that I can take it, and I won't give in.
I will hold on if it kills me.

I must remember that the darkest hour is just before the dawn."

Now, there is something noble in that,
    something praiseworthy in that attitude.
But the oyster does not do that,
because the oyster is at one and the same time a realist as well as an idealist.
There is no point in trying to deny the reality that tortures every nerve, so the oyster doesn't try.

In spite of all the denial, nothing can change the fact that the grain of sand is there.

Nor would grumbling or rebelling do any good,
for after all the protests and complaints, the grain of sand would still be there.

No, the oyster recognizes the presence of the grim intruder, and right away begins to do something.
Slowly and patiently, with infinite care, the oyster builds upon the grain of sand—layer upon layer of a plastic, milky substance that covers each sharp corner and coats every cutting edge . . .

    and gradually . . . slowly . . .
        by and by a pearl is made . . .
            a thing of wondrous beauty wrapped around trouble.

The oyster has learned—by the will of God—to turn grains of sand into pearls
    cruel misfortunes into blessings . . . pain and distress into beauty.

And that is the lesson that we are to learn along this pilgrim way. The grace of God, which is sufficient, will enable us to make of our troubles the pearls they can become.
It is no mere figure of speech.
It is something more than a simile to say that one enters heaven through pearly gates.

One enters into the presence of the Lord through gates bedecked with pearls,
and every pearl—a trouble

a pain
a heartache
a misfortune

which, by the grace of God, has been changed into a beautiful,
lovely thing.

No wonder they speak of pearly gates!

O UR FATHER, give us the faith to believe that it is possible
for us to live victoriously even in the midst of crisis. Help
us to see that there is something better than patient endurance
or keeping a stiff upper lip, and that whistling in the dark is
not really bravery.

May we have the faith that goes singing in the rain, knowing
that all things work together for good to them that love Thee.
Through Jesus Christ, our Lord, Amen.

The Touch of Faith

"And his disciples said unto him, Thou seest the multitude thronging thee, and sayest thou, Who touched me?" (Mark 5:31).

That is an electrifying question when you realize who asked it, and under what circumstances. You cannot escape the thrill of it—the tingle of excitement that grips you when you think of Christ stopping in response to the touch of a poor nameless woman.

The words of this question are not cold
      abstract
    inanimate
  dead words.

They do not form a hook on which one could hang theories or finely spun philosophies. No, they are too vital for that. They march into the vestibule of your heart and knock on the door.

They suggest all kinds of daring thoughts to your weak faith. They are like sparks falling into dry grass.

The setting of this text is a vivid picture—colorful, appealing, and of absorbing interest.

The incident takes place in a city street. It is a narrow, twisted street packed with a crowd of gesticulating, excited people, surging past its bazaars and pavement stalls with all the noise and confusion of an Eastern marketplace.

A murmur of conversation grows louder as the procession pushes its way through the narrow street. There is a sound like the chanting of some mysterious dirge that frequently rises to an excited crescendo. Here and there a voice rises distinctly out of the medley in what might have been a prayer; but it is lost in crackling laughter, rudely interrupted and drowned in the barking of dogs and the argument and discussion of a crowd that loves to talk.

They are caught up in the infection of curiosity, and walking along in their very midst, wedged in the tightly packed procession, is Someone . . . .

It is His face that will hold your gaze—and will haunt you long after the sun has gone down, and the purple night, cool and starlit, has stilled every noise in the city, while only the Syrian stars wink unsleeping.

One is aware of that face even in such a crowd. Having once seen it, one sees it everywhere, for it is a haunting face—an expression that will not fade . . . eyes whose fires never die out . . . a face that lingers in memory. Farmers were to see it as they followed the swaying plow, and fishermen were to watch it dancing on the sun-flecked water.

This One who walks like a king is named Jesus. They called Him the Nazarene or the Galilean. He called Himself the Son of man.

The common people speak of Him softly, with deep affection, such as the shepherds know, who carry the little lambs in their bosoms.

The beggars whisper His name in the streets as they pass, and the children may be heard singing about Him. His name has been breathed in prayer and whispered at night under the stars. He is known to the diseased, the human flotsam and jetsam that shuffle in and out of the towns and drift hopelessly along the dusty highways of human misery.

His fame has trickled down to the streets of forgotten men, has seeped into the shadowed refuges of the unremembered women. It is Jesus of Nazareth.

Any outcast could tell you of Him. There are women whose lives have been changed who could tell you of Him—but not without tears. There are silent men—walking strangely as if unaccustomed to it—who speak of Him with lights in their eyes.

It is Jesus whom they are crowding to see. They want to look
on His face to see the quality of His expression that seems to
promise so much to the weary and the heavy-laden; that look
that seems to offer healing of mind and soul and body;
forgiveness of sin;
another chance—a beginning again.
His look seems to sing of tomorrow—a new tomorrow—in
which there should be no more pain
no more suffering
nor persecution
nor cruelty
nor hunger
nor neglect
nor disillusionments
nor broken promises
nor death.

At the request of one Jairus, a ruler of the synagogue, He is on
His way to restore to complete health a little girl.

He is on a mission of restoration, and the crowd is following
Him in order to see Him perform this miracle.

Speculation is rife.
Opinion is divided.
There is argument and excited discussion.

Some are declaring that He can do it; others are doubtful.
Some frankly say the attempt is bound to fail.
However, their curiosity is aroused, and it promises to be an
interesting experiment.

There is in the crowd another face—the face of a woman.
Strange that it should be so noticeable—yet not strange, for it
is a face that portrays great depth of human emotion.

There is so much in it—pale, pinched, and wan. Great lines of
suffering mar its beauty and sweetness, and even now her lips
are drawn in a thin line of agony.
The face is streaked with pain.
Her body is racked with acute suffering.

Who is she? Well, some say her name is Martha

and some say Veronica.
Tradition gives her various names, but I cannot tell who she
was.

It does not matter.
Is it not enough that she was a woman in pain?
      Call her Martha . . . or Mary . . . or Margaret . . .
         or mother . . . or sister . . . or wife.

She is typical of countless cases of endless pain and suffering.
For twelve years she had suffered
      and twelve years is a long time!

Her malady seems to have been a pernicious hemorrhage
      or a form of bleeding cancer.

She had gone to many physicians and was none better—
      but rather worse.

She had spent all that she had, and every new day was another
hopeless dawn. Every sunset was stained with the blood of
her pain.

She is typical of human despair—not only physical despair
but spiritual despair as well. For her the world could offer no
healing—so she represents all the people who look everywhere for peace of mind and heart—for hope and comfort—
and find none. She represents them all—whatever their
wants
            their fears
         their hopes
      their pains.

For her apparently, there was no relief, no human aid. Hers
was a hopeless case—incurable!

After twelve years of treatment—she was no better. What
would *we* do?

We would probably send her to some home for the incurables,
and visiting clergymen would be embarrassed to know what
to say to her.

Now, this woman had heard of the Great Teacher
      of His wonderful works

She had heard the lepers talk and them that had been blind from birth and now had thrown away their sticks, and looked around them with eyes that flashed or filled with tears as they spoke His name.

She had heard what He had done for others.
Surely He had power to bring into the haven of health the lost explorers of the vast treasuries of pain!

Surely He had power to lift from the dust of disease the flowers whose stems had been crushed or withered in the mildews of human misery!

As this thought burned itself into her mind her faith was curiously stirred as it wrestled in the birth-throes of a great resolve.

It was daring—fantastic, perhaps.
Her heart thumped
  but it was worth trying.
    It could only fail
and she was no stranger to failure.

There came to the woman the assurance that if she could but touch Him—even only the hem of His garment—she would be healed of her awful malady.

Cannot you imagine her nervous reasoning?

"Touch Him . . . yes . . . just to touch Him—
There would be no harm in that!

"I do not think He will harm me . . .
They say He is so kind
  and gentle
    so full of sympathy.

"Besides, here is my great chance.
  He is coming this way
    soon He will be gone.
Why not touch Him as He passes?

"On the head!—no, that would be irreverent!
I would not dare!
Well, on the hand!—no, that would be too familiar!

But there cannot be any harm in touching His robes as He passes.

"It would be enough—just to touch the border of His robes. I *must* touch Him. I *must* get some of that power."

Thus reasoning, she pushes her way through the crowd and with the pertinacity of despair she struggles in that dense throng
    nearer and nearer
        pushing and crushing.
People get in the way—not knowing her need.

Now she is desperate. He must not pass so near and yet so far away. Was she to lose this opportunity?
    She must touch Him.

Now just a little farther. He is drawing nearer. Now she can almost reach Him—another moment—at last just as He passes, she is able to reach out her hand, and with the tip of her finger touch His robe.

It was enough! She had actually touched the Great Doctor!

With a trembling finger she had touched Him with the touch of a mighty faith! Like an electric shock there surged back into the shrunken veins
      the panting lungs
    the withered muscles
  and the bloodless flesh
the rich glow of health and vitality.
Once again a body had been redeemed and given life.

She had touched Him with secret and trembling haste and thrilled with the change that had come to her, she retreated back into the crowd
unnoticed, she thought.

No one had noticed her—
    no one—but Christ!

Recognizing the one magnetic touch of faith amid the pressure of the crowd, He stopped and asked that *terrific* question:
"Who *touched* me?"

The question seemed absurd to those who heard it.

Impatiently, brusquely, almost with sarcasm, the disciples asked:
"How should we know?
There are hundreds of people here—pushing all about you.
Look at the crowd—
and yet you ask, 'Who touched me?' "

But, looking around Him, Christ stood still—His kind, but searching, glance fell at last on the face of the woman who had done it.

His gaze held hers. Something passed between them, and she told Him her story while His eyes were fixed upon her; His eyes gave her confidence. They seemed to promise all that she desired. Her fear disappeared.

Then He answered her:
    not in scorn at her action
        not in resentment
            not in anger at her presumption
            not in ridicule at her faith
    not in indignation at her audacity
but in the sympathetic tones of understanding love.

"Daughter, thy faith hath made thee whole.
Go in peace . . . and be healed of thy plague."

That is the record. These are the facts.
                    It is a matter of history.

She had no money—only faith.
    She did not meet Him in a house of worship.
        She met Him on the street.
She had no private audience with the Lord.
    She touched Him in a crowd.

She touched Him in faith—in desperate believing faith and He stopped!
The touch of one anonymous woman in a crowd halted the Lord of glory. *That is the glorious truth of this incident. She touched Him. So can we.*

Let us take it into our apathetic hearts,
   let its glorious significance thrill our jaded souls.

The human touch has the power to arrest God.
Yes, to stop Him
   to halt Him
      to make Him aware of your problems
         your pain
            your petition.

"Oh," you say, "that's impossible. God is not interested in me.
What does He care what happens to me—one tiny individual
in all this creation?
Who am I—or what am I that God should take special notice of
me?"
Well, there is the record.
   There you have it in black and white
that, stopped by the touch of a sick woman, He turned
about—
   He who conquered death
      He who defeated Satan
         He whom all the legions of hell cannot stop
            He who is King of kings.
He stopped just because a sick and nameless woman touched
the hem of His garment.

We need to touch Him—O how much we need to touch Him!

Most of us are thronging Him—just like the crowd . . . It is
easy to throng the Lord and never touch Him.
A great many people in the churches, and perhaps a great
many outside the churches, are thronging Jesus
   seeking Him
      coming close to Him
         but never actually touching Him.

In this matter of eternal importance, coming close is not
enough. It is like missing a train . . .
   You may miss it by one minute—and that's pretty close—
but you have lost the train . . .
   It is gone, and you are left behind.

Thronging saves nobody.

Coming near to Jesus will not bring healing.
We have to touch Him for ourselves.

One can feel close in the crowd without touching the Lord.
And that is exactly the trouble with most of us. We are following the crowd
    thronging the Lord
but not many of us are actually in touch with the Master.

And because we are not in touch, there is no vitality in our
spiritual life.
There is no thrill in our prayers
    no tingle of contact with the infinite resources
        no flush of reality about our religion.

Because we are out of touch with the Lord,
    we are lost in the crowd
        have become separated from the Master.

We preach the immanence of God.
Our creeds set forth our belief that the Lord is with us
        near us
    in this very place.
The Old Book records for us some amazing promises
    some startling assurances if we would
        only believe them.

He promised that we should have power
    power—to do amazing things
    grace—to do unnatural things, such as
to harbor no grudges and to forgive those who hurt us
    to love even those who treat us unjustly or unkindly
        to pray for those who give us pain and grieve us
            to confess our own private and secret sins
        to try to make right situations that have been
wrong, even if it means humbling ourselves, swallowing our
pride, and risking a snub or a slight.
We can have grace to do these things, and we know perfectly
well that it takes a lot of grace to do them!

He who made these promises is here with us now.

But you may ask: "How can I touch Christ?"

It was one thing for that woman long ago, for she saw Him with her eyes, and could touch Him with her fingers.

She heard His voice,
    saw the sunlight dance on His hair.

He was in the flesh then, and she could touch Him.

How can I, today, touch Him with the same results?

Some of you may seek healing of body or mind or of soul.
Some of you may seek guidance on some problem.
Some of you need faith to stand up under the tensions and suspenses of life.
Some of you seek forgiveness and a new beginning.

All of us need to touch Christ for some reason or other.

As the Church offers this wonderful new life—this peace of mind and heart—this healing of mind and soul and body in Christ's name—perhaps she ought more and more to give instructions with her soul medicine.

You are justified in looking for directions on the lid
    or some instructions for taking
        a manual of operation.

Perhaps I can make some suggestions which will be helpful.

First, give God a chance. Take your problem, whatever it may be, to Him in prayer. Tell Him all about it—just as if He didn't know a thing. In the telling be absolutely honest and sincere. Hold nothing back.

Our minds are sometimes shocked when we permit our hearts to spill over, but it is good for our souls when we do.

If we would only have the courage to take a good look at our motives for doing certain things, we might discover something about ourselves that would melt away our pride and soften our hearts so that God could do something with us and for us.

Then the second step is to believe that God will hear you. Remember that He heard the poor woman who only touched the hem of His garment. Believe with all your faith that He cares what happens to you. You must believe that. You can't doubt it when you look at the cross.

Next, you must be willing to wait patiently for the Lord. He does not answer every prayer on Sunday afternoon. You may have to wait until Friday. But wait. God is never in a hurry.

Then when He speaks to you—as He will—do what He tells you. He may not tell you audibly. You may not hear your voices—as did Joan of Arc. You may not see any writing in the sky and have any unusual experience. God *could*, if He wanted, send you messages in that way, but that is not His usual method.

It generally comes through your own conscience—a sort of growing conviction that such and such a course of action is the one He wants you to take. Or it may be given you in the advice of friends of sound judgment—those who love you most.

God speaks sometimes through our circumstances and guides us, closing doors as well as opening them.

He will let you know what you must do, and what you must be. He is waiting for you to touch Him.
The hand of faith is enough. Your trembling fingers can reach Him as He passes.

Reach out your faith—touch Him.
He will not ask, "Who touched me?"
He will know.

T EACH US, O LORD, the disciplines of patience, for we find that to wait is often harder than to work.

When we wait upon Thee we shall not be ashamed, but shall renew our strength.

May we be willing to stop our feverish activities and listen to what Thou hast to say, that our prayers shall not be the sending of night letters, but direct conversations with God. This we ask in Jesus' name, Amen.

<small>BOOK II</small>

Let's Keep Christmas

Man cannot comprehend Infinity.
Yet the crumb of our pity comes
from the whole loaf of God's compassion.
The milk of human kindness
comes from the dairies of God's love.

Soon after Peter Marshall came to the United States, he had an experience he never forgot. It happened on Christmas Eve, when newfound friends opened their hearts and their home to the immigrant boy from Scotland. Joyously, Peter helped to decorate a fragrant spruce tree. Then he sat on a kitchen stool and carefully cut out cookies, decorating them with cherries and nuts. Then around the piano came a family sing of beloved Christmas carols, bringing the unmistakable feeling of a Presence, as if Christ Himself had entered that home and quietly joined the family circle.

Suddenly Peter was filled with a wistfulness that brought tears to his eyes. For in other parts of the world there was anything but music and laughter—instead, hunger marches and rebellion and bloodshed.

The thought in Peter's mind became a prayer on his lips: "O God, why can't more people, all of us, open our hearts to the wonderful spirit abroad in the world tonight—not just on Christmas, but every day? What a happy place this old earth could be if—O God, if only we would keep Christmas the whole year through!"

Following is the entire text of Peter's much-loved message *Let's Keep Christmas*, the little book that for a quarter of a century has been heard at Yuletide over radio stations, from church pulpits and in homes all around the world. The words are a moving expression of gratitude that the Christ-child came into the world, and a plea that we keep the wonder of this ancient miracle in our hearts.

C. M.

C hanges are everywhere.
   Many institutions and customs that we once thought
sacrosanct have gone by the board.
Yet there are a few that abide, defying time and revolution.

The old message "For unto you is born this day in the city of
David a Savior, which is Christ the Lord" is still the heart of
Christmas.
It can be nothing else.
And this message can neither be changed—nor quite forgot-
ten
   although there are many things that tend to make us forget.

The idea of Santa Claus coming in a helicopter does not ring
true.
No interior decorator with a fondness for yellow or blue could
ever persuade me to forsake the Christmas colors of red and
green.

I must confess that modernistic Christmas cards leave me
cold.
I cannot appreciate the dogs and cats
      the galloping horses
   the ships in full sail . . .
or any of the cute designs that leave out the traditional symbols of the star . . .
      the manger . . .
   the wise men on their camels.

Angels there must be—but they need not be modernistic
angels in evening dress with peroxide permanents.

There is no need to search for stories new and different. There
is only one after all—and no modern author can improve it:
   "And there were in the same country shepherds
   abiding in the field, keeping watch over their
   flock by night,
   And, lo, the angel of the Lord came upon them,
   and the glory of the Lord shone round about
   them: and they were sore afraid.

   "And the angel said unto them,

Fear not: for, behold, I bring you good tidings
of great joy, which shall be to all people.
For unto you is born this day in the city of
David a Savior, which is Christ the Lord."

We all feel the pressure of approaching Christmas. The traffic
is terrible.
  You can't find a parking space . . .
    The stores are crowded . . .
      Mob scenes make shopping a nightmare.

You are thinking about presents—wondering what in the
world you can get for so-and-so.
You think of friends and loved ones who are so hard to shop
for.
You can't think of anything they need (which is rather strange
when you take time to think of it).

Maybe there is nothing in a store that they need.
But what about some token of love—what about love itself . . .
  and friendship . . .
    and understanding . . .
      and consideration . . .
        and a helping hand . . .
      and a smile . . .
  and a prayer?

You can't buy these things in any store, and these are the very
things people need.

We all need them . . . Blessed will they be who receive them
this Christmas or at any time.

Let's not permit the crowds and the rush to crowd Christmas
out of our hearts . . .
  for that is where it belongs.
Christmas is not in the stores—
  but in the hearts of people.

Let's not give way to cynicism and mutter that "Christmas has
become commercialized."
It never will be—unless you let it be.
Your Christmas is not commercialized, unless you have commercialized it.

Let's not succumb to the sophistication that complains:
"Christmas belongs only to the children."
That shows that you have never understood Christmas at all,
for the older you get, the more it means, if you know what it
means.
Christmas, though forever young, grows old along with us.

Have you been saying, "I just can't seem to feel the Christmas
spirit this year"?
That's too bad.
As a confession of lack of faith, it is rather significant.

You are saying that you feel no joy that Jesus came into the
world . . .
You are confessing that His presence in the world is not a
reality to you . . .
Maybe you need all the more to read the Christmas story over
again,
   need to sit down with the Gospel of Luke
    and think about it.

I thank God for Christmas.
Would that it lasted all year.
For on Christmas Eve, and Christmas Day, all the world is a
better place,
   and men and women are more lovable.
Love itself seeps into every heart, and miracles happen.

When Christmas doesn't make your heart swell up until it
nearly bursts . . .
   and fill your eyes with tears . . .
    and make you all soft and warm inside . . .
then you'll know that something inside of you is dead.

We hope that there will be snow for Christmas.
Why?
It is not really important, but it is so nice, and old-fashioned,
and appropriate, we think.

Isn't it wonderful to think that nothing can *really harm* the joy
of Christmas . . .
Although your Christmas tree decorations will include many

new gadgets, such as lights with bubbles in them . . . it's the
old tree decorations that mean the most . . . the ones you save
carefully from year to year . . .
   the crooked star that goes on the top of the tree . . .
   the ornaments that you've been so careful with.

And you'll bring out the tiny manger,
   and the shed,
   and the little figures of the Holy Family . . . and lovingly
arrange them on the mantel
   or in the middle of the dining room table.

And getting the tree will be a family event, with great excitement for the children . . .

And there will be a closet into which you'll forbid your husband to look,
And he will be moving through the house mysteriously with
bundles under his coat,
   and you'll pretend not to notice . . .

There will be the fragrance of cookies baking
      spices and fruitcake . . .
and the warmth of the house shall be melodious with the
lilting strains of "Silent Night, Holy Night."

And you'll listen to the wonderful Christmas music on the
radio,
Some of the songs will be modern—good enough music,
perhaps—but it will be the old carols,
   the lovely old Christmas hymns that will mean the most.

And forests of fir trees will march right into our living
rooms . . .
There will be bells on our doors
   and holly wreaths in our windows . . .

And we shall sweep the Noël skies for their brightest colors
and festoon our homes with stars.

There will be a chubby stocking hung by the fireplace . . .
   and with finger to lip you will whisper
and ask me to tiptoe, for a little tousled head is asleep and
must not be awakened

until after Santa has come.

And finally Christmas morning will come.
Don't worry—you'll be ready for it—
    You'll catch the spirit all right,
or *it will catch you, which is even better.*

And then you will remember what Christmas means—the beginning of Christianity . . .
    the Second Chance for the world . . .
        the hope for peace . . .
            and the only way.
The promise that the angels sang is the most wonderful music the world has ever heard.
    "Peace on earth and good will toward men."

It was not a pronouncement upon the state of the world then
Nor is it a reading of the international barometer of the present time . . .
but it is a promise—God's promise—of what one day will come to pass.

The years that are gone are graveyards in which all the persuasions of men have crumbled into dust.
If history has any voice, it is to say that all these ways of men lead nowhere.
There remains one way—The Way—untried,
        untested,
        unexplored fully . . .
the way of Him who was born a Babe in Bethlehem.

In a world that seems not only to be changing, but even to be dissolving, there are some tens of millions of us who want Christmas to be the same . . .
    with the same old greeting "Merry Christmas" and no other.

We long for the abiding love among men of good will which the season brings . . .
believing in this ancient miracle of Christmas with its softening, sweetening influence to tug at our heartstrings once again.

We want to hold on to the old customs and traditions because
they strengthen our family ties,
      bind us to our friends,
     make us one with all mankind
for whom the Child was born,
and bring us back again to the God who gave His only begot-
ten Son, that "whosoever believeth in Him should not perish,
but have everlasting life."

So we will not "spend" Christmas . . .
   nor "observe" Christmas.
We will "keep" Christmas—keep it as it is . . .
   in all the loveliness of its ancient traditions.

May we keep it in our hearts,
that we may be kept in its hope.

G OD OF OUR FATHERS and our God, give us the faith to
believe in the ultimate triumph of righteousness . . . .
We pray for the bifocals of faith that see the despair and the
need of the hour but also see, further on, the patience of our
God working out His plan in the world He has made. In Thy
sovereign name we pray, Amen.

BOOK III

Praying Is Dangerous Business

Church members in too many cases
are like deep sea divers, encased in
the suits designed for many fathoms deep,
marching bravely to pull out plugs in bathtubs.

In the preface to *A Man Called Peter* I wrote that, among my many dreams of Peter after his death, one stood out. I dreamed I was allowed to visit Peter briefly in his new setting, and I found him working in a rose garden, surrounded by the flawless hybrid tea roses he had always wanted to grow.

"I know perfectly well what you've been doing, Catherine," he told me playfully. "You're writing a book. Now, now—no exposés! What you're doing to me shouldn't happen to a dog!"

Then he became more serious. "It's all right, Kate. Go ahead and write it. Tell it all, if it will prove to people that a man can love the Lord and not be a sissy . . . . "

I think Peter would be pleased with the many lives changed through his story and the number of men who went into the Christian ministry after seeing the Twentieth Century-Fox movie version of *A Man Called Peter*, which is still appearing on television 28 years after it was made. Since publication of the book in 1951, sales of all editions have topped the two-million mark.

Whenever I recall the impact of Peter's teaching, I think of letters received and see a procession of pictures: A blind woman in Atlanta, laboriously typing a letter, with many mistakes. A sixteen-year-old girl writing on pink paper at four in the morning. A senator dictating his letter in his office. An interne in his Baltimore rooming house: "I'm in the eye section of Johns Hopkins Hospital . . . ." A Boston shoe manufacturer, en route to Washington by train, reading in his roomette until almost dawn. A soldier near the front lines in Korea, sitting on an upturned keg, laboriously printing his letter: "I'm not sure you will ever receive this . . . ." An Iowa housewife writing in her farm kitchen. A Japanese girl in her college dormitory room: "I am a foreign student from Tokyo . . . ." An Illinois businessman: "I handle auto parts. For the past several years I have been groping for God . . . ." A prisoner in the Insular Penitentiary of the Philippines: "I am a terrible sinner, but I am trying to seek and know God like your Peter did. Humans like you can help me . . . ."

At the end of *A Man Called Peter* there appeared six of Peter's memorable sermons. Four are reprinted in the following pages, under the general title of his classic "Praying Is Dangerous Business."

C. M.

The American Dream

D uring the Second World War, I met on the train a lieuten-
ant who had just returned from fighting in Italy.
He had been in the North African campaign.
  He had fought in Sicily.
    He wore the Purple Heart ribbon with his campaign
    ribbons.

I asked him what he thought of America.
It was a hard question to ask a man who had been gone so
long,
  who had been fighting for his country . . .
    who had been wounded in action . . .
It was almost an impertinence.

He said that after what he had seen in North Africa and in
Italy, he appreciated America more than ever.
He described the filth and the squalor of the cities he had
seen . . .
He spoke of Tunis and Bizerte . . .
He told me of his impression of the Arabs and the natives of
North Africa.
  He had been deeply impressed with their misery and their
slums.

I asked him some rhetorical questions, not expecting answers
but rather to make him think, and to divert his attention from
the bottle of rum in his raincoat pocket which, he had told me,
he intended to finish between Roanoke and Washington.
"What is America?" I asked.
  "What were you fighting for?
Did anyone in North Africa ever ask you that question?
If they had, what would you have said?"

I venture to say that deep down in the hearts of the men who
fought the bitterest battles—of them who died—there was a

glimmering of an understanding that the things for which
they fought were somehow all tied up in one bundle of ideals
  of concepts
    of principles
that we call the American Dream.
It is a Dream that has shone brightly at times
  and that has faded at other times.

World events today are forcing us, whether we realize it or
not, to rediscover the meanings and the significances of the
things that make America different from other nations . . .
  the hope of a world weary of war, heartsick and hungry.

What is the American Dream?
What is it that makes our country different?

Do you know . . . you who fought for it overseas . . .
    who braved the sniper in the jungle,
   who flew through flak-filled skies,
  who waded through the mud of Italy,
who knew the heat of the desert sun and the cold of the
North Atlantic?

Do you know . . . you who made your speeches in Congress
and waxed eloquent on the stump?

Do you know . . . you who boast of your ancestry and your
membership in patriotic societies?

What is America?
Where is our country going?
Let no answer be lightly made . . . .

We cannot speak with any truth or realism about the future
unless we understand the past.
What has America to give the rest of the world?
If only grain
  or money
   or clothing
    or armaments . . .
then we have already lost the war and the peace . . . and our
own souls.

Ours is a Covenant Nation . . .

The only surviving nation on earth that had its origins in the determination of the Founding Fathers to establish a settlement

"to the glory of God and the advancement of the Christian faith."

That was what William Bradford and George Carver had in mind when, beneath the swinging lantern in the cabin of the *Mayflower*, they affixed their signatures to the solemn declaration which established the Commonwealth of Massachusetts.

They had come from the Old World and were seeking refuge in the New.

They had come from tyranny and oppression . . .

They had come from fear and coercion . . .

They had come from famine and from difficulty . . .

from wars and threats of wars . . . .

And they sought a new life in a new land.

Religious liberty to worship God according to the dictates of one's own conscience

and equal opportunity for all men . . .

These are the twin pillars of the American Dream.

Now a Covenant Nation is one that recognizes its dependence upon God and its responsibility toward God.
This nation was so born.
God was recognized as the source of human rights.
The Declaration of Independence says so.

A Covenant Nation is one which recognizes that God and His purposes stand over and above the nation . . .

that the highest role a nation can play is to reflect God's righteousness in national policy.

That is what Bradford and Carver certainly intended.
That is what Roger Williams sought, when he set up his settlement in Providence, Rhode Island.
That is what William Penn was striving after in Pennsylvania.
That is what they wanted in Maryland, when, in 1649, the Maryland Act of Toleration set it down in writing.

That is what Thomas Jefferson was striving after when he wrote the Declaration of Independence.

That is what they fought for, too.
You can trace it from Bunker Hill
  from Lexington and Concord
    down through Valley Forge . . . .
They were concerned about rights.
  These free men who had burlap wrapped around their feet,
  as they marched through the snow,
      who carefully hoarded their gunpowder and clutched
      their muskets under their tattered uniforms to keep them
      dry . . . .
They were concerned about the rights of free men.

They made the first down payments there—down payments
that have been kept up to this good day . . .
  through Château-Thierry and the Argonne . . .
    to Anzio and Cassino . . .
      at Saint-Lô and Bastogne . . .
        at Tarawa and Iwo Jima
          at Saipan and Guadalcanal . . . .

There have been periods in our history when the American
Dream has faded and grown dim.
Today there is real danger that the American Dream will
become the Forgotten Dream.

For freedom is not the right to do as one pleases
  but the opportunity to please to do what is right.
The Founding Fathers sought freedom . . .
  not from law but freedom in law;
  not freedom from government—but freedom in government;
  not freedom from speech—but freedom in speech;
  not freedom from the press—but freedom in the press;
  not freedom from religion—but freedom in religion.
We need to ponder these things today.

Our standard of values is out of focus.
We boast that many of our national leaders came out of country schoolhouses.

Yet the average country schoolteacher makes a fraction of
what we pay big league baseball players.

I, for one, enjoy baseball, but is hitting homeruns more important than giving boys and girls an education?

It is a strange commentary on our standard of values that lobbyists who try to influence legislation get more money than the men who write it.

There is something wrong with a standard of values that gives a comedian a million dollars and a high school teacher two thousand.

The reward is greater for making people laugh than it is for making people think.

Again, no nation on earth has more laws, and yet more lawlessness than this nation.

There exists a current philosophy which you and I have accepted, more or less, that

If we don't like a law, we need feel no obligation to keep it.

Any philosophy which thus makes the will of the people its norm for morality and righteousness is a false philosophy.

The test, after all, is not whether a certain law is popular but whether the law is based upon fundamental justice

fundamental decency and righteousness

fundamental morality and goodness.

What we need is not law enforcement—but law observance.

In a modern society there is no real freedom *from* law.

There is only freedom *in* law.

Our government is in danger of control by corrupt party machines, and even by gangsters—

cynical

ruthless

self-seeking lovers of power . . .

a fact which should challenge every true patriot and summon all who love America to roll up their sleeves and make this once again a "government of the *people*

by the *people*

for the *people.*" . . .

For what is freedom?

Is it immunity for the unreliable and the despotic?

Is it freedom to take what you want regardless of the rights of others?
Is it a matter of getting yours while the getting is good?

The story of the waste of this nation's riches, for example, is a sad story of the misuse of "freedom."

Consider the philosophy which for far too long pervaded the thinking of those who settled and developed our southland. Their philosophy was "plow and plant
     plow and plant
   plow and plant, until the land is exhausted,
and then we'll move farther west and repeat the process."

Consider the philosophy of those who went into our forests to cut timber, feeling no responsibility to replace what they took by reforestation, so that we cut into vast tracts of good timberland and left it open,
   with no windbreak . . .
      with no barrier against erosion . . .
with nothing to prevent dust-bowl storms . . . and the removal of hundreds of thousands of acres of irreplaceable topsoil, which year after year was washed into the Gulf of Mexico.

Only now is the Department of Agriculture meeting with any success in persuading our farmers to adopt contour plowing
   to put in windbreaks
      to sow crops, grass, shrubs, and trees
that will tend to hold the soil together, and keep on the face of America that irreplaceable fertility which, in the past, has been her wealth.

I needn't say anything about the extravagant misuse or abuse of our wildlife.
There are many of you who, as hunters, know perfectly well that only the stupidity and greed of so-called sportsmen are responsible for the elimination of so many duck and wildfowl, once so plentiful, now nonexistent . . . .

All because somebody said: "This is a *free* country. I have a *right* to hunt and shoot and kill."

Surely freedom does not mean that people can do as they like
with the country's resources!

There are so many things that are wonderful about America—
   things that are gloriously right and well worth defending.
But there are also things that are deeply and dangerously
wrong with America, and the true patriot is he who sees them
   regrets them
and tries to remove them.

The Bill of Rights applies to all men equally . . .
Yet where is the man who considers others equal to himself . . .
   who feels that other men are his brothers . . .
      who is ready to agree that liberty, except for himself, is a
      good thing?

The modern man will hardly admit,
   though in his heart he knows it to be true . . .
that it is only by the grace of God that he was not born of a
different race or creed.

"All men are created equal," says the Declaration of Independence.
"All men are endowed by their Creator with certain unaliena-
ble rights." . . .
And this applies to red men
   and yellow men
      and black men
as well as white men.

There is nothing in the Bill of Rights that says:
   "This applies only to men with white skins
   or to people from Virginia."

But we must confess with troubled heart that not yet are the
black men in our land wholly free.
They are even yet half-slave in this "land of the free and home
of the brave."

*A democracy that boasts of freedom and still keeps some of its citizens
in bondage is not worth defending.*
Let the implication of this sink into every American heart.

Again, while we know that the lot of the working man in America is better than that of the working man in any other nation, yet we seem to have more difficulty in labor relations here than in anyplace else in the world.
That is a paradox.
It is something very hard to understand.

Now before you get me wrong, I want to make it clear that I was a member of a union.
When I left Scotland I was a mechanical engineer.
I have worked in machine shops, and for three years I worked alternately night and day . . .
one weekday shift and one weeknight shift . . . .

I know what it is to be unemployed,
to be out of work because other men are on strike.
I know what it is to work on time rate.
I used to average 10.48 pence per hour by time rate.
I know what it is to work piecework.

I know about incentive plans, and I know about slowdowns.
I want it clearly understood that I not only believe in, but I am willing to defend labor's right to organize
labor's right collectively to bargain
labor's right to strike.

But I am also prepared to defend the right of a man to work, if he would rather work than strike.
I am also prepared to defend the right of an employer to hire whom he will, and to fire those who are no longer necessary to his operation, or who, by laziness or disobedience, or by any other cause, are no longer acceptable to his employ.

I am also ready to defend the right of a man to join a union, if he wants to, and also the right of another man to stay out of it, if he would rather. I believe that is concerned with fundamental rights in the American Bill of Rights.

In the first few months of living in this country, I went to New York City to try to get a job on a steel-construction job.
They were building a skyscraper, and I was told that I could get a job, but there were two things I would have to do.

One, I would have to go to the hiring hall that night and join the union. That was all right, I could do that.

And then I was told, "You see that guy over there and pay him $50." If I would do that, I would be all right.

And I decided I would not do that.

I decided that that was not my understanding of the American way of life,
> that I was not going to buy a job . . .
>> that I was not going to bribe anybody,
>>> nor was I going to recognize the right of one man to collect at the expense of other men who needed work.

The paradox is that labor in this country does not realize how well-off it is.

Nor do the leaders of labor unions seem to realize that with power comes responsibility, and that these two things are joined together by the eternal laws of God.

Apparently some labor union leaders, together with some employers, do not seem yet to have learned that to every right there is attached a duty,
> and to every privilege there is tied an obligation.

We, in America, are today enjoying the greatest freedom the world has ever known—
> a freedom that staggers all who will consider it—
> *for we are free in these days to ignore the very things that others died to provide.*

We are free, if we please, to neglect the right of franchise . . .
> free to give up the right to worship God in our own way . . .
>> free to set aside, as of no consequence, the Church's open door . . .
>>> free to let the open Bible gather dust.

We are free to neglect the liberties we have inherited.
Surely there can be no greater freedom than that!

Significantly, religious liberty stands first in the Bill of Rights. It is the most essential, the foundation of all the other freedoms. Take that away, and eventually all freedom crumbles.

But the Constitution and the Bill of Rights would seem to imply that we *will* worship God *in some way.*

Now, this generation has distorted religious freedom to mean freedom from religion.

We find our Supreme Court now declaring it unconstitutional to teach our children that this nation was founded under God to His glory and for the advancement of the Christian faith . . .

   unconstitutional to include in the curriculum of our children's education any knowledge of God.

Today a large percentage of our population are without even a nominal connection with any church, children and young people entirely without religious training of any kind.

But our children are souls—made in the image of God.
These souls are immortal and will live forever, and the human brain is but a tool and an instrument which the human soul shall use.

In the name of God . . .

   in the name of truth . . .
teaching about religion must be demanded and provided for the children of today, if this democracy and this civilization are to survive.

The idea may be abroad in some quarters that democracy is the thing that must be preserved . . .

   and that God is to be brought in as its servant.

We must not get the cart before the horse.

The plea of the Church today is not that people shall call upon God to return to democracy and bless it . . .

   But rather that we shall together cause our democracy to return to God and be blessed.

Let us remember that we are a republic under God.
Let us remember that each of the metal coins we jingle in our pockets bears the inscription
                    "In God We Trust."

Is that just blasphemy?
What does it mean to trust in God?

Certainly no conception of trust in God can make any sense which assumes that He will prosper our ways or bless us,

until our ways become His ways . . .
until we begin to keep the conditions He has specifically laid
down for national blessing.

The blessing of peace is *not* a product of politics—but a fruit of
righteousness.
God's order is always righteousness and peace—
    not peace and righteousness.
The Bible has been telling us that for centuries.
When will we learn it?

Desperately we need a return to government by principles
rather than by politics.
But where are the principles evident in the events of this
present hour?

Peace is not made by compromise.
It does not grow out of expediency.
Peace is not a flower growing in the world's formal garden.
It is rather a product of the blacksmith's forge—
    hammered out on the anvils of sacrifice and suffering . . .
        heated in the fires of devotion to righteousness . . .
            tempered in the oil of mercy and goodness . . .
Peace is a costly thing.

Now, there are only two nations in the world today capable of
shouldering world responsibility for peace.
One of them, the United States of America, shies away from it.
She does not want it . . .
    She does not seek it . . .
The idea is distasteful; her instinct is to withdraw.

The other, the Union of Soviet Socialist Republics, is eager for
it, plotting and planning for it, and has openly announced its
intention to have it at whatever cost.

Now the choice is clear.
Either we withdraw and let the Russians do it, or we assume
it, unwilling and reluctant though we are.

But the price of world leadership is high.
Deep in our hearts we know that we are not good enough for
it.

The call is therefore for Christian men and women, of every communion, to become fighters for peace
　　practitioners for righteousness.

Every Catholic and Protestant, who owns the name of Jesus, must fight together to make America good enough to lead the world,
　　to make the American Dream of equal opportunity for all men come true.

Nonetheless, I believe that the dream has been glimpsed by enough people
　　and is deep enough in the heart of the average citizen to shape America's future and make the dream come true.

We have already done a great deal for the rest of the world.
Let no man minimize our gifts.
But they are not enough.

We have to give more, and I do not mean more dollars.
I do not mean more tractors.
I do not mean more guns.

We have to give more of the only thing, after all, that makes our life different from theirs, namely, our ideals
　　　　　our faith
　　　　our philosophy of life
　　　our concept of human dignity
　　our Bill of Rights
　our American Dream.

That is what we have to export—
That is what we have to give to the French
　　　　and the Italians
　　　and the British
　　and the Belgians
　and the Dutch.
That is what we have to give to the Czechs
　　　the Poles
　　the Bulgars
　and the Slovaks.

If we can somehow sit down with their governments and say, "Now, look here, rich American blood was poured out to make possible your establishing this kind of government. We don't mean that you have got to copy ours, but you have to make it possible for a man living within the borders of Greece to have the same opportunities that a man has in the state of Missouri."

Three hundred thousand Americans did not die in the second World War merely to see conditions develop again that will make necessary another war.
God forbid.

That is what we fought for, because we found out that if there is a denial of personal liberty in Athens
      or in Prague
    or in Amsterdam
  or in Edinburgh,
there is a restriction of personal liberty in Boston and Charleston.

We found out that what happened on the banks of the Yangtze River affects the farmer over in Stark County
  or the man who makes shoes in St. Louis or Massachusetts.

    It affects Joe Doaks, with a cigar stuck in his mouth, sitting out there in the bleachers in the ball park yelling for his club.

These are the things America has to export, and perhaps that is the reason why almighty God, with the hand of Providence, guided this nation.
He has made and preserved our nation . . .
    maybe that is the reason . . .
in order that this republic, in a federal union, might save the rest of the world, by giving back to them the new life that was forged from the anvil of sacrifice and daring adventure in this country . . . .

America may be humanity's last chance.
Certainly it is God's latest experiment.

But we cannot fool God about our individual or national goodness.
Let us not be deluded into thinking we can fool ourselves.

And so I come to my text—II Chronicles 7:14.
It is God's word for America today—

"If my people, which are called by my name, shall humble
themselves, and pray, and seek my face, and turn from their
wicked ways; then will I hear from heaven, and will forgive
their sin, and will heal their land."

L ORD GOD OF HEAVEN, who hath so lavishly blessed this
land, make us, Thy people, to be aware that the good
things we enjoy have come from Thee, but that Thou didst
only lend them to us.

Impress upon our smugness the knowledge that we are not
owners but stewards. Remind us, lest we become filled with
conceit, that one day a reckoning will be required of us.

Sanctify our love of country, that our boasting may be
turned into humility and our pride into a ministry to men
everywhere.

Help us to make this God's own country by living like God's
own people. We ask these things in the name of Jesus Christ,
our Lord, Amen.

Sin in the Present Tense

T he three chief causes of death in the United States are, in statistical order, diseases of the heart
cancer
and disorders of the nervous system.

Two of the three are obviously diseases brought on by the strains imposed on the human body by worry
anxiety
nervousness
and the tensions of life in our modern world.

Our lives are so geared these days that any contemplation is difficult.
I have tried it on the top of the Washington Monument and found it impossible even there.

I well remember leaning out of one of the windows—550 feet above Washington—wondering how the city must have looked in the time of John Quincy Adams
or Thomas Jefferson . . .
when Pennsylvania Avenue was a muddy road, rutted with carriage wheels.

As I stood there, lost in reverie, trying to recapture Washington's past, I was interrupted by a brusque voice at my elbow saying,
"Keep moving, please . . . move right on round."

Try standing for five minutes anywhere on the main shopping street of any city,
or on the loading platforms for streetcars during the rush hours in the evening.

Observe the surging, seething mass of humanity flowing past you.

Notice the furrowed brows
  the faces lined with anxiety and worry
    the haggard, hurried look.

Above all, notice the tenseness of the people,
  the feeling of tension in the very atmosphere.

Its symptoms are obvious—irritation, short temper, frowns,
nervousness, impatience . . .
  fighting to be waited on . . .
    struggling against time . . .
Everywhere is this tension that is just on the verge of hysterics
      bitter tears
    screams of impotence and rage
  and actual conflict.

Now, at this moment, when you are quiet, you know in your
heart that God did not mean us to live like that.
We were not made for that sort of struggle for existence.
It is against every law of health, every law of God.

The essence and core of Christianity is *Trust in God.*

As Christ traveled up and down the dusty roads of Palestine,
He was constantly amazed that human beings did not really
trust His heavenly Father.
  "Why are you afraid?" He would say.
    "How little you trust God!
      Why are ye so fearful?
        How is it that ye have no faith?
          O men, how little you trust Him!"

By every gentle word,
  by every act of compassion and pity,
Christ was trying to show men that God is not only all-
powerful, but also all-loving . . .
  nearer to each of us than we know . . .
always ready and willing to make His power available to meet
our needs.

Christ was constantly admonishing men to trust this loving
Father, to pin all their faith on Him.
  "Have no fear, only believe," He said to one seeking heal-
  ing.

"Have faith in God," He said to a distraught father.
"All things are possible to him that believeth" (Mark 9:23).

Now why was it that Christ considered faith—trusting God—
so all-important?
And exactly what did He mean by "trusting God"?

This is fundamental to Christian faith.
It has to do with our understanding of life.
It has to do with that basic selfishness, which is so often
mistaken for grief.

If you are in financial straits and have turned to God for help,
  as you are expected to do . . .
    as God wants you to do . . .
but you still continue to worry and don't see how you can
make both ends meet,
  then you are not really trusting God to help you.

Why do we worry about these material things?
Our heavenly Father knows perfectly well that we need them
and is more willing to send them to us than we are to ask for
them.
  "If ye then, being evil, know how to give good gifts to your
  children, *how much more* shall your Father which is in heaven
  give good things to them *that ask him*" (Matthew 7:11).
God has pledged His word to supply all our needs.

Paul could testify that God keeps His promises.
I myself know that this promise is true.

God may not supply all your wants, because sometimes we
want things that are not good for us.
Parents don't supply all that their children may want.
But you have every need supplied.
What more can we ask?

Why is it that Christ considered anxiety and worry a sin?
Because worry and anxiety are really lack of trust in God.
And this lack of trust shows that we do not really believe the
promises of God.
We believe in God—but may not *believe* God.

If you doubt God's ability to help you in a given difficulty, you
are doubting either His power

His ability to help you . . .
or you are doubting His willingness to help you.

To doubt either God's power
    or God's love
is to say by our actions:
    "Lord, I do not believe Your promises.
    I do not think they really apply to me.
    I do not think You will do it.
    It might have been all right for Palestine in the long ago,
    but Lord,
    You just don't know Washington."

Surely it is perfectly evident that to doubt God in that way is to sin against Him, and to cut ourselves off from His help.

Thus one of the greatest sins of Christian people is the sin of tension and worry.
It is characteristic of all our people, that we, as a nation, need to learn *how* to relax.

We have permitted ourselves to be stampeded into a life of unnatural and dangerous high pressure.
    We try to cover too much ground.
    We are always in a hurry.

I gave my mother's address to some of our boys who were going overseas, in the hope that they might be able to call upon her. Some of them did, and commenting on the first visit she received from these American soldiers, Mother said,
    "They came in a Jeep, and they were in a hurry."

That, I think, is a typical commentary on our American way of life.
    We are always in a hurry.

We hate to miss one panel of a revolving door. Some bright soul has defined a split second as "that interval of time between the changing of a traffic light from red to green, and the honking of the horn in the car immediately behind you."

Whereas our grandparents could make a gracious ceremony and devote a whole evening to a game of Parcheesi, we now feel frustrated unless we can, in a single evening,

combine a dinner date
take in a movie
make a couple of telephone calls
visit somebody on the way downtown
and maybe do some shopping on our way to the
show.
We try to do too much in too short a time.

We are compressing our lives into capsules that are quite
indigestible.

That this sin of tension is taking a terrific toll among the
people of the nation cannot be denied.
The incidence of functional diseases
neuroses
mental illness
and heart trouble
increases year after year.

Medicine has made great strides.
It has learned how to combat infectious diseases, but what has
happened is that we have merely exchanged the types of
disease.
The citadel of disease has simply retired to other strongholds
further in, and more difficult to root out.

Fewer people now die of infectious diseases, but more die of
degenerative diseases.
The years of life which we have *gained* by the suppression of
smallpox
diphtheria
and scarlet fever
are *stolen* by the chronic diseases such as cancer
diabetes
ulcers
and heart disease.

Thus, disease still has not been mastered.
It simply has changed its nature.
As modern medicine seeks the cause of all this, it has made
some startling discoveries.
The British Medical Journal (June 18, 1910) put it this way:

"There is not a tissue in the human body wholly removed from the influence of the spirit."

In other words, we are discovering that there is a closer relationship between our minds,
    our emotions,
        the state of our spiritual health, and our bodies than doctors thought possible a few decades ago.

To illustrate:
It is a well-known fact that the hyperacidity often leading to stomach ulcers is directly caused by emotional stress and, generally, a sense of frustration.
I can vouch for that out of my own experience.

But physicians are now discovering that the same thing is equally true of other diseases.
Dr. Loring T. Swaim of Boston, a nationally known specialist of arthritis, says that:

> It has been increasingly evident, as pointed out by doctors everywhere, that physical health is closely associated with, and often dependent upon, spiritual health.

> No constitutional disease is free from the effects of mental strains, which are part of life. Rheumatoid arthritis is no exception.[9]

If tension and worry are the great sins of our day,
    and if they affect not only our spiritual health,
        not only our peace of mind and happiness—but even our physical health,
it is certainly worthy of our greatest efforts to learn how to overcome them.

This is where Christianity has the answer.

God has designed us for happiness.
He has created us for peace and joy.
It is His will for each of His creatures that life shall be free and lived to the utmost for His glory.

Now, worshiping and serving God is a solemn thing,
    but it can be happy.

We have confused being solemn with being sad,
   being dignified with being depressed.

Have you ever wondered why going to church
      working in the church
   taking part in its activities
is done with a sigh instead of a smile or a song?

Why is it that so few people find in it fun
         fellowship
       good company
     good times
     good humor
   and happiness?

Christ's invitation into the Kingdom of God as a joyous affair is
like an invitation to a feast of good things, and an invitation to
happiness.

Does your religious experience fit into that?
If not, there's something wrong.
People refuse the offer of Christianity, because they never
dream that what they want can be found there.

Christ offers us what we are really hungering for, but we don't
believe it, because we mistake what we really want in life.

How often Jesus used words that make the new life as attrac-
tive as a feast!
   The Prodigal Son is received with music, dancing and a
   banquet.
   The faithful servant is invited to enter into the joy of his
   Lord.
   The wise virgins go into supper with the bridegroom.
There is only one conclusion.

Either Jesus was wrong—
   or we have missed something.
Jesus did not intend that following Him should be sad.
It is true that He was "a man of sorrows, and acquainted with
grief," but that was in order that our joy might be full.
   "Come unto me, all ye that labour and are heavy laden, and
   I will give you rest. Take my yoke upon you, and learn of

me; for I am meek and lowly of heart: and ye shall find rest
unto your souls.
For my yoke is easy, and my burden is light" (Matthew
11:28).

The yoke He imposes is an easy one.
It does not chafe
  or hurt
    or hold you back.

On the contrary—
It takes away pain
  gives you freedom
    drives you on to a fuller and happier life.

But we won't believe it.
We won't give Him a chance.
We prefer to attempt to carry our burdens and, as if we did not
have enough, we try even to carry God's burdens also.

Now what shall we do, who are seeking peace of mind and
heart? How can we find it?

First, let us try to clear our thinking about the nature of God.
Let us make a study, a serious study—for it merits our best
efforts—to find out the nature of God.

Most of our difficulties, our lack of trust in God, spring from
our basic misunderstanding of what God is like.
We are dismally ignorant of the love and the power of God.
  No wonder we do not trust Him!

Have you ever set out to read your New Testament to find out
about God?
How do you expect to know what God is like if you never read
intelligently the only Book that professes to tell you these
things?
Get a good modern translation, like Moffatt's or Goodspeed's,
and read it intelligently.
Christ came to reveal God.
He said to one of His disciples:
  "Have I been so long time with you, and yet hast thou not
  known me, Philip? he that hath seen me hath seen the
  Father" (John 14:9).

If you want to know what God is like, look at Christ.
Study what Christ said.
Notice what Christ did.
And remember—
   He is "the same yesterday, and today, and forever."

Next, study the lives of some others who have been personally
acquainted with Him.
Read the letters, journals, and biographies of men like
   Francis of Assisi
      Thomas à Kempis
         Wilfred Grenfell
            George Müller of Bristol
               Brother Bryan of Birmingham
                  William Pulmer Jacobs of Thornwell Orphanage
                  and Dr. George Washington Carver.
Find out how God dealt with them, and thus you will begin to
find out about God.

The second step is to become personally acquainted with God
yourself—
   in your own way,
      according to your own needs and circumstances.
"Practice makes perfect" in the realm of the spiritual, as well as
in other things.

You see, your real trouble is spiritual, so that the remedy must
be spiritual, too.
All of which means . . . "Take your burdens to the Lord . . .
and leave them there."
"But how?" . . . you ask.

Get off by yourself . . . somewhere . . . and tell God your
fears—
   what you are afraid of . . .
Tell Him what you are worried about . . .

And then ask Him . . . very simply . . . to take care of you.
Let all your fears go—give them to God.
He will not let you down.
Try to let yourself go . . . to God.

If you feel that you haven't enough faith to do that . . . ask
Him to give you the faith too.

He will do that—exactly that.
> *He will give you what it takes.*

The man or woman who really trusts God is not spiritually
rigid . . .
    afraid of what may happen tomorrow . . .
rehearsing in imagination all the terrible things that could
happen.
No, as believers in God, we must relax.

When you are weary and sit down in a chair, you do not sit
rigid, expecting the chair to collapse beneath you—that is,
unless the chair is an antique . . .

When you lie down on your bed, you do not lie like a poker—
tense, rigid.
You trust the bed to hold you.
You do not worry about the possibility of your bed collapsing
and depositing you on the floor.
I have had that happen to me . . . and it's not so bad, really.

But you don't lie there speculating about the possibility of its
happening. You don't lie there all tense . . . listening for the
sound of a burglar at the window . . .
    or the crackle of flames from the basement . . .
        or the smell of smoke . . .
            or the trembling of the earth in a possible earthquake.

If you did, you would not get much sleep.
You trust your bed.
You trust your precautions against burglars.
You trust the police force . . .
    and the fire brigade . . .
    and trust yourself to sleep . . .
which is another way of saying you trust yourself to God.

The believer trusts himself to God . . .
    believing that God will watch over him.
Will you relax spiritually today?

Will you leave with God—now—the troubles you have been
carrying around for so long?
Will you ask Him—now—to take them away from you?

and let you relax in simple trust . . . just like a little child?
Will you?

"There was once a fellow who, with his father, farmed a little piece of land.
Several times a year they'd load up the ox-cart with vegetables and drive to the nearest city.

"Except for their name and the patch of ground, father and son had little in common.
The old man believed in taking it easy . . .
   and the son was the go-getter type.

"One morning, they loaded the cart,
   hitched up the ox and set out.
The young fellow figured that if they kept going all day and night, they'd get to the market by next morning.
He walked alongside the ox and kept prodding it with a stick.

"'Take it easy,' said the old man. 'You'll last longer.'

"'If we get to market ahead of the others,' said his son, 'we have a better chance of getting good prices.'

"The old man pulled his hat down over his eyes and went to sleep on the seat.
Four miles and four hours down the road, they came to a little house.
'Here's your uncle's place,' said the father, waking up. 'Let's stop in and say hello.'

"'We've lost an hour already,' complained the go-getter.

"'Then a few minutes more won't matter,' said his father. 'My brother and I live so close, yet we see each other so seldom.'

"The young man fidgeted while the two old gentlemen gossiped away an hour.
On the move again, the father took his turn leading the ox.
By and by, they came to a fork in the road.
The old man directed the ox to the right.
'The left is the shorter way,' said the boy.

"'I know it,' said the old man, 'but this way is prettier.'

*'Have you no respect for time?' asked the impatient young man.

*'I respect it very much,' said the old fellow.
'That's why I like to use it for looking at pretty things.'
The right-hand path led through woodland and wild flowers.
The young man was so busy watching the sun sink he didn't notice how lovely the sunset was.
Twilight found them in what looked like one big garden.
'Let's sleep here,' said the old man.

*'This is the last trip I take with you,' snapped his son.
'You're more interested in flowers than in making money.'

*'That's the nicest thing you've said in a long time,' smiled the old fellow.
A minute later he was asleep.

*A little before sunrise, the young man shook his father awake.
They hitched up and went on.
A mile and an hour away they came upon a farmer trying to pull his cart out of a ditch.
'Let's give him a hand,' said the father.

*'And lose more time?' exploded the son.

*'Relax,' said the old man.
'You might be in a ditch some time yourself.'

*By the time the other cart was back on the road, it was almost eight o'clock.
Suddenly a great flash of lightning split the sky.
Then there was thunder.
Beyond the hills, the heavens grew dark.
'Looks like a big rain in the city,' said the old man.

*'If we had been on time, we'd be sold out by now,' grumbled his son.

*'Take it easy,' said the old gentlemen, 'you'll last longer.'

*It wasn't until late in the afternoon that they got to the top of the hill overlooking the town.
They looked down at it for a long time.
Neither of them spoke.

Finally the young man who had been in such a hurry said, 'I see what you mean, father.'

"They turned their cart around and drove away from what had once been the city of Hiroshima."[10]

F ORGIVE US, O GOD, for the doubting suspicion with which we regard the heart of God.

We have faith in checks and banks, in trains and airplanes, in cooks, and in strangers who drive us in cabs. Forgive us for our stupidity, that we have faith in people whom we do not know and are so reluctant to have faith in Thee who knowest us altogether.

We are always striving to find a complicated way through life when Thou hast a plan, and we refuse to walk in it. So many of our troubles we bring on ourselves. How silly we are.

Wilt Thou give to us that faith that we can deposit in the bank of Thy love, so that we may receive the dividends and interest that Thou art so willing to give us. We ask it all in the lovely name of Jesus Christ, our Savior, Amen.

Letters in the Sand

. . . I came not to judge the world, but to save the world
(JOHN 12:47).

T here are many startling verses in the New Testament . . .
This one for instance,
   " . . . let us not criticize one another any more."
No more criticism of any kind?
Can you imagine living like that?
Yet that is exactly the spirit in which Jesus looked at men and
women.
He knew that even when one has sinned grievously . . .
   when things are desperately wrong in a human life
it is love—not criticism—that helps
   and heals
      and redeems.

"But Christ *did* criticize the scribes and Pharisees," you may
say. Yes, He did . . .
   That is an exception . . . .

But that was condemnation of an attitude of mind and heart.
It was a solemn warning of the wrongness of the spirit shown
by these religious leaders—
         their self-righteousness
      their hypocrisy
   their concern about ritual and form
   their making religion a legal matter.

You will remember what He said to the nameless woman who
was brought before Him by the very same Pharisees.
They had caught her in the act of adultery, and in the coldness
of their hard hearts they would use her case as a trap for Jesus

I do not know the woman's name.
Tradition does not name her.

The incident takes place in the early morning in the Temple court.
The eastern sun—already up—casts short purple shadows among the great pillars.
Jesus is seated, teaching a large group of devoted followers gathered round Him.

Suddenly, a group surges forward, pushing their way roughly through the morning worshipers.
Christ's face clouds for a moment, and pain looks out from His eyes.

The scribes and Pharisees thrust their way toward Christ.
In the midst of them is a woman—being dragged roughly by strong men whose faces are hard and stern.

They are pulling her along.
She struggles feebly now and then.
She winces and cries out with the pain of their strong grip on her arms.
With all the strength of their contempt they throw her down at Jesus' feet.

Then they spew out their accusations . . .
In voices honed on hate they shout the vile names reserved for such women.

There are voices hot, like scorching blasts from a furnace . . .
  and others cold, as if they came from frozen hearts.

The woman lies before Christ in a huddled heap,
  sobbing bitterly
    trembling in her shame
shivering as she listens to the indictment.

Her head is bowed; her face covered with her hands.
Her disheveled hair falls over her face.
Her dress is torn and stained with the dust of the city streets along which she has been dragged.

His disciples look into the face of Christ and see in His eyes an infinite sadness, as if the load of all the sin since the world began has already been laid on Him.

His steady eyes take in the situation at a glance.
He sees what they try to hide from Him—
    the hard faces that have no pity or mercy in them
      the looks of satisfaction and self-righteousness with
    which they finger the stones they have picked up.
Every hand holds a stone and clutching fingers run along the sharp edges with malicious satisfaction.

Their shouting ceases as the piercing look of Christ travels round the circle questioningly, and they fall to muttering, as one of their group shouts out the accusation again.

The woman has been caught in the very act of adultery.

Christ looks beyond the woman sobbing at His feet,
    perhaps in search of the man who shares her guilt.
But the woman alone is accused.
There is no man sharing her shame.

It seems to His disciples that Christ does not look at her at all.
He is watching those men who try to hide the stones they carry in their hands.
They are ready—her self-appointed judges—to throw them at the poor defenseless creature on the ground, for it is the Law—the sacred Law of Moses—that such shall be stoned to death.

They have brought her to Christ as a vindictive, malicious afterthought, not for formal trial—for they have already tried her—but in a bold effort to trap Him, either by setting aside the plain commandment of the Law, or by tacitly consenting to a public execution.

If He chooses to repudiate the Law, the priests can accuse Him of being no prophet.
He had said that He came to fulfill the Law, not to *destroy* it.

If He permits the woman's stoning, He will clash with the Roman authorities.

In this little occupied country, Rome alone retains the power of life and death.

If the Nazarene condemns the woman, He will lose His popularity with the multitudes who love and follow Him.
"Be ye therefore merciful," He has often said to them, "as your Father also is merciful" (Luke 6:36).
How can He condemn the woman and still be merciful?

Every form of sin is repulsive to Him,
    and although at times it seems that He thinks the sins of disposition and attitude more to be detested than the sins of the flesh,
yet He nowhere—at any time—condones evil and the doing of wrong.

The circle of bearded men wait impatiently for His answer.
Will His verdict be justice—or mercy?

It is a clever trap.
Surely the Nazarene can find no way out of this one!

But Jesus stands there calmly, quite unruffled by the dilemma so neatly framed.
He well knows that, in the eyes of the Pharisees, *He* is the real enemy—not the woman.
Therefore, He will appeal the case to a Higher Tribunal.
He will lift the issue from the level of human law to that of divine law.
He will appeal to the bar of conscience.

He does not speak.
Stooping down, He slowly, deliberately begins to write in the dust at His feet.
This is the only time we know of His writing anything . . .
    and no one knows what He wrote.

Some ancient scholars believe that He traced there in the dust a catalog of human sin.
Perhaps He looks up at a tall man, with graying hair and piercing blue eyes, and traces the word "Extortioner"—
    and the man turns and flees into the crowd.

Christ looks up into the faces of the men standing in the circle, and steadily—with eyes that never blink—He speaks to them:

"He that is without sin among you,
let him first cast a stone at her" (John 8:7).
His keen glance rests upon the woman's accusers one by one.
Then He writes in the sand at their feet—letter after letter.
They watch His finger—fascinated, as it travels up and
down—up and down.
They cannot watch without trembling.

The group is thinning now.
They think of the recording angel.
They think of judgment.
They have howled for it.
Now it has descended on them.

Looking into their faces, Christ sees into the yesterdays that lie
deep in the pools of memory and conscience.
He sees into their very hearts, and that moving finger writes
on . . .

> Idolater . . .
> Liar . . .
> Drunkard . . .
> Murderer . . .
> Adulterer . . . .

There is the thud of stone after stone falling on the pavement.
Not many of the Pharisees are left.
One by one, they creep away—like animals—slinking into the
shadows . . .
    shuffling off into the crowded streets to lose themselves in
    the multitudes.

"He that is without sin among you, let him first cast a stone at
her."

But the adulteress could not have been unfaithful had not a
man tempted her.
There would be no harlots if men had no evil passions.
Another should have stood with her in condemnation, but she
was alone.

The first lesson Jesus taught that day was that only the guilt-
less have the right to judge.

"Judge not, and ye shall not be judged.
Forgive, and ye shall be forgiven" (Luke 6:37).

But no stones have been thrown.
They lie around the woman on the pavement.
They have dropped them where they stood, and now she is left alone at the feet of Christ.

The stillness is broken only by her sobbing.
She still has not lifted her head . . . .

And now Christ looks at her.
He does not speak for a long moment.

Then, with eyes full of understanding, He says softly:
"Woman, where are those thine accusers?
Hath no man condemned thee?" (John 8:10).
And she answers,
"No man, Lord."

That is all the woman says from beginning to end.
She has no excuse for her conduct.
She makes no attempt to justify what she has done.
And Christ looking at her, seeing the tear-stained cheeks and her eyes red with weeping,
seeing further into her heart,
seeing the contrition there,
says to her:
"Neither do I condemn thee: go, and sin no more" (John 8:11).

What a strange verdict for the Nazarene to pass . . .
There has been no doubt of her guilt, and likewise there is no doubt about His attitude toward it.

What He here says is not that He acquits the woman, but that He forgives her.

Not that He absolves her from blame, but that He absolves her from guilt.
Not that He condones the act, but that He does not condemn her for it—He forgives her instead.

His soft voice is like a candle at twilight,

like a soft angelus at the close of the day . . .
    like the fragrance of a rose in a sickroom . . .
        like the singing of a bird after the storm . . .
It is healing music for a sin-sick heart.

All is quiet for a while.
If she breathes her gratitude, it is so soft that only He hears it.
Or perhaps it is a silent prayer which He and the angels in
heaven alone can interpret.

Perhaps He smiles upon her, as she slowly raises her eyes, a
slow, sad smile of one who knew that He Himself has to pay
the price of that absolution.

And it may be that His finger writes again in the dust, tracing
this time the outline of a cross or the shape of a hill—
    a hill shaped like a skull.

No, we do not know her name
    nor where she lived
        nor who she was.
But of this we can be sure—she was never the same again.
She was a changed woman from that moment. Of that we can
be sure.

She has looked into the eyes of Christ.
She has seen God.
She has been accused
    convicted
        judged but not condemned.
She has been forgiven!

And now her head is up.
Her eyes are shining like stars, for has she not seen the
greatest miracle of all?

It is more wonderful than the miracles of creation . . .
    more beautiful than the flowers . . .
        more mysterious than the stars . . .
            more wonderful than life itself . . .
that God is willing, for Christ's sake, to forgive sinners like
you and me.

For we are *all* sinners . . . guilty of different kinds of sin, no
doubt.

For there are sins of the heart
  and sins of the mind
    and sins of the disposition
as well as sins of the body.

We, too, may be forgiven, no matter what type or kind of
transgressions we have committed.
That we may be forgiven is the greatest miracle of them all.

God is willing to forgive us,
  to cleanse us from all unrighteousness,
because the blood of Jesus Christ, His Son, cleanseth us from
all sin.

That is the basis and the only basis for our forgiveness.

Therefore, "be kind one to another, tenderhearted, forgiving
one another, even as God for Christ's sake hath forgiven you"
(Ephesians 4:32).

We have no greater need today than this—the need of forgiv-
ing one another.
The whole world cries out for forgiveness . . .
Nations need it.
  Society needs it.
    Business, capital, and labor need it.

Homes need it.
  Individual human hearts need it.
    Friends need it.
      Aye—and enemies, too.
We need forgiveness—to be forgiven and to forgive—for with-
out forgiveness, our troubled hearts can know no peace.

But there is a stern condition to be met, if you and I are to be
forgiven . . .
There must be no malice in your heart against anyone in the
whole world.
There must be no refusal on your part to forgive anyone
else . . .
      whatever he or she may have done . . .
    no matter how wrong they were . . .
  or how innocent you were.

If you hug to yourself any resentment against anybody else, you destroy the bridge by which God would come to you. If you do not forgive other people, you yourself can never *feel* forgiven, because you will never *be* forgiven.

How can I be so sure about that?
Simply because Jesus said so . . .
> "But if ye forgive not men their trespasses, neither will your Father forgive your trespasses" (Matthew 6:15).

Jesus was not sentimental about the alternatives.
He was blunt and honest.
In other words, if you will forgive others when they offend you, then your heavenly Father will forgive you too.
But if you refuse to forgive others, then your heavenly Father will not, indeed cannot, forgive you your offenses.

So—if you would have peace in your heart—
   if you would know the forgiveness of God—
it is a case of forgive—or else.

FORGIVE US, LORD JESUS, for the things we have done that make us feel uncomfortable in Thy presence. All the front that we polish so carefully for men to see, does not deceive Thee. For Thou knowest every thought that has left its shadow on our memory. Thou has marked every motive that curdled something sweet within us.

We acknowledge—with bitterness and true repentance—that cross and selfish thoughts have entered our minds; we acknowledge that we have permitted our minds to wander through unclean and forbidden ways; we have toyed with that which we knew was not for us; we have desired that which we should not have.

Make us willing to be changed, even though it requires surgery of the soul and the therapy of discipline.

Make our hearts warm and soft, that we may receive now the blessing of Thy forgiveness, the benediction of Thy "Depart in peace . . . and sin no more."

In Thy name, Amen.

Praying Is Dangerous Business

A few months ago I heard a talk by a university professor, who addressed a civic club.
When the professor had finished, the men were thoughtful and quiet. They went back to their offices and their places of business in a chastened mood, for the professor had sketched a very grim picture.

He was talking about a formula a Jewish professor of mathematics had written on a blackboard in 1913 for the amusement of his students.
Einstein had written this:
$$E = MC^2$$
Energy equals mass multiplied by the square of the speed of light.

Of this formula, *Time* magazine, 32 years later, said that man could forget all that he learned up until now, for this formula had changed everything.
This formula was the first key to the doors leading to atomic power.

The potentialities of this new power are such as to stagger the imaginations of men.
Clearly we are on the threshold of a new world . . .
    with terrific implications.
It all depends on how we use this new energy—
    whether for good or for evil . . .
        whether for humanity or against it.

Man found fire when he learned how to make a spark.
Now fire can be directed by a flame thrower to burn human bodies—
    or it can be used as steady lights gleaming on tall tapers on an altar.

When explosives were discovered, the world shuddered in apprehension at the implications of this dreadful power. Explosives can blow men to bits—when packed inside a shell casing.
   Or they can also be used in a coal mine to dig out coal to keep people warm in winter.

Gasoline drives a tank . . .
   It also drives an ambulance.

Electricity can toast your bread at the breakfast table.
   It is also used in the death house in Sing Sing.

Because thieves have walked in darkness, shall darkness be called a thief?

Not a single one of the new powers discovered by man possesses any redeeming force.
   Neither fire
      nor steam
         nor explosives
            nor electricity
               nor atomic energy
can change his nature.

Man got one power after another . . .
   but they never turned him toward God or made him like God.

As Mr. Fulton Oursler said in a radio address on *The Catholic Hour:*
"It would take another kind of power altogether to make an unhappy man happy
   a bad man good
      a cruel man kind
         and a stupid man wise.

"Yet there is such power freely available in this world, and unless it is used, the atomic bomb,
   like all other useful inventions of man,
will be turned to evil.

"Every Christian knows that redeeming power.
For two thousand years it has been at man's disposal."[11]

The greatest force ever bestowed on mankind streamed forth
in blood
                    and sweat
                    and tears
            and death on Calvary . . .
when Jesus of Nazareth was crucified on the cross.

It was a power so great that it shattered the last fortress—
death.
It was a power so great that it made atonement for all the sin of
all the world.
It was a power so great that it provided for those who would
accept it the ability to live victoriously like children of God,
    in fellowship with Him who made the world and the sun,
    the moon and the stars.

It was a power that would enable believers to do the mighty
works of Christ,
    and to experience, flowing in and through their own lives,
    the energy of God.

Here is a power so tremendous that with it nothing is impossible;
    and without it, nothing we do has any eternal value or
    significance.

It is a power so simple that a child may use it . . . .
Yet we reach for that power only when our hands are clasped
in prayer.

The prayer of faith can move mountains.
It can heal the sick.
    It can overcome the world.
        It can work miracles.
            It "availeth much."

It is like the atomic bomb in at least two particulars:
    It may be just as dangerous . . .
        And it certainly is as little explored.
In very truth, prayer may be our only defense against the evil
implications of the atomic bomb.

Prayer generally is an unexplored field.

Believers have not experimented with prayer, regarding it as
an emergency measure or a conventional practice to be main-
tained,
    much as one's subscription to a series of cultural lectures.

It is culture—and not conviction— that keeps some people
praying.

The whole field of prayer,
    and praying as laying hold on unlimited power,
is unexplored, with the result that spiritual laws still lie un-
discovered by the average believer.

There is an element of danger and risk in all exploration into
new fields.
Every scientist knows that.
Every explorer into the realm of the spiritual will find it just as
true.

In a little pamphlet, I saw a story about a former missionary
who had been stricken by illness and bedridden for eight
years.
During these eight years, she had steadily and persistently
asked God: "Why?"

She could not understand why this incapacitating illness
should lay her aside when she had been doing the Lord's
work.
There was some rebellion in her heart,
    and the drums of mutiny rolled every now and then.

The burden of her prayers was that the Lord should make her
well in order that she might return to do His work.
But nothing happened.
    Her prayers seemed to get nowhere.
She knew that they were not answered,
    and they seemed to be rising no higher than the ceiling.

Finally, worn out with the failure of her prayers, and with a
desperate sort of resignation within her, she prayed:
    "All right, Lord, I give in.
    If I am to be sick for the rest of my life, I bow to Thy will.
    I want to yield to Thy will more than I want anything else
    in the world—even health.

It is for Thee to decide."

Thus leaving herself entirely in God's hands, she began to feel a peace she had not known at any time during her illness. In two weeks she was out of bed, completely well.

Now why did this prayer unlock the very gates of heaven,
    to pour down blessings and health,
whereas the other three thousand prayers had produced no results?

The answer is that somewhere within this missionary's experience is revealed a little-known and rarely understood spiritual law, which, if followed, always works,
    just as the law of gravity works.

The spiritual law in this case is that we must seek and be willing to accept the will of God—
    whatever it may be for us.
Our prayers must not be efforts to bend God to our will or desires—
    but to yield ourselves to His—whatever they may be.

We forget that God sometimes has to say, "No."
We pray to Him as our heavenly Father, and like wise human fathers,
He often says, "No,"
    not from whim or caprice,
        but from wisdom and from love, and knowing what is best for us.

Christ Himself, in the agony of the Garden of Gethsemane, prayed with the certain stipulation that God's will—not His—be done.
It is this factor of divine decision which the skeptic cannot comprehend,
    and which the believer must accept,
that produces answered prayer.

It is this matter of the surrender of our wills to God's will that is hard for us.
It is this unknown factor—sometimes not knowing what *is* God's will in a particular case—that makes praying dangerous

business. Usually we learn how wonderful God's will really is only through experience.

Starr Daily tells of a boy who was desperately ill with infantile paralysis. The mother arrived at the church, weeping—full of fear.
Her minister, Pastor Brown, drew her to one side and asked: "If you knew that it was God's will, would you be willing to let Billy go to heaven?
Could you give him up, if you knew God wanted him?" . . .

After a long struggle with her emotions, she said, "Yes, if I knew for certain it were God's will I'd be willing to release the boy."

Pastor Brown then lifted the child up to God in prayer, surrendering him completely to the mercy and wisdom of God. Three days later the boy was discharged from the hospital with no sign of paralysis left in his body. [12]

Dr. Glenn Clark, who has probably experimented more with this type of prayer—
    the prayer of relinquishment—
than any other contemporary, says that Starr Daily's story is not unusual. The prayer of relinquishment has in it amazing power.

But, you see, it's a dangerous prayer in a sense.
Praying that kind of a prayer is a big adventure.
It's a dangerous business.

Just as soon as we are willing to accept God's decision in the matter about which we are praying,
    whatever it may turn out to be,
then, and not until then, will our prayers be answered.
For God is always far more willing to give us good things than we are anxious to have them.

If we know spiritual laws and pray *with* them,
    instead of *against* them,
the results are certain.
But it is here that we enter into an almost totally unexplored realm.

Men have explored and ferreted out the so-called natural laws
. . . have harnessed them and used them even to making
water to run uphill
   iron to float
     and man to fly.

Very few of us have done any exploring in the hinterland of
spiritual laws.
We do not know them . . .
   so that our praying, for the most part, is a hit-or-miss
   proposition.

Sometimes, in our desperation, we hit upon the right way to
pray, and things happen—
   our prayers are gloriously answered.
But for the most part, our praying is very haphazard,
   and the results are often disappointing.

It is also dangerous business to pray for something unless you
really and truly mean it.
You see, God might call your bluff,
   take you up on it . . .
and would you be surprised!

It is for this reason that it were better for most of us not to sing
some of the hymns we used to sing in Sunday school . . .
   or at revival meetings.

Do you remember when you sang, "I'll go where you want me
to go, dear Lord . . .
   over the mountain,
     or plain,
       or sea.
I'll say what you want me to say, dear Lord.
I'll be what you want me to be"?[13]
Suppose the Lord had taken you up on that one!

Or here is another . . .
   a couple of lines in one of our hymns of consecration:
     "Take my silver and my gold;
     not a mite would I withhold." [14]

Probably you have sung that many a time.

What a shock it would have been if the Lord had taken you up on that one!

Suppose He said, "All right, go, sell your property, cash in your bonds, and give Me that money to use for My needy children." Suppose He did!

Real praying—
    that is, talking with God—
and maintaining communications with Him as Director of your life and activities—demands real honesty.

If our prayers are to avail anything at all, we have to open up every corner of our hearts and minds to Him.
We dare not say one thing with our lips and mean another thing in our hearts.

Being really honest with God does not come easily to any one of us. Sometimes we do not know ourselves very well.

A woman had been ill in bed for a long time.
She had constantly prayed that God would make her well.
She thought she wanted health more than anything in the world.

But one day, as she prayed, it seemed to her that God said, just as He had to the impotent man at the Pool of Bethesda—
    "Do you really *want* to be made well?"

As the woman pondered this strange question, suddenly she realized that there was a sense in which she had grown fond of her quiet life
        no dishes to wash
    none of the petty details of living
all the time she wanted to read and think . . . .

She saw that God's will for her was health, all right, but that it was actually going to stretch her to attain it.

"Climb out of bed," Christ said to her.
    "As you take up active life again, you'll get well."
And she did get well.

Yes, it is very hard really to be honest.

But when we are honest with God, He is equally honest with us.
He will take any promises or pledges we make to Him at their face value.

He has a way of calling our bluff.
That is why praying is dangerous business.

I once heard about a man who knew that he needed patience more than anything else.
He knew that impatience was his worst fault.
And it kept him perfectly miserable.

So he began to pray for patience.
What do you think happened?

He secured a new secretary . . .
    and lo and behold, she was the slowest secretary the man
    had ever seen or heard of.
The girl almost drove him crazy.

The poor businessman was almost frantic when, one day, it occurred to him that this was God's answer to his prayer for patience.
And when he understood how God had answered his prayer, he began to learn patience.

But God—who surely must have a sense of humor—had used an exasperatingly slow secretary to teach the lesson.
The businessman learned patience all right.
He also learned that you had better mean what you say when you ask God for something.

Another reason why praying is dangerous business is that when God answers prayer, we have to follow His guidance
    or take the consequences.

A friend of ours in a nearby city had been out of a job for several months.
Finally, there came an offer from a firm in Michigan.
They asked him to come out for an interview.
He decided to go.

Meanwhile, he prayed that if God did not want him to take this position, He would close the door in his face.

This was to be the sign.

Well, God heard the prayer and took it at simple face value.
Our friend had the interview.

The deal was not closed just then,
    for the president of the firm wanted more time to consider
it.
A week passed by.

Then the offer came,
    with a very attractive salary.
But our friend was confused with the week's silence, so that he
was not sure that it was God's will that he take it.

Then came a telegram substantially raising the salary.
Finally, completely confused by side issues, he turned it
down.

Now what was the result?

In the end he accepted a local position at half the pay,
    with an employer who had an ungovernable temper,
        and made his life completely miserable.
Now he clearly sees his mistake.

He had asked God to use a particular sign . . .
    namely, that the door would be closed, if it was God's will
    that he should not go to Michigan.
Instead of that,
    the door was opened very wide,
        and every inducement offered him to go ahead.

But apparently our friend simply couldn't believe that such
was the case.
The result was that he spent the most miserable months of his
life living out his mistake.

That is why I say praying is dangerous business.

Here again is a matter that many of us overlook when we ask
God to do something.
We forget that God may require something of the one who
prays.
Often He wants us to help answer the prayer.

The answer to a particular prayer may involve some real effort . . .
  maybe even some sacrifice.

I have yet to see a seriously threatened marriage in which all the blame was on one side.
Sometimes a wife, as she prays about her marriage, asks God to change her husband—
and is promptly shown something that *she* must change.

Prayer can help to make us clear-eyed about our own short-comings.
  That isn't always pleasant.

You've got to be ready to be shown uncomfortable things
    to do your part
  to do anything God tells you
if you really want your prayer answered.

God's method in answering almost any prayer is the head-on, straightforward approach.

It calls for courage as well as faith.
It's the march-into-the-Red-Sea-and-it-divides method . . .
  or march-right-up-to-the-walls-and-they-fall-down
  technique.

You've got to have faith for that sort of venture . . .
  and courage too.
That's why some prayers may be dangerous.

You set out, under God's guidance, on a course that seems almost foolhardy . . .
But you keep going,
  if you really mean it . . .
and God works His wonderful works.

But there are times when you are "sweating it out," as they said in the Air Force.

Yes, praying can be dangerous business . . .
For God expects us never to question that He is a God of love . . .
  who loves us each one individually.

It is a wonderful idea, once it gets hold of you, that God loves
you,
    whoever you are . . . for yourself.
You are precious to Him.
    He loves *you*.
        He wants you to be happy.
            He wants to give you good things.
It is His will for you that life should be full,
        abundant . . .
    and rich.

He expects us to believe that He holds us in the hollow of His
hand,
    and that we are safe for all eternity.

This does not mean that no trouble shall come to us—
    or that we will never get sick—
        or that no sorrow shall ever touch us.

On the contrary, we are told very bluntly by Jesus Himself that
in this world we shall have trouble.

But then He says:
    "Cheer up! I have overcome the world.
    My grace is sufficient for you.
    I am with you always, even unto the end of the world"
    (Matthew 28:20).

In the words of Paul:
    "We know that all things work together for good to them
    that love God . . . " (Romans 8:28).
God will not permit any troubles to come upon us, unless He
has a specific plan by which great blessing can come out of the
difficulty.

To believe this calls for strong faith and no little courage . . .
    but it shuts out all bitterness and rebellion against our
circumstances.
And when trouble comes,
    no matter what form it takes,
we can then turn it over to Him and ask Him to open the door
in the wall.

Nothing gives the Lord greater pleasure than to help His children.
But unless you really mean it,
    praying can be dangerous business.

Inventions can never save mankind.
Redeeming grace will come
    not from a laboratory . . . but from an altar,
        in your home and in your heart.

"The hope of the world in this atomic age lies," as Mr. Oursler said,
    "not in physics
        but in prayer."

$E = MC^2$ . . .
Yes, that may be true.

But this is the truth that will save us all—Psalm 37:4 and 7.

"Rest in the Lord . . .
wait patiently for Him . . .
And He shall give thee the desires of thine heart."

O GOD, OUR FATHER, history and experience have given us so many examples of Thy guidance to nations and to individuals that we should not doubt Thy power or willingness to direct us. Give us the faith to believe that when You want us to do or not to do any particular thing, You will find a way of letting us know it. In Jesus' name, Amen.

Book IV

Heaven Can't Wait

*We need a faith that is as real as fire
. . . and prayer that is as real as potatoes.*

While the sermons in this section will be of particular interest to the young, the book from which they were taken was not directed exclusively to them. It could not be, because Peter Marshall never segregated young people, never talked down to them or patronized them. Rather, his appeal to the young, as well as to those of any age, was the ever-zestful, youthful exuberance of his own inner spirit.

Peter Marshall had not long been pastor of the New York Avenue Church before the old-timers were afraid that the staid and historic Washington church was being turned into a youth center. Twenty-five young voices in the chorus-choir. A canteen all during World War II. A Sunday evening youth service. A young adult Sunday school class which Dr. Marshall himself taught. Busloads of students from private schools for the regular Sunday morning service.

"We kids liked Peter Marshall," one high school student commented, "because he spoke our language. And he put the responsibility of what we made of our lives directly on us."

Today the hunger in young people for answers may be even greater than when Dr. Marshall was alive. Today's young want the truth—even when it hurts.

The truth was what Peter Marshall always gave them. That must be a big clue as to why the young in heart continue to clamor for more of the man—his insights and wisdom, his ability to make God pertinent to everyday life.

The title of this volume, *Heaven Can't Wait,* is not based on the Hollywood film released several years ago. Peter's sermon of this title, itself borrowed from a popular song, preceded the film by several decades! The name under which the book first appeared, *John Doe, Disciple,* is taken from another sermon (one of seven included in this section), and is meant to challenge every one of us, old or young: "Would you, John Doe, be a disciple today were Christ to reappear? Would you have the courage? Would you make the sacrifices?"

Indeed, more than thirty years after Peter's death, the Lord he served is still looking for recruits.

C. M

Under Sealed Orders

I do not know what picture the phrase *under sealed orders* suggests to you.
To me it recalls very vividly a scene from the first World War, when I was a little boy spending vacations at a Scottish seaport.

I saw a gray destroyer slipping hurriedly from port in response to some urgent commands . . .
I watched the crew hurry their preparations for sailing,
    watched them cast off the mooring hawsers . . .
saw the sleek ship get under way, as she rose to meet the lazy ground swell of a summer evening . . .
Her Morse lamp was winking on the control bridge aft, and I watched her until she was lost in the mists of the North Sea.

She was a mystery vessel.
She had sailed under sealed orders.
Not even her officers knew her destination or the point of rendezvous.

We all start out in life, going—we know not where.
It will be revealed later.
But meanwhile we must go out in faith—
            under sealed orders.

So, in like manner, all the pioneers of faith have gone out—
and all the explorers—
    Abraham of old
      Columbus
        Magellan
          John Smith
            Peary
              Lindbergh
                Byrd.

Abraham stands out among the Old Testament heroes as the leading example of this kind of faith.

In the Epistle to the Hebrews we are told:

"By faith Abraham . . . went out, not knowing whither he went" (Hebrews 11:8).

Here was Abraham, a mature and successful man, having established himself in Ur of the Chaldees.

Then God spoke to him:

"Get thee out of thy country, and from thy kindred, and from thy father's house, unto a land that I will shew thee: And I will make of thee a great nation, and I will bless thee, and make thy name great . . . and in thee shall all families of the earth be blessed" (Genesis 12:1-3).

Try to imagine what was involved in obeying this guidance.
Abraham had to sever all his business connections,
    uproot himself
procure supplies for a new and strange way of life.
He was giving up the comforts and conveniences of a world he knew to live as a nomad under canvas with no settled abode.

From a common-sense point of view, it was crazy.
Doubtless Abraham had many friends who told him just that.
Where was he going?
Well, he did not know exactly.
What was he going to do?
He was going to found a new nation somewhere else.
Found a new nation?
What was he talking about?

He and his wife did not even have any children, and they were getting on in years.
Abraham himself was seventy-five!
What kind of crazy talk was that?

Nevertheless,
Abraham carried out his decision.
He left Ur of the Chaldees.
He did it because of a spiritual insight—an insight which for him had the authority of a direct command from God.

And God kept His part of the bargain.

Abraham was led to Canaan.

In their old age, he and his wife Sarah had a son—Isaac.

"I will multiply thy seed as the stars of the heaven . . . and in thy seed shall all the nations of the earth be blessed," God had promised.

And it came to pass.

For this pioneer of faith became the father of the Hebrew nation.

And through him, all men everywhere have been blessed— for Jesus Christ Himself was to be one of Abraham's descendants.

Some people find it difficult to believe that human beings like us, like Abraham, can get direct guidance from God,
        can have their lives ordered by Him.

They ask, "But surely you don't believe that God speaks directly
    specifically
as I am speaking to you now?
You don't mean that God sends telegrams?"

Now the Bible always speaks of God saying to His children this and that . . . "And God said unto Abraham . . . "
            "God said unto Moses . . . "
Was that just for Bible times?

If you have never had an experience of God's guidance in your life, you may question how it comes.

No doubt it comes in various ways to different people.

I cannot fully explain it, but I have to believe it, because I have had many experiences of God's guidance which were for me just as dramatic and critical as the guidance that came to Abraham.

I was given an opportunity to leave Scotland and come to this country, and I asked God what I should do about it.

I asked God in the only way we have to ask Him—through prayer.

I prayed and waited for the answer.

I believed that the answer would come; I did not know when or how.

For three weeks I waited with some impatience, I must confess, and at the end of that time, the answer came, and God told me to go.

I could not accurately describe what was a subjective experience.

I did not see the answer written in the sky, nor yet upon the wall of my room.

But I knew—positively, definitely, that God had said, "Yes, go."

I remember well the spot where the answer came.
It was on a beautiful Sunday afternoon outside Glasgow.
I was walking down a path lined with rhododendron on the Sholto-Douglas estate when I heard the voice.
Now, whether it sounded like a voice outside of me or inside of me, I cannot tell.
But I knew it was the voice of God.
I was positive that the answer for which I had prayed had come, and I acted upon it immediately by making application for a visa to enter the United States as a quota immigrant.

Well do I remember on the nineteenth of March, 1927, standing on the afterdeck of the *Cameronia*, watching with moist eyes the purple hills of Mull of Kintyre sinking beneath the screw-threshed waters of the Atlantic, when every turn of the propeller was driving me farther from the land of my birth—from all I knew and loved.

And then—I walked slowly and wonderingly for'ard until I was leaning over the prow.
I stood looking into the west,
    wondering what lay beyond that tumbling horizon—
    wondering what the unknown tomorrow held for me.

I, too, was going out in faith, not knowing whither I went.
I was leaving the tube mill, where I had been working in the machine shop.
I was coming to the United States to enter the ministry, because I believed with all my heart that those were my orders from my Chief.

But I did not know how
         or when
         or where.

I could not foresee the wonderful way in which God would
open doors of opportunity.
I could never have imagined the thrilling way in which God
was to arrange my life . . .
                    order my ways
                    guide my steps
                    provide for all my needs
                    give me wonderful friends, generous helpers
until, at last, I would achieve His plan for me, and be ordained
a minister of the gospel.

It is an amazing adventure simply to be born upon this wan-
dering island in the sky, to make a temporary home on this
rolling ball of matter . . .
To go to school
   to make friends
      to marry
         to choose a career and to develop it,
to rear children and assume life's responsibilities;
to face life with its swift changes of circumstances that no man
can certainly predict an hour ahead—
      These are all adventures.
And it is an adventure to leave it when death calls and "Taps"
sounds for you at the close of life's day.

Each new day is like an hitherto unvisited country which we
enter— like Abraham leaving Ur for a strange land—
      "not knowing whither he went."
And every new year we begin a tour of exploration into twelve
months where no man's foot has ever walked before.

If we all love tales of pioneers, it is because from the time we
are weaned until the time we die—life is pioneering.
With all his science, with all his new insights and tools for
conquering the unknown, man must face each day as Paul
faced his journey to Rome—"not knowing the things that shall
befall him there."

As you stand peering into the future—you cannot see what
tomorrow will bring.
You cannot even tell as you look upon Grandfather Time
whether his indistinct features are smiling or frowning . . . .
And his hand behind his back—does it hold a bouquet
                                          or a brickbat?

Is there no way, then, that we can know the future?
Shall we go—you and I—to some wizened old hag, cross her
palm with silver, and permit her to spread fanlike before us a
deck of cards so that she may tell us what the future holds?
Shall we listen to her as she interprets a fair lady or a dark
knave as the message of a deuce or a trey?

Can it be that the drawing of a card will signify
the career we shall follow,
     or the girl we shall marry,
          or the family we shall have?
Nonsense!
There are so many things that even the most educated among
us do not know!
Things that no faculty can teach us . . .
     that no textbooks can contain . . .
          that no man can foresee or prophesy.

I urge you then simply to go out in faith—even as Abraham
                              Columbus
                    or the Pilgrim Fathers
and all the host of pioneers of the centuries.

Yet this is not easy.
Today we must send young people into a changing world
     where old concepts are being discarded,
          old theories exploded,
               where standards are constantly changing—
into this unknown they must go, whether they like it or not.

But then is everything so uncertain, you ask?
Is there nothing on which I can rely?

Yes, there is an assurance that can help you to confidently and
successfully face the unknown vistas of all the tomorrows.
It is an assurance given to us in the old Book:

"But I trusted in Thee, O Lord:
I said, Thou art my God.
My times are in Thy hand" (Psalm 31:14-15).

If you trust in God, if you are willing to give your life to Him,
then, and only then, will you have no fear.
For no matter where you go, He will be with you.
You can never wander from the pathway, for He will lead you.

Some people speak of *luck* and accord it a great and determin-
ing place in their lives.
>   They trust to luck,
>   they count on it, live by it.
>   They cross their fingers, knock on wood,
>   look for four-leaf clovers and carry rabbits' feet.
But I would not dare wish you or anyone else "luck"
because there is no such thing as luck!
Others speak of "accidents"—and make allowance for the
happening of accidents—regard certain events as purely accidental. Yet are there really such things as accidents?

Was the creation of the world an accident?
Are the laws that maintain the universe accidental?
Ask Eddington
>   or Jeans
>   or Milliken
>   or Einstein.

Were the prophecies of the Old Testament accidental?
Was the birth of Jesus Christ an accident?
It was no accident that Judas printed the kiss of betrayal on the
fair cheek of Jesus!
The old rugged cross was no accident!
Paul's conversion was not an accident!
The work of Martin Luther was no accident!

Was it an accident that John and Charles Wesley were rescued
from a burning house, as they themselves described it, "like
brands from the burning"?

Is this nation of ours an accident?
Were George Washington and the Declaration of Independence,

Abraham Lincoln and the Emancipation Proclamation purely accidental?

Is a rose an accident—merely the coming together of ca-
pricious factors in nature?

I shall not soon forget the words of Dr. W. R. Whitney, a past
president of the American Chemical Society,
    fellow of the American Academy of Arts and Sciences,
        director of many vast electrical researches, as he made the
        simplest of all experiments.

Dr. Whitney picked up from his desk a small bar magnet. He
brought this near a steel needle, and the needle leaped to the
magnet.
Why?
Dr. Whitney said:
    "We have worked out elaborate explanations.
    We speak learnedly of lines of force.
    We draw a diagram of the magnetic field.

"Yet we know that there are no lines there and the *field* is just a
word to cover our ignorance.
Our explanations are only educated guesses.

"Or consider," Dr. Whitney continued, "the beam of light that
comes speeding from a star, traveling hundreds of years.
Finally it reaches your optic nerve, and you *see* the star.

"How does that happen?
We have our corpuscular theory of light,
    our wave theory,
        our quantum theory.
But they are all just educated guesses.

"So," explained Dr. Whitney, "after we are all finished with
our theories and our guesses, we are still backed up against
the fact of God—the will of God at work in what we call
'science.'"

Thus an eminent scientist looks beyond science (that some
still think infallible and the source of all answers) for guidance.

Many of our scientific theories and explanations are only
educated guesses.

The day before yesterday, the atom was thought of as whirling particles but that is outmoded now.
Yesterday the atom was described as a wave in space, according to Schrödinger's theory; that too is outmoded.

Today the atom has been split and developed into the greatest explosive force in the history of mankind.
No, the theory of relativity is not final.
No scientific concept stands still.

All is in motion, because we are forever in the process of discovering more of what God has placed in this world.

But the will of God, the laws we discover
            but cannot always understand
        or explain,
the will of God alone is final.

No, there are no accidents.
God is still the ruler of His universe and of our lives,
                            yours and mine.

So, even though you go out, not knowing whither you go,
        you can go confidently, like Abraham,
provided you can say with the psalmist:
    "My times are in Thy hand."

God knows each one of you, and He has a plan for *you*.
God made one you—and only one.
Nobody who ever lived was quite as you are now.
God gave you life for a purpose, and if you fail to fulfill it, that purpose will never be realized.

I long for all you young people to know the full fellowship of the Christian life . . .
    what it is to be guided by the Lord into the very place where He wants you to be . . .
        to know when you make decisions that you are doing what He wants you to do.

Not only ministers can find God's will; so too can clerks
                            and secretaries
                        and engineers
                        and waitresses

and salesmen
and bus drivers.

If you only knew the peace that comes with the conviction that
you are in the place where God wants you to be . . . and that
you are doing the thing for which He created you.
What a difference it makes!

To Abraham, God spoke directly and specifically.
Nowadays, since the advent of Jesus Christ, I believe that God
speaks to you and me through the Holy Spirit.
Indeed, we are told in the Scriptures that it is the function of
the Holy Spirit to guide us,
    to lead us into all truth.

So the Holy Spirit is available to guide us in everything:
    A young man into his life work,
        A young woman into the friendship out of which will
        grow love and marriage to the man of God's choice for
        her.
            A family can be led to the city where God wants them to
            live . . .
            A businessman can be guided to make the right
            decisions.

No, that is not silly, it is not fanaticism.
Nor does it do violence to human responsibility.
As soon as you try living this way, you will find that God's
purpose for your life is maximum creativity, achievement, and
responsibility—not less.

Others object to the idea that the Lord of the universe could
possibly be concerned about the details of millions of lives. Yet
this glorious truth could never have been imagined. Jesus said
it was so, and He would never raise false hopes in a human
heart.

Jesus' emphasis was always upon the one—the single soul.
Consider His parables—the story of the lost coin,
                of the one lost sheep,
            and of the lone lost boy.

    " . . . the very hairs of your head are all numbered"
(Matthew 10:30).

" . . . your heavenly Father knoweth that ye have need of all these things" (Matthew 6:32).

In this viewpoint, Jesus was being realistic about human life. The truth is that our lives are made up of the sum of the small decisions
 the little turnings
  the minute choices.
If we do not let God into these everyday details, practically speaking we are not letting Him in at all.

Would you like to have God's guidance for your life?
If you would, first you have to believe that He can guide you.

But faith is not belief.
Faith is belief plus what you do with that belief.

I might have believed intellectually that God could guide me, indeed, that I had heard His voice that afternoon in the park. But that would have counted for nothing, had I not gone on to act on that belief by applying for my number as a quota immigrant.
Belief becomes faith only at the point of action.

First of all, if you want to hear God, you will have to face up squarely to the question,
 "Am I willing to follow His plan wherever it may lead?"
 "Am I willing to do whatever He tells me to do?"

This is a decision that must be resolved before you can receive any guidance from God,
 before your Christian adventure can begin.

How hard it is for our proud wills to bow the neck and call Him "Master and Lord"!
Yet bow we must, if we are to understand what life is all about, if we are to take even the first step toward maturity,
       or fulfillment,
     or greatness.

Understand that this is no craven slavery Christ asks of us:
 "Henceforth I call you not servants; for the servant knoweth not what his lord doeth; but I have called you friends . . . "
 (John 15:15).

A friend of Jesus!
No knight of old ever had a greater privilege.
He who bows before this One—joyously to hand over his life
and his future—
    finds himself raised to knighthood,
       received into the inner circle,
          immediately heir to all the rights and privileges of the
          King.

But the move is ours . . .
Are you willing to tell God now that you will follow His plan
wherever it may lead?

This is important because God has given us free will, and this
He will never violate.
He holds in a more profound respect than any of us could the
sanctity of every human personality.
Therefore He requires the consent of our wills before He will
enter our hearts and lives.

And it is just at this point that many of us are in the grip of a
terrible conflict:
We want to hear God speaking to us . . .
    but we are afraid of what we might hear.

We want to be made clean . . .
    but there is still a hunger for the husks the swine eat.
We would follow Christ . . .
    but we don't want our friends to think us odd.
We want God's way . . .
    but we also want our own way.

There is an answer to our dilemma . . .
Tell Christ honestly about our divided will . . .
              our divided self.

Ask Him to take that over and make it whole.
And He will!

It may be that His plan for you will not be revealed for some
time.
You will have to keep close to Him, keep listening for His
signals.

His plan for you may be a gradual development.

There are a thousand ways in which He may use you.
You may have to make some changes in your life,
        break with some of your present companions,
      change some of your habits . . .
I cannot tell you that—but He can.

He will send His power surging into you,
      to give you power to defeat temptations.
    to chase away your fears,
  to give you a quiet heart,
to make you joyous and free.

We are living in a hazardous epoch of history.
The wind . . . the earthquake . . . and the fire of old are here,
in fact, the threat of more terrible fire than man ever thought
possible.

It would be tragedy indeed if the still, small voice of God's
wisdom and direction is not heard at such a time.
You are leaving port under sealed orders and in a troubled
period.
You cannot know whither you are going or what you are to do.
But why not take a Pilot on board who knows the nature of
your sealed orders from the outset,
  and who will shape your entire voyage accordingly?

He knows the shoals and the sandbanks,
        the rocks and the reefs.

He will steer you safely into that celestial harbor where your
anchor will be cast for eternity.
Let His mighty nail-pierced hands hold the wheel, and you
will be safe.

Now is a splendid time to entrust your life to Him, *now, as you
begin.*
Give Him your life.
He will treasure it, even as you.

Then, though you may not know what will be your harbor,
you will know your Pilot . . .
And all will be well.

John Doe, Disciple

T here are many of you who think of Christ as someone
who belongs to history—like Caesar,
                    or Washington,
                    or Napoleon.
You think of Him as one who lived on earth and passed away.
A great man, to be sure, but nothing more.

Perhaps you look on His life as an affecting sacrifice,
                              a great inspiration.
He was a Wise Teacher, you say, but beyond that Christ is not
really significant for you.

Or do you have an inner contempt for the mild, suffering
Jesus so often pictured?
It is a curious thing that the artists whose brushes have traced
His form on canvas have largely portrayed His gentleness,
                              meekness
                              compassion
                              suffering . . .
rather than the other, equally true sides of His personality . . .
                    strength
                    tireless energy
                    uncompromising will.

Perhaps it is this one-sided picture of the meek and long-
suffering Christ that you and I *want* to see.
Perhaps it is the picture that more nearly suits our generation
with its broadmindedness
    its easygoing compromises
        its scorn of hell
            its denial of the reality of sin.

But when we throw away our preconceived ideas and turn to
the New Testament for ourselves, we come away with an
altogether different conception.

There is a true picture of Christ in the Gospel of John—a dramatic scene in the Temple of Jerusalem near the beginning of Jesus' public ministry.
It is His first appearance before His nation as the Messiah.

No one could forget it . . . Jesus walking through the colonnade with its marble forest of great Corinthian pillars a hundred feet high, then on into the Court of the Gentiles.

It is early morning, but already the Temple court is a bedlam of activity and noise.
Among the tables of the moneychangers, the cages of doves and the stalls of cattle, people crowd about
                    chatting with their friends,
                    selecting a dove for sacrifice,
or getting their money from Tyre or Persia or Egypt or Greece changed into the sacred half-shekel of the sanctuary.
It is convenient to buy sacrifices on the spot instead of having to drag them from a distance.
It is helpful to be able to exchange money bearing upon it the head of the emperor, a graven image and therefore unacceptable in the Temple, for the statutory half-shekel.

And so, convenient for all and profitable to many, the Temple huckstering has become a recognized institution.
Shrill voices bargaining
    swearing angrily
      bickering
the metallic tinkle of coins as they drop into the moneyboxes on the table . . .
all the signs of greed can be heard just outside the Holy Place.
There is no serenity—no peace.
No one can pray there.

Suddenly there is a lull in the confusion.
Startled at the sudden quiet, we look up to find a strange yet hauntingly familiar figure standing between two of the gigantic stone columns, His eyes burning with intensity,
              His face magnificent in its wrath.
Poor peasants are being bled in the name of God.
Has He not watched His own mother patching clothes,

skimping on food
to save one denarius after another for the Temple dues?

As He steps forward with a resolution and firmness born of
the terrible conviction that shines in His face, there is a look in
His eyes before which men break away.
His lips are drawn into a thin line . . .

Stooping, He picks up some binding cords which the merchants have discarded.
Deftly He knots them into a whip.

There is something in His attitude,
                in His eyes,
              in His face,
in that ominous silence in which He stands watching, which
makes men look at Him with uneasiness in their eyes.

And then the full fury of His wrath breaks.
In a few long strides He is across the court.
Picking up the boxes filled with money—scornfully and deliberately—He empties them on the stone floor . . . and the coins
spill with a clatter and go rolling in a hundred directions.

The tables too go crashing to the floor, and the moneychangers rush to gather up their coins from the filth.
In their greed—made all the more frantic because of their
fear—they grovel in the dirt, pouncing upon their money and
screaming in protest as the Man with the whip stands over
them.

And then He drives out the terror-stricken cattle.
The muscles of His arms stand out like cords;
    lights dart from His eyes.

Not a voice is heard in protest . . .
    not a hand is raised against Him.
Even the Temple guards only stand and watch helplessly.
His magnificent figure dominates the scene.

His voice rings out, echoing among the stone pillars, and it
sounds like the voice of doom . . .

like the voice of God Himself . . .
"It is written, My house shall be called the house of prayer, but
ye have made it a den of thieves."

Who is this Christ?

He is a Man whose impact on people who listened to Him
must have been more like dynamite than dew.
One cannot read the Gospels without reaching the conclusion
that there was something disturbing about the march of the
Galilean through the land.
Everywhere He went there was anything but peace.
  Debates and arguments buzzed around Him.

If men did not come to Him with questions,
He challenged their thinking with questions of His own.
He made men wonder about themselves . . .
look into their hearts and see things they had not seen before.
He made them ponder about life and what it meant.

Who is this Christ?

In talking to young people I have the feeling that there is
confusion about Jesus . . . .
To many, He is a dim shadowy figure . . . almost a stranger.

You have heard echoes of His Person . . .
  rumors of His movements in the hearts and lives of people
  around you.
But again and again you have missed Him—as though He
were some romantic figure moving about the pitched tents of
an army at night.
You have heard stories of Him whispered around the camp-
fires before which young people seek to warm their souls.

Yet, always you miss Him and grow weary in the search until
you question in your heart His mysterious Person. The fact is
that you really have not met Him face-to-face.
An introduction may help.
John Doe, I would like you to meet One who means everything to me . . .
John Doe, meet Jesus of Nazareth.

This Christ—whence did He come?

His home was in an obscure village of an occupied Roman province.
He was born in a stable where animals from the inn were kept.
His parents were poor working people.
The only records we have of Him are silent about the greater part of His life.
This remains one of the most intriguing historical mysteries of all time.

There are hints that after Joseph's death He took over the family carpentry shop—first in Nazareth, then in Capernaum.

His formal education was in the local synagogue school, and it stopped when He was twelve.
He left no writings.
Indeed, the only record of His having written anything is one of finger tracings in the sand . . . and the eddies of wind that swirled around the pillars of the Temple porch soon covered it up.

He spoke Aramaic, the traditional Hebrew, and probably a smattering of Greek and Latin, for He lived in a trilingual world.
Never did He travel more than a hundred miles from home.
Standing on the Mount of Olives He could look over the length and breadth of His country . . . which He never left during His life.

When He began His public ministry and took to preaching, His family tried to talk Him out of it, thinking and saying that He was mad.

His friends were mostly as poor as He was—fishermen and peasants.
See Him mingling with the forgotten men,
        talking to the outcasts,
      knowing no social barriers,
    caring nothing for money or material things,
  going about with publicans and sinners
until many of His contemporaries were scandalized.

He attracted great crowds, for He walked among the sick,

> touching here a blind eye
> there a palsied limb
> here a running sore
> there a crippled leg.

Even His enemies were later to admit these miracles.

But finally the crowds drifted away, for His counsels were too difficult; men were not ready to accept this hard way of love.
And so the sands ran out and His three-year ministry drew to its close.
At one point, He feared His own followers might also melt away.
In the end, most of them did flee in fear, caring more for their own safety than for Him.

He died a criminal's death, reviled and mocked . . .
> tormented and laughed at,
> hanging between two thieves.
> They buried Him in a borrowed grave.

But the story was not finished.
Suddenly His disciples, the same men who had run away, came back boldly into the streets of the city which had crucified Christ, proclaiming that He was not dead at all—
He was alive.

The body with the marks of the nails and the spikes had disappeared.
On this everyone was agreed.
There were many attempted explanations, but somehow none was adequate.
All that His enemies had to do to silence forever the rumor of this resurrection was to produce the body—but they could not.

Whatever anyone else in Jerusalem thought, it was obvious that Christ's disciples were convinced beyond any doubt that their Master was alive.
For they were different—not the same men at all.
They were no longer afraid.
They spoke boldly.
Threats did not intimidate them.

They said fantastic things—that the living God had once and for all, in a brief life on this earth, given a full and final revelation of Himself in Christ.

In Jesus—God had come!

They said that, within thirty-six hours of Christ's death, the dead body had become alive,

had walked out of the grave,

appeared to many human witnesses—to *them*.

Among the pillars of the Temple porch itself, their ringing assertions echoed and reverberated:

"This Jesus whom ye crucified is risen from
the dead and now demands that every man repent."

As you would suppose, such a message was laughed at.
"These men are drunk" was the first popular verdict.
Then, "They must be mad."

The wild story traveled fast . . . to Asia Minor . . . to Rome. There was derisive laughter—"Just another superstitious cult." Was not the world of that day satiated with cults and bizarre manmade religions?

But then this Jesus began to be talked about too much and the Roman Empire tried to stop the story's spreading by force and threats.
"Don't tell these tales again," the disciples were told, "if you value your lives."

But they did not stop.
The threats only made them more eloquent and bold.

Thrown into prison, they made the cell a pulpit and the dungeon a choir.
Stoned, they rose from the dust bleeding and bruised, but with a more convincing testimony.
Lashed with whips, they praised God the more.

Nothing could stop them.
The Romans made human torches of believers to light the arenas on their holidays.
Yet in death, these Christian martyrs made converts to their strange preaching.

Hunted and persecuted,
   thrown to the lions,
      tortured and killed,
still the number of those who made the sign of the cross
grew . . .
   and grew.
Rome could not stop Jesus.
Her grandeur toppled and fell; Jesus lived on.
What the Empire had regarded as a ripple on the wide sea of
polytheism became a tidal wave sweeping over the world.
Incredibly, in A.D. 325 under the Emperor Constantine,
Christianity won official recognition from the Empire which
had once vowed to crush every last follower of the Nazarene.

In all of history, has there ever been such an extraordinary
sequence of events?
Who is this Jesus?
What is the explanation of His power?

Etched against the skyline of every city,
   carried in the forefront of every human endeavor,
   the cross on which He died has become a haunting
symbol of a haunting Person.
Christ is an end . . . and a beginning.
All secular history is divided into two great divisions:
                  before Christ—
                  after Christ.

In an old document, Celsus—a Roman historian— trying to
explain the strange power of Christianity in his day, wrote:

   "The importance of Christianity is the excessive value it
   places on every human soul."

Jesus insisted that God's interest centered on the individual.
His is the power that sets the prisoners free, in whatever
bondage they languish.
Testimonies are without number.
Changed lives all ascribe the glory to Him.
It is to Him that credit belongs for the newness of life and the
victories that men and women have achieved.

How many are there who will testify to this power?

The power that saves
that forgives
that leads and guides through life.
There it is . . . a mystery and a power!

But it is more than the power of an idea or a philosophy; more
than the memory of a good and great Man.
He is a Presence now—even now.
"Lo, I am with you always," He once said—and many of us
have found it true—gloriously true.

Part of the mystery is this: that He lived nineteen centuries
ago, in the faraway little land of Palestine.
He wore Oriental robes and sandals.
Yet His words and His presence are as real and as relevant as if
He had spoken last night on the radio in English
from New York or San Francisco.
Even in our days of neon signs and penthouses, of skyscrap-
pers and fast air travel, He is authoritative, the last word for
us.

There is no shortage of evidence that the ethical teaching of
Christ is eternally and everlastingly right.
Our best minds today are willing to admit that a great many
things on which we pinned our hopes have failed us misera-
bly.

Man has supposed that his new heaven and his new earth will
come through materialism . . .
having two cars for every garage,
a television set in every living room
an electric dishwasher and clothes drier.
Somehow these have not brought about the desired results.

Nor has secularism made life happier or easier.
We are all becoming aware with a sickness of heart that a
civilization whose art ends in surrealism . . .
whose music ends in discord,
whose literature ends in the airing of sexual license and
sexual deviations,
whose science ends in the power to destroy civilization . . .

can never satisfy the soul of the world or the hunger of the
human heart.

An assistant of Thomas A. Edison once tried to console the
inventor over the failure to achieve in a series of experiments
what he had set out to find.

"It's too bad," he said, "to do all that work without results."
"Oh," said Mr. Edison, "we have lots of results. We know
seven hundred things that won't work."

By this time we ought to know a good many things that will
not work in our world . . .
You and I have even found out one or two philosophies of our
own that have not brought us peace or happiness.

Still that haunting Figure stands in our midst.
Read the New Testament for yourself and see if this same
Jesus does not step out of the pages to stand beside you
     with His piercing eyes and His quiet vibrant voice—
                         like the voice of God—
"Follow Me," He says. "Follow Me . . . "
"Whom say *ye* that I am?"

What then are you to reply, John Doe?
Have you answered that question in your own mind?
Has your heart whispered its response?
It is a question you cannot dodge forever.

It is today as it was in His day.
When He walked the trails of Palestine, men tried to be neu-
tral and found that they could not.
Try as they might to brush Him aside—on whatever pretext
                         they could not have done with Him.

There has always been a quality about Jesus that was urgent.
It had to be accepted—or rejected.
He forced the issue because of the claims He made for Him-
self.

Consider those claims . . .
He claimed equality with God . . .

   "I and my Father are one" (John 10:30).
   "He that hath seen me hath seen the Father" (John 14:9).

He claimed to be the fulfillment of Old Testament prophecy.
He stated that before Abraham was born, He had lived . . .
  He said that He had come from God in heaven, and that
  He would return to His Father.

Such talk was not misunderstood by the Jews.
Jesus meant that it should be understood, and it was.
Knowing full well the meaning of what He had claimed,
they howled for His death . . . .

  "Therefore the Jews sought the more to kill him, because
  he . . . said also that God was his Father, making himself
  equal with God" (John 5:18).

Christ accepted the worship of men.
He took it as His right, accepted it as His prerogative.
When Simon Peter or Thomas or many another worshiped
Him, He did not say, "Stand up on your feet, for I am like
yourselves."
He took their worship and breathed upon them His benediction.

He affirmed His sinlessness.
The challenge He hurled, "Which one of you accuseth Me of
sin?", found none to speak against Him.
It is the testimony of the friends who knew Him best,
  of the enemies who loved Him least.

"I find no fault in this Man," said Pontius Pilate wonderingly.

"This Man hath done nothing amiss," cried the thief dying
beside Him.

Christ has been under the microscope for twenty centuries.
Philosophers
  scientists
    reformers
      poets and statesmen
        cynics and saints
have examined Him for blemishes and found in Him no flaw.

He claimed the right to forgive sin—a prerogative of God. This
was no mechanical formula, no hocus-pocus or black magic,

for in every case His pronouncement of pardon was accompanied by a peace of mind and a cleanness of soul that expressed itself in a transformed life
   a changed outlook
    a fresh beginning.

He claimed to have the right and the authority to tell men how to get in touch with God.
He told them what to do to find peace and happiness and eternal life.
He gave them new commandments with the authority of God.
He predicted that later He would judge men everywhere.
He claimed to be doing the will of God.

Now as you read the audacious claims made by this Jesus, you are forced to a simple conclusion:
   Either the claims are true—or this Man was a charlatan.

If they were false, did He hope to convince people simply by making more stupendous claims than any other human being had ever made?

Men have laughed at fools before . . . have been amused, entertained.
But Christ did not affect them like that.
"Never man spake as this Man," even His enemies admitted.

He placed Himself at the center of His ethic and His message.
He did not come to us to point the way.
He said, "I am the way . . . I am the door . . . I am the truth."

Calmly He obtruded Himself—yet so convincingly that men were shocked.
Thus Christianity is more than the religion of Jesus:
                       It is the worship of Christ.

Christ is not only the center; He is also the circumference.
Take Zoroaster out of the religion that bears his name, and you will still have Zoroastrianism.
Take Mohammed out of Islam, and you will still have the worshipers of Allah.
But take Jesus Christ out of Christianity, and you have absolutely nothing left

           Christianity is Christ.

Now what shall we make of all this?

Either it is sheer nonsense—or it is true.

Either anyone who speaks as Christ did was a mumbling idiot,
    a deranged megalomaniac who thinks that he is a teapot
    . . . or Joan of Arc's horse . . . or Napoleon—

or else Christ was, and is, who He claims to be.

The alternative that He did not leave us is to believe that He
was merely a great moral teacher.

To say this is to betray our ignorance.

For one who made the claims that Christ did—if they were
fraudulent—could scarcely be a great moral teacher.

He would be a maniac, or at the least a consummate liar.

Yet His sanity has never been questioned, for His life and His
teachings were too obviously normal and sensible and clear-
headed.

In fact, as the relatively new science of psychology is progres-
sively finding out, His teachings of love and selflessness lie at
the heart of an integrated personality.

And the suspicion of fraud has no foundation, for the
swindlers always use their ability to fool people to gain wealth
or power.

Jesus asked nothing.

He taught unselfishness and indifference to the treasures of
this world, and His own life is the proof of His sincerity.

Did He then speak the truth?

Was He God come down to earth to show us the loving heart
of the Father?

As a matter of fact, there could be no greater proof of the truth
of His claims than that I—some nineteen hundred years later—should even be asking the question: "John Doe, what do
you think of Christ?"

Perhaps no one has ever confronted you with the fact that
what you decide about Him will be the most important decision of your life.

You cannot go on dodging the issue.

You must be either for Him—or against Him.

Even if you try to be noncommittal, that is an answer too.

A man in a burning house to whom the firemen throw a rope ladder may have difficulty deciding whether or not to risk using it.

Should he hesitate too long, he *has* decided.
The notice of his death in next day's newspaper will leave little doubt of his decision.
What are you going to do with Jesus?

There are stern facts which Christ Himself asks you to consider before you decide.
Few men have ever recruited disciples on such hard-hitting terms . . . .
He warned that following Him might divide families . . .
alienate friends.
He said that it would mean a shift in values,
a turning away from materialism.
It would involve sacrifice, because you would no longer be able to put yourself and your own comforts first.
For some, hatred, persecution and death would follow

Let us not deceive ourselves that these warnings were just for first-century Christians.
If Christ were to reappear—dressed in a modern business suit—on Main Street or Madison Avenue, would we react any differently than did the inhabitants of Jerusalem in A.D. 30?

Would we have enough dedication and stamina
to accept Him and His audacious claims
to make known our allegiance to Him
under the pressure of an unpopular cause and ostracism?
The sad truth is that purity and sacrifice are unpopular in every century.

At the moment, we are in a period when church membership is socially acceptable and on the rise.
It is not hard to decide for Christ so long as He stays safely in the pages of the New Testament,
or smiles at us on a Sunday morning from a stained-glass window.
But as materialism and secularism accelerate, our civilization may yet, in our time, go full circle.
In that case, we may see a new conspiracy against God,

a modern version of Christian persecution,
   even of Christianity having to go underground.
These are possibilities you should consider, John Doe.

What then *does* He offer you?
His friendship—the most wonderful friendship in the world.
   His strength for your weakness . . .
      His forgiveness for your sins . . .
         His comfort for your sorrow . . .
            His light for your darkness . . .
               His guidance for your way.

For, start wherever you will in an honest search to find out this truth about this Christ, sooner or later God in Christ will find you.
And then you will have the final, complete proof of His deity—in your own experience.

Whenever you look into your own heart, you will find His haunting Presence.
He will show you a love that will never let you go.
"Come after Me," He still calls, asking for recruits,
                                        for disciples.

Are you ready to answer Him, John Doe?
Are you ready to be—John Doe, Disciple?

M AY OUR PRAYER, O CHRIST, awaken all Thy human remi-
      niscences, that we may feel in our hearts and bodies
what Thee felt while walking this earthly vale. Thus we will
better know what it is to be tired, what it is to know aching
muscles, as Thou didst work long hours at the carpenter's
bench. Thou hast not forgotten what it is to feel the sharp stabs
of pain or hunger or thirst. Thou knowest what it is to be
forgotten, to be lonely. Thou dost remember the feel of hot
and scalding tears running down Thy cheeks.

We are thankful that Thou wert willing to come to earth and
share with us the weakness of the flesh. Now we know that
Thou dost understand all that we are ever called upon to bear.

So bless each of us, not according to our deserving, but
according to Thy riches in glory, Amen.

Heaven Can't Wait

E ach one of you has a philosophy of life.
You may not realize it . . .
You may not even know it, but you have one nevertheless.

It may be sound—or it may be false.
It may be positive—or it may be negative.
It may be Christian—or it may be pagan.
Perhaps you could not expound it in so many words,
    but you have one just the same.

It lies back of every decision you make . . .
    It colors every opinion you hold . . .
It suggests every action you take . . .
            and it shows itself in a hundred different ways:
                The type of amusements you seek . . .
                The kind of pictures you prefer . . .
            The magazines and newspapers you read . . .
            The television programs you watch . . .
                The slang you use . . .
                Your favorite songs . . .

All these things are indicative of the tenor of your thinking
and are clues to your philosophy of life.

Such a clue, I believe, is the title of a song of some years ago,
"Heaven Can Wait."
It is indicative of a prevailing idea to which a great many of us
subscribe . . .
"This is paradise enough" is a philosophy which says,
"We're only young once, let us have our fun while we can.
There's plenty of time for responsibility and serious thoughts.
We're not ready to settle down yet . . . .
We're out for a good time, so don't be a wet blanket by asking
us to be serious.

This is the time to be gay—so come along, let's dance.
Have another drink . . . you're only young once."

This idea is not new, nor is it modern.
You and your parents and your grandparents have been saying it down through the ages.
Always there have been young people who have fallen victims
to this pagan philosophy and have expressed it in many
different ways.

It was this idea that Robert Herrick expressed in the seven-
teenth century when he said:

> "Gather ye rosebuds while ye may,
> Old Time is still a-flying:
> And this same flower that smiles to-day,
> To-morrow will be dying."

You see, there is nothing new about the idea of sloughing off
responsibilities or duties
   or thoughts of a future life.
There is nothing new here—but there is also nothing good
about it.

I wonder why it is that so many young people are afraid of that
which is high—afraid of high ideals
        of high thoughts
        of high morality.

Is it because so many grew up in homes saturated with
                    cynicism
           and helplessness
           and defeatism
now that we have a bomb of such awesome destructiveness?

Some of you grew up in an age when not only big sisters and
brothers—but fathers and mothers took to drinking and stay-
ing out nights . . .
When young girls were trained to serve liquor in barrooms no
better than the old saloon . . .
When American women were persuaded by brilliant advertis-
ing that it was fashionable to drink . . .
When Hollywood and Freudian psychology were making us
sex-conscious as never before.

It is not surprising, therefore, that so many of you young
people have lost your moorings . . .
    are confused and bewildered . . .
And have the feeling that no one—not even God—
    cares about you.

Yet behind the "so-what" indifference—the cynicism, the
boredom, all of you want challenges and jobs.
All of you want to make your own way in life . . .
unless you have been softened and spoiled by parental indulgence.

Most of you want to get married—and deeply and sincerely
desire your marriage to be a success . . . .

You want to have a home and a family
    and you want to see some light ahead for your children.

You would like to give yourself to something worthwhile,
    perhaps a hospital project . . .
        work with children . . .
            the church.
Inside are stirrings and longings and a hunger for the real
meaning of life.
You are in search of happiness but don't know where to find
it, or even how to look.

So meanwhile you say, "Let's not worry or think about it. Turn
on the record player, and fill the room with jazz.
Live for today, do what comes naturally . . . .
This doesn't take thought
        or hard work
    or being different.
    Heaven can wait."
But will young people, by postponing serious thoughts and
refusing to think of spiritual things, eventually stumble upon
some satisfying beliefs?
Will you one day—without thinking about it— find a satisfying experience of God?

Will you manage to find the happiness you seek by drifting
along, day by day, "gathering rosebuds while you may"?
Is it true that "heaven can wait"?

Does heaven wait?
Will heaven wait?

Youth is the period of the most important decisions of life for
which the Lord's guidance is particularly needed.
It is in youth that we form our basic ideals and philosophies . . .

It is in youth that we come to crossroads where decisions are
made between right and wrong:
    To do homework—or to sneak out the sexy magazine . . .
    To take a low grade—or cheat . . .
    And when caught doing something wrong to tell the truth
    fearlessly—or lie cravenly—
    perhaps even shifting the blame to someone else.

These are the crossroads . . .
Here is where greatness begins its journey
    or weakness and evil take over.

Habits are begun in youth that solidify like concrete:
    Putting off assignments until it is too late . . .
    Telling little lies that grow into bigger lies
                    that trap
                  enmesh
                entwine
              imprison . . .
Giving away a priceless treasure a little at a time until it is all
gone, and you are soiled, distraught, bitter,
    and desperately disillusioned that love can turn so dirty . . .
Choosing friends that help lift your thinking,
    or lower it by feeding your ego, tempting you to do the
    things that deep inside you know are wrong.

It is in youth that we decide upon a life work.
Either we just drift into something as the only thing we could
get, or we carefully prepare at home and in school for that
niche in life which we feel is specifically ours.
But whether we drift or whether we steer a direct course, we
achieve that place we choose in youth.

It is usually in youth that we select a life partner. And in this,
the most important decision of our whole life, we need the
help and guidance of a Wisdom greater than our own.

The prophet promised that it was the young who would see visions . . .
   the old who would dream their dreams.

Joan of Arc was only seventeen when she was riding at the head of the army that liberated France from the English.

John Calvin was twenty-six when he published his *Institutes*.
John Keats died at twenty-six.
Shelley was thirty when he was drowned, leaving English literature his undying *Odes*.

Sir Isaac Newton had largely discovered the working of the law of gravitation when he was twenty-three.
Henry Clay was sent to the United States Senate at twenty-nine, and was Speaker of the House of Representatives at thirty-four.

Raphael painted his most important pictures between twenty-five and thirty—he died at thirty-seven.
Van Dyck had done his best work before he was thirty.

Jesus Christ was not quite thirty-three when He died. For the most part, His followers were young men.

Those who gathered at Pentecost were young people.
The movement that started when the winds of the Holy Spirit blew through the streets of old Jerusalem was essentially a youth movement.
It is for all these reasons, you see, that heaven can't wait.
The visions that are to be granted are given to youth.

But voices that are unheeded have a way of being heard no more.
And visions that shine through the fogs and above the mists have a way of fading and disappearing as time goes oozing out.

"Heaven Can Wait"?

"Well," you may say, "it sounds fine. I do want to be happy with a lasting kind of happiness.
I do want to get the most out of life.
I do want to be successful.

I would like to feel that there is a God who is interested in me
and my life.
Of course, I don't want to make any big mistakes that will mar
my life—that will mess it all up.

"I would like to believe that it is not simply a lot of sentimental
pious nonsense to say that God cares whom I marry . . .
     that marriages are still made in heaven
    that somewhere there is a particular person for me
   that I can feel close to God in my daily life
but—let's be practical.

"Suppose I am ready to call your bluff!
Suppose I am willing to give it a trial.
How does God become real to me?
What do I do?"

These are legitimate questions—if asked by an open mind.
All right, let's be specific . . . .
If you want anything in this life, you must reach out for it,
                         the right job . . .
                     the ideal marriage partner . . .
                 achievement in any area.

Just so, if you desire the treasures in the Christian life, they
will not come to you unless you seek them.
Christ said, "And all things, whatsoever you shall ask in
prayer believing, ye shall receive."
Notice that the *ask*—which is action on your part—has to come
first of all.
He also said:

  "Ask, and it shall be given you;
  seek, and ye shall find;
   knock, and it shall be opened unto you" (Matthew 7:7).
The key words here are action words: *ask* . . .
                    seek . . .
                    knock.

Jesus never said that there was plenty of time.
He never said to take it easy now and things would work out.
He never suggested that you can sow your oats while young,

because there will always be a chance later on
to straighten out your life.
He never told us, "Heaven will wait while you make up your
mind about Me."

Jesus Himself was a Man of action.
He did not want publicity
             praise
           comforts
success as the world measures it . . .
He wanted lives—all or nothing.
He has never changed.
He wants your life committed to Him
now—not tomorrow.

And you would be surprised at the wonderful changes that
can come into the life of anyone who is willing to say to Jesus
Christ:
   "Yes, I do want to give myself to You today. Here I am.
   Please take over the direction of my life in every area."

That was the case back in the eighteenth century in the life of
the British parliamentarian, William Wilberforce.
I first learned of him in my history textbooks in Scotland.

As a teenager, Wilberforce had idled through Pocklington
School, and then through St. John's College, Cambridge.
After that, he had spent several years enjoying London's
society life.
Later he was to comment that he "could not look back without
unfeigned remorse" on all the opportunities he had neglected
during those years in school.

Then in 1784, he went to Nice, France, with an old friend,
Isaac Milner. During the trip, Milner talked seriously to
Wilberforce about what he was going to do with his life . . . .
   Was he going to drift with the tide of London society?
   What did he intend to do about the talents God had given
   him?

The result of this talk was that before he got back to England,
William Wilberforce did hand his life
             his dreams

        his future
        his potential over to God.

Changes in the young man's life came thick and fast.
Within three years he knew that God had given him a special
assignment . . . .

It was a prodigious one, breathtaking:
He was to end forever the vicious slave trade of the then
farflung British Empire.

How could one man achieve that?
The slave trade cut directly across some of the most powerful
financial interests of the Empire.
Wilberforce knew that since God had given him the assign-
ment, God was in the fight, too.
So this young man rolled up his sleeves and soon became a
voice to reckon with in Parliament.
His days of drifting were over.
   Now his life had a goal.
     He was on God's side.
And he found within himself unflagging zeal for a fight on
those terms.

The fight took forty-six years in all, but God and Wilberforce
won it.
By act of Parliament, the British emancipated every slave in
the Empire twenty-two years before we achieved the same
end in this country with the bloodshed of the War Between
the States.

Do changes take place in a life handed over to God? Yes,
always . . . .
Adventure? Decidedly.
Does a goal emerge and with it an understanding of that goal?
Yes. But it begins for each of us with an act of commitment.

I knew a girl named Jane who came to Washington from a
small town in the Midwest.
She was excited about her nation's capital . . .
   stirred by the monuments to greatness she saw . . .
    awed by the famous names.

She was a wholesome girl—the type you would like to have
for a daughter
   or a sister
    or a friend.
She dreamed of serving her country, of filling a need.
Her story is, in a way, the story of all quiet, lonely girls in a
new city.

Jane became a typist in an office with many girls, in a govern-
ment office on Constitution Avenue. She soon discovered that
one can be lonely in the midst of many.
A shy girl can get lost in a big city . . .
A girl with ideals may not immediately attract men.
Jane became a steady worker, reliable, conscientious.
In a simple, wholesome way she was attractive, and she did
receive invitations to a few parties.

At first she accepted these invitations eagerly.
But when she saw what went on, she felt sick inside . . .
      the constant drinking
     the petty gossip
    the blatant sexuality
    the lack of sincerity.
It was hard to refuse invitations, because she needed friends.
Yet she felt soiled and unclean when she came home.

There were times when the pressure of it all made her wonder
why she held on to her ideals, when other people seemed to
be having a good time without scruples,
   without being bothered by ideals.

After some of these parties, Jane made concessions, compromised with her conscience.
It seemed the thing to do.
Yet the memories of what happened made her blush and feel
miserable.

She knew she could never be happy that way—not really
happy. But Jane was puzzled, because neither was she happy
as she was now—in her loneliness.

Then came a sudden new temptation, worse than the others
because it devastated her at the center of her greatest need—
her loneliness.

She was torn, seared by the desire to do something she knew was completely wrong.

All that she believed, all her ideals stood in her path. She longed to thrust them ruthlessly aside, to say "Yes" to a young man's proposition.
He liked her; she liked him. Why not?
Heaven can wait!

Jane went to her room to think it over.
There the four cold walls of the drab one-room apartment,
the comfortless furniture,
her aloneness and confusion overwhelmed her.

She buried her head in her hands, sobbing, "Oh God—
Why am I so miserable? Oh God—help me!"
And although she heard nothing, something made her look up.
Jesus was there by her side.

Jane was startled, but she did not feel fear.
Something about His presence calmed her,
dried her tears:
His compassionate face . . .
understanding eyes . . .

It was His eyes that seemed to phrase the statement:
"You called for Me!"

How universal the appeal—man loses the way and cries for his Maker.
He comes in many ways . . .
Through the gentle illumination of a thought . . .
In the soothing coolness of understanding that dissolves hot emotion . . .
In the brilliance of light that pierces foul darkness.
And He comes also as a Presence—a living Presence.

Jane found herself pouring out to Him all her unhappiness . . .
Her disappointments
Her loneliness
Her fears
Her temptation.

She was ashamed as she spoke, but the look of love never left
His eyes.
And suddenly she realized that Jesus already knew every-
thing about her.
But that had not changed His love.

Finally Jane phrased the question: "Why am I so unhappy?"
Quietly came the answer: "He who loseth himself for My sake
will find himself. Follow thou Me."
And then with a smile of amazing tenderness, He said:
"Lo, I will be with you always."

And then suddenly He was gone.
Yet there was still that strange and wonderful warmth in the
room.
The furniture did not seem so drab . . . .
Something was different inside her, too . . . .
          She felt new hope . . .
             new determination to stand on principle . . .
          an inner buoyancy, a zest for life . . .
      and a new love for the girls whom she had envied
      and even despised.

But most wonderful of all, she knew that never again could
she doubt that Jesus cared about her—even her.

There is a place in the heart of God for you, too . . . .
It is reserved in your name.
Is it empty still?
Then it is empty only because you have not claimed it.

When you do, you will be home.
You will know for yourself His warm and wonderful love,
                 how He will guide you,
                    and help you,
        give you joy you have never had before.

Isn't it worth trying?
   Heaven can wait?
Ah, but when we can have the joy of heaven now—
   who wants to wait?

The Chains of Freedom

T he great yearning of youth is for freedom.
      To be free . . . to be on your own . . .
   to be your own master.
Does not your blood tingle at the thought of it?

But wait a minute—
If you had the freedom to go where you wanted . . .
If you had the money, and your parents would not stop
you . . .
and you could take off tomorrow . . .
Where would you go?
What would you do?

This was exactly the situation confronting a young man whose
story I once heard . . .
Robert Duvois wanted his freedom.
He did not like the slow tempo of country life, even though
"Twin Oaks" was a large plantation in South Carolina.

He thought his older brother stuffy.
His father, while kind and sympathetic enough, had some
old-fashioned ideas.
Only his mother might have understood, but she had died six
months before his twenty-first birthday.
I have no freedom here, Robert kept telling himself.
Life seemed a cramped sort of thing,
   always in the same old groove,
      no excitement.

John, the elder son, had inherited his father's business ability
and steadfast character.
Gradually his father had let John take over the management of
the plantation.

Robert had his mother's artistic, restless temperament.
He wanted to go to Paris to study art.
He wanted to be free to paint—to live, really live.

Finally he could stand it no longer.
"Give me," he said to his father as he sought to get his hands
on his inheritance.
"Give me," he said to life, as his young blood tingled with
anticipation.
"Give me," he said to the world, and his eyes danced with the
excitement of it.

There were entrancing worlds and fascinating people beyond
the discipline of home.
He was of age now, old enough to live his own life.
He had money coming from his mother's estate.
"A man has to do what he has to do," he told his father.

The father recognized that he could no longer hold his younger son at home.
He would merely chafe, grow resentful, and eventually leave
anyway.

So the father turned over the inheritance to his son.
Some of the money was sent to a Paris bank.
And Robert had his freedom . . . .
    He was twenty-one . . .
        with enough money to be his own boss.
What more could anyone ask?

At first, all went well in Paris.
Robert took his art studies seriously.

He wrote his father that several of his oils had been hung in art
exhibits.
Then, gradually, the gay life of the French capital began to lure
him.
He moved to a fine apartment, bought a sports car.

As he experimented with life, soon on all sides he found
himself faced with restrictions on his freedom.
For example, as he drove his car along the Rue de Rivoli he was
halted by stop signs and red lights.

Even with Robert's tendency toward self-pity, he knew that
the traffic lights were impersonal
                    unfeeling
                    playing no favorites.

He was free to drive through a red light . . .
    but he was not free to avoid the subsequent collision.
He was free to eat whatever he liked in his favorite Paris
restaurants, but if he ate too much of exotic foods in combina-
tion, he was not free of the gastronomical consequences.

In the realm of his art, his freedom was limited by his ability or
lack of it.
He would see wraithlike mists rising from the Seine . . .
    gay colors of sidewalk cafés under their awnings,
        cypresses bathed in shimmering light . . .
but he was not free to capture on canvas what he saw because
there was a limit to his talent.

He was free, free to be a traditionalist
                    or an impressionist
                    or to turn to cubism or surrealism . . .
yet whatever art he chose was held in bondage by his own
limitations.

In order to overcome these limitations, he would have to sit at
the feet of those who knew more than he did,
    study techniques,
        paint . . . paint . . . paint, hundreds of hours.
It was easier to neglect his studies for the theater,
                    gay parties
                    night life in the cafés.

There was a procession of women upon whom Robert lav-
ished gifts
    jewels
        furs and perfume.
"Monsieur Robert's" fame soon became well-known, even in
Paris, for wealth and extravagance and dissipation.
At last he felt really free.

This was the life, he thought.
And the "substance" which represented years of hard work,

of sacrifice
and saving on the part of his parents
was scattered to gratify passing whims, to try to satisfy greedy
desires that were fed but never fulfilled.

One morning, the young man woke to the bitter realization
that his money was gone.
He was in debt to his clothier
his landlord
his clubs
his jeweler.
All his creditors were hounding him.

Hurriedly he left Paris for a small town in Normandy.
There he lived for a few months—guiltily—at a small country
inn where he tried to go back to his painting.
But the joy and inspiration had gone out of it.

Besides, he scarcely had enough money even for paint supplies.

Finally his past caught up with him.
All his possessions, even his clothes, were confiscated.
There was nothing for him to do but to seek work with one of
the local farmers.

At first he was made an overseer for a wealthy landowner, but
he had little business ability, and what he had was drowned in
the unquenchable thirst for drink to which he was now a
slave.
Years passed.
He had long since lost touch with his home.
Things went from bad to worse, until finally he ended up a
hired hand, herding the sheep and tending the pigs.
The vestiges of the sensitive, artistic nature that had once been
his recoiled from every sight and smell of the barnyard and
the pigsty.
He loathed his surroundings,
his work
and most of all—himself.

Then somehow the boy came to himself.

Memories of home came surging back before the jaded and
bloodshot eyes of the playboy turned ragged swineherd.
Something—the wooing of God's Spirit in his heart,
    the early training of his father and mother,
        the inherent quality of the boy's nature—
something brought him back to himself.

He thought of "Twin Oaks" and the gracious, orderly life he
had left behind.
Wistfully he compared his days with those of the workers on
his father's plantation.
Nostalgically he remembered Christmas back home.
The roast turkey with chestnut stuffing . . .
    the platters of fried chicken
        the beaten biscuits
            watermelon-rind preserves
                pecan pies
                spoon bread
and cold floating island.

He rembered the look in his father's eyes as he had stood at the
head of the table carving the turkey,
    the look of tender pride as he had surveyed his family.

Once again he could feel his father's strong arms around
him . . .
    a big hand laid tenderly on a little boy's head that day his
    puppy had been killed.
Dimly he recalled certain moments of growing up when he
had thought his father stuffy, old-fashioned.
Now everything in him cried out for some of that old-fashioned love.

That night he crept away from the farm, and on foot made his
way to Cherbourg, where he worked his way back across the
Atlantic on a freighter.
He was going home . . . .

Yes, the story does have a familiar ring. You have heard it
before.
It is the old, old story of the Prodigal Son,
                    as old as man's sin,
as new as God's forgiveness for every man who thinks that
freedom means the license to do what he pleases.

All of us have to begin by discovering what freedom is . . .
and what it is not.

The first valuable revelation is that freedom is not rebellion,
not anarchy.

Sometimes the act of rebelling . . .
throwing off parental restraints
flouting accepted conventions of society
renouncing old and accepted beliefs
gives the exciting illusion of freedom.

Thus every country and every generation has its equivalent of
the Latin quarter
its Montmartre
its Shepherds' Market
or its Greenwich Village
and the hot-blooded radicals who live there.

The problem is that a man cannot live negatively,
just in terms of what he is *against*.
The more pertinent question is,
what is he *for*?
Once all parental restraints are withdrawn, then what?
Around what will the "free" one build his life?

Many of the moralities and proprieties against which the
younger generation of the "roaring twenties" revolted and
against which the young writers and painters crusaded seem
trifling now.
Today as then, the trouble with the nonsense verse and the
abstract paintings which flow out of these apostate hearts is
that once you subtract the rebellion—
no matter how artfully expressed—
you have little or nothing left.

The same mistake of confusing anarchy with freedom is made
over and over by political or racial groups struggling to cast off
shackles.
See the Marquis de La Fayette standing on the balcony of the
Château of Versailles beside Louis XVI and Marie Antoinette
pleading . . . pleading with his rioting fellow countrymen not
to fall into this trap.

But they would not heed; La Fayette could not stem the tide.
   The heady wine of anarchy was already brewed.
So blood flowed in rivers down the gutters of the Place de la
Concorde from La Guillotine.
Liberté . . . Egalité . . . Fraternité. . . .

Ah, but in the end, murder
                    drunken mobs with heads on pikes
                         lawlessness
                              frenzied promiscuity
                                   anarchy
turned out to be not freedom—but chaos.

Of course you can see it in such extreme instances.
But in the ordinary course of our lives, each of us has to find
for himself that there is more to this freedom than rebellion.

It is also true that freedom is not planlessness.
I am reminded of the child in kindergarten who grew tired of
having the play period planned and supervised.
He rebelled at having to play group games.

So the teacher finally told him to find his own amusement,
                         do whatever he wanted to do.

It was not long before the rebel was back, grumbling,
"What can I do now? I don't want to do what I want to do."

On a more adult level, a recent spokesman of the school of
self-expression and self-indulgence made the same confession: "We took what we wanted, and now we find we no
longer want what we took."
There you have the disillusionment that inevitably follows
liberty without restraint or plan.

In genuine freedom the plan comes from inside a man. In the
case of Robert Duvois— given his time to use it as he chose—
what did he choose to do?

He was on the right track, so long as he was attempting to
express his true inner self through his painting.
But as soon as this trailed off into irresponsibility . . .
   "wasting his substance in riotous living . . ."
then this young man had betrayed freedom.

The more irresponsible he became, the less freedom he had,
the more hemmed in he was by poverty,
 the more he was shackled by the tyranny of habits,
  the more he was confined by the laws of man and God
that play no favorites and will step aside for no one.

And then—at a crisis moment—Robert Duvois turned himself
around to take his first good look at what freedom really is.
 True freedom is finding oneself . . . choosing oneself.
Always in that process, one or more false concepts of what he
thought he was must die.
That is why Jesus' "For whosoever will save his life shall lose
it . . ." is found today to be an incisively penetrating psycho-
logical insight.

Then, once the self is found, for the first time man accepts full
responsibility for that self . . .
 for the choices he makes
  the disciplines he imposes upon himself
   the way he relates to other human beings.

No longer does he interpret freedom as rebellion against
realities.
Now he accepts himself, other people, and circumstances *as
they are* and uses his freedom to shape his circumstances
creatively.

At this point he discovers the paradox at the heart of all truth:
 We want our freedom in order to give our love and our
 loyalty away to something bigger than ourselves.

Michelangelo wanted to be an artist, but his father objected.
He wanted no son of his to be "a stonecutter."
But the passion to create was in Michelangelo's blood, so at
age thirteen—over his father's stubborn opposition—the boy
left home.
He was free now . . . yet what a bondservant to art Miche-
langelo became!
Long hours of work . . .
 pinching hardship . . .
  superhuman labor . . .
Two years, three months of grueling toil to complete the statue
"David" . . .

Over four-and-a-half years to paint the ceiling vault of the
Sistine Chapel . . .
Free—yet voluntarily bound.

We can watch the same pattern with many a scientist.
See Marie Curie in her laboratory—her fine mind,
                              all her training in physics,
              every moment she could spare, day or night,
                                        utter devotion
given to refining from pitchblende a new substance—radium.

In the end, Marie Curie laid down her life on the altar of
science because, during those long days and nights of work,
she had been exposed to radium too often.
A free woman, but she had given her love and her loyalty
away. Yet we can never doubt that this is real freedom, because
it is the heart's voluntary loyalty,
      the man's or the woman's own choice.

Long centuries before, God's first direct word on behalf of His
chosen people had been the thundering "Let my people go,"
to the pharaoh who held them in bondage.
After that, through the long years of Israel's history
      through wanderings and captivities
            through times of obedience and
                  through times of falling away—
God's word never changed—"Let my people go."

Finally, the word came to Jesus.
It is no accident that Jesus Christ is so concerned with freedom.
That day in Nazareth when He stood in the local synagogue to
announce His Messiahship to His astounded relatives and
friends, a major portion of the platform of His Kingdom was
      "deliverance to the captives."

Then He proceeded to live this out episode by episode . . .
      He freed many a one bound by sin.
            Everywhere He went, He released the captives of pain
            and disease.
                  With gladness, He threw open the dark dungeons of
                  hate to the sunlight of God's love.

He struck the shackles from tortured minds and personality compulsions.
Moreover, He went on to more dangerous liberties:
He declared war on the bondage of ossified traditions
and manmade dogmas.
Almost every point of the Sermon on the Mount begins with "It hath been said of them of old time . . .
But I say unto you . . . . "
Tangling with entrenched religious tradition . . .
Dangerous! Of course it was dangerous!

Yet if you read the accounts of Christ for yourself, you will see that He had no trace of fear of public opinion.
Physical fear seems to have been unknown to Him:
He never hesitated to touch any loathsome leper . . .
On more than one occasion He walked through the midst of a rioting mob . . .
He slept through a violent storm on the Sea of Galilee . . .
He faced spies and inquisitors, Temple authorities, King Herod, or Pontius Pilate
with an equanimity nothing could shake.

"Fear not them which kill the body," He advised His disciples.
His words were prophetic.
Finally, His was the supreme freedom:
He was free even to go to His cross.

This point He made over and over, so that no man could mistake it.
"I lay down my life . . . .
No man taketh it from me . . . .
I have power to lay it down,
and I have power to take it again" (John 10:17-18).

Yes, Christ was the freest Man who ever lived.
Yet—here is the paradox again—He was free because He had given His love and His loyalty away.
Voluntarily, He had made His Father's will supreme:

"I seek not mine own will," He said repeatedly,
"but the will of the Father which hath sent me" (John 5:30).

Out of such freedom and such loyalty always comes intense
joy.

Just here, we do violence to the New Testament narratives if
we imagine Christ to be a melancholy recluse.
Isaiah prophesied that He would be "a man of sorrows and
acquainted with grief."
Yes, but that was in order that *our* joy might be full.
A Christ who with trembling lower lip and tear-filled eyes
looked wistfully at human joy is a caricature that belies the
records.

On the contrary, the picture of Jesus in the Gospels is of a
radiant, laughter-loving Friend whom everybody loved, save
the cynical . . . the hard . . . the hating, who had lost the art of
loving anybody.

He was a guest at the wedding feast at Cana because He
enjoyed human fun and fellowship.
He was criticized because of the company He kept . . .
    sneeringly referred to as "a friend of publicans and sinners
    . . . even called "a winebibber."

The humble folk heard Him gladly, indeed idolized Him.
Children flocked to Him eagerly, and children never go to the
austere, stern person sunk in perpetual gloom.

Always Christ's message is that His Father has designed you
and me for freedom and for happiness.
Having counted the word *joy* 191 times in the Scriptures . . .
glad or *gladness* 125 times, at that point I gave up counting.

God is a God of laughter as well as of prayer . . .
    a God of singing as well as of tears.
God is at home in the play of His children . . .
    He loves to hear us laugh.

Every one of Jesus' Beatitudes begins with the words
    blessed or *happy.*
He came to give you the secrets of living, He said,
    so that "your joy might be full."

"Your joy no man taketh from you," He insists (John 16:22).
Indeed, so much does He cherish our liberty and our joy that if
we will let Him—He will see to it that no one takes it from us.
He will stand shoulder to shoulder beside us
   and battle for our freedom.
This is the point at which turning to Him can be dangerous
business.
For when we get right down to it, most of us *like* some of our
shackles,
   feel so comfortably secure in some of our prisons that we
   resist final maturity and ultimate responsibility.
But Christ will tolerate no compromise with our liberty.

The tyranny of lust or greed cannot abide His presence.
   The despotism of jealousy flees before Him.
      Always He opens the door to the dungeon of judging.
      He can heal the bindings of painful memories and
      bitter remorse.
         He sets Himself against the dictatorship of standard-
         ization and social conformity.
         He had specific words to speak against parental or
         family domination.

Now will you listen to Christ when He says:
   "The Spirit of the Lord is upon me because . . .
   he hath sent me to . . . preach deliverance to the captives"?
   (Luke 4:18).
The captives are you and me.

Yet with Christ Himself as our example—we, like Him, have to
give our love and our loyalty away.
In the end, there is only One into whose hands we dare
entrust the keys to our personal freedom.

Once we put those keys in Christ's hands, we have a surprise
awaiting us.
We had feared that giving Him our loyalty would cramp us,
   that He would give us a long list of forbidden pleasures.

That is not His way.
"Where the Spirit of the Lord is, there is liberty," the apostle
Paul exults (II Corinthians 3:17).

All during his ministry, Paul battled "the false brethren who come to spy out our liberty in Christ Jesus" by setting up moral and ritualistic restrictions.

Augustine was right:
Christ's way is "Love God, and do as you please."

As you grow to love God, what you "please" will change. This is where the surprise comes in.
God gives the inner man a new set of goals and passions. It would be bondage indeed to obey God when we do not want to; it is delightful freedom to do what we most want to do. And that is the wonderful way that God works it out for us.

It is at that point that, like Robert Duvois, we come to ourselves, experience for the first time real freedom. For like Robert Duvois, every one of us has misused the freedom that God gave us.
The story of the Prodigal Son is the story of every man.

And when the sands of the desert grow cold . . .
   when the stars go out one by one . . .
      when the earth is rolled up like a carpet . . .
         and thrown over the high balconies of heaven . . .
            when our clever sciences have been forgotten . . .
when the proud boasts of men have been carried away on the hurricanes of time,
   this story will still speak to us . . .
Of a boy who lost his way
Of a father who freely forgave him.

It will still have the power to soften our hard hearts and bring tears to our eyes.
It will still point the way to the heart's true home,
   still unfold to us the love of God.
For this story that Jesus told contains the most appealing picture of God ever drawn.
This parable contains the heart of the gospel:
   That God is willing, indeed eager, to forgive sinners like you and me,
   that the moment we turn around to take the way back home,
   the Father will come running down the road to meet us . . .

That He is the One who alone holds in His hands the keys to
our freedom.

> "Make me a captive, Lord,
> And then I shall be free;
> Force me to render up my sword;
> And I shall conqueror be . . . "[15]

F ATHER, forgive us all that we talk too much and think too
little. Forgive us all that we worry so often and pray so
seldom. Most of all, O Lord, forgive us that, so helpless
without Thee, we are yet so unwilling to seek Thy help.

Give us grace to seek Thee with our whole heart, that
seeking Thee we may find Thee, and finding Thee may love
Thee, and loving Thee may keep Thy commandments and do
Thy will. Through Jesus Christ, our Lord, Amen.

Get Out of Step

O ne of the memorable scenes in an English novel of some years ago[16] describes how a little boy named Bron goes to church for the first time with his governess.

He watches with interest every part of the service and then the preacher climbs into the high pulpit and Bron hears him give out a piece of terrible news.

It is about a brave and kind Man who was nailed to a cross . . . ferociously hurt a long time ago . . . who feels a dreadful pain even now, because there was something not done that He wants them all to do.

Little Bron thinks that the preacher is telling the story because a lot of people are there and they will do something about it.

Bron is sitting impatiently on the edge of the pew.
He can scarcely wait to see what the first move will be in righting this injustice.
But he sits quietly and decides that after the service someone will do something about it.

Little Bron weeps . . . but nobody else seems at all upset. The service is over, the people walk away as if they had not heard such terrible news,
     as if nothing remarkable had happened.

As Bron leaves the church, he is trembling.
His governess looks at him and says:

   "Bron, don't take it to heart—someone will think you are strange."

Strange—to be alive and sensitive in one's spirit!
Strange—to show emotion!
Strange—to listen to what is going on in God's house,

       really to hear,
      to respond . . .
Strange—to take Jesus Christ seriously!

What does *strange* mean?
The dictionary says, "Differing in some odd way from what is ordinary."

Ought not the Christian, then, to be strange?
He should not be satisfied with the ordinary in life.
Christ was not ordinary, and He did not call His followers to be ordinary.

Yet so many people who call themselves Christians today are living ordinary lives.
There is nothing about them that makes them any different from others who make no profession of belief, acknowledge no faith, and assume no obligations.
In fact, like Bron's governess, what they fear most in life is being "different."
We are becoming an assembly-line society.
The days of rugged individualism that explored the American frontier have been left far behind.

While this pattern of conformity can be seen in every age group, I want to speak about it especially to you young people, because as you huddle together—
  each of you trying to be like everyone else—
You are not finding the satisfactions you seek.

You are still hungry and thirsty on the inside, you still have problems unsolved, questions unanswered.
I want to tell you where you can find some of the answers you seek.

With many of you, conformity has become a creed.
You are terrified at being set apart.
Your own teenage definition of sin is to be out-of-step with your friends.

You must wear clothes like everyone else . . .
  collect and listen to the same records
   learn the same dances

know the latest teenage slang.

The desire to look and act like everyone else affects all of life:
                    your study habits
                    your dating patterns
                 how you spend your time
               what you buy with your allowance
your attitude toward parents . . . your nation . . . God . . . the church.

In order not to be different, you have to be content with a low standard of achievement . . .
    a conformity to mediocrity rather than a desire to excel.

Are you, for example, content with average grades, because to excel would be to be thought "a grind"
                    "a square"
                 just plain strange?

Why read for yourself and draw your own conclusions when it is far safer to adopt the philosophy of your friends
                    or favorite columnist
                 or television commentator?
The editorial page of our newspaper is ignored by too many readers who turn to the sports page or the comic strips for their reading, because they do not wish to do any serious thinking.

The teen years are the years for discovering "the real you,"
    the time when you should be shaping your own tastes.
Yet the temptation with all thoughts, activities, and goals is to keep right in step,
    marching along like robots,
        fearful of ridicule . . . criticism . . . isolation . . .
if you should, perchance, get out of step with the crowd.

Take the matter of social drinking.
More and more this is motivated by the desire to satisfy the requirements of sociability—and too many young people are facing the ultimatum:
    "Drink . . . or be left out . . .
    No drink . . .

no dance . . .
no date!"

If you decline a drink, you are accused of assuming a "holier-than-thou" attitude,
you are not a "good sport."
You are a wet blanket.
The refusal to drink is often interpreted as a boorish criticism of the occasion and those conducting it.

Social pressure is a dreary fact of our day, and you young people who try to buck it run into embarrassing situations and feel certain tensions that result in strained relationships.

Now it is a natural human desire to be congenial with the group and to act in harmony with prevailing customs, and the liquor trade is exploiting it to the limit.

It is this social pressure that induces you to begin drinking.
It is not because you are thirsty
or like the taste of alcohol
or the smell of it
but simply because you lack the conviction that will enable you to be "different."
You don't want people to think that you are "strange."
The drinking which is required by the powerful pressure of an authoritative social code is a type of tyranny.
This tyranny of the crowd is actually a flagrant interference with your personal liberty and a gross repudiation of the democratic principle and spirit.

Why is it that people who want to imbibe alcoholic beverages insist that you take one too, just to be sociable?
But do they likewise insist that you are
a spoilsport
a wet blanket
a prude
if you decline a cup of coffee or prefer a cup of tea?

I am not suggesting that you isolate yourself from social situations to avoid the embarrassment of refusing a drink.
Not at all! This was not Jesus' viewpoint.

He Himself was criticized because He associated with all types and manner of people.

No . . . instead refuse that drink and then show the others that you can have as much fun as anyone.
In fact, the nondrinker should have more fun, for alcohol eventually dulls the brain and acts as a depressant.

I can never understand why the person who acts on principle should be considered dull.
There is excitement in taking a stand . . . in being different.
It brings a sparkle to the eyes.
  The mind is alive.
    The spirit sings.
      True values come into sharper focus.

Yet when one falls into line . . . going along with the crowd, conforming to the group pattern, nothing new is happening!
                There is weary repetition,
                  dull compliance
                lack of initiative
              boredom.

And that is exactly what so many of you are feeling
  and why so many of you are dissatisfied with life.
Have you ever stopped to wonder *why* you have not wanted to be different?
Is it because you have not found yourself . . .
              who you are . . .
            why you are here . . .
          where you are going?
So you think that your protection and security lies in huddling together with your friends,
  losing your unsure self in the group.

The problem is that by losing yourself in the group, you can go through your whole life and *never* get the answers to what you are supposed to do with your life.

Then, too, what "everyone else" is doing may be quite wrong.
Many students cheat, but that does not make cheating right.
Remember that it is the *mob* that lynches an innocent man.

Entire nations have swallowed evil propaganda which was all falsehood.
The fact that millions believed it did not turn falsehood into truth or avert disaster.
In fact, what governments decide can be—and often has been—quite wrong.

Henry Thoreau—a rugged New England individualist of the nineteenth century—once went to jail rather than pay his poll tax to a state which supported slavery.
During this period he wrote his essay "Civil Disobedience"—now famous the world over.

Thoreau's good friend, Ralph Waldo Emerson, hurried to visit him in jail, and peering through the bars exclaimed:
    "Why, Henry, what are you doing in there?"

The uncowed Thoreau replied, "Nay, Ralph, the question is, what are you doing out there?"
Who is the strange one—Little Bron or his governess?
                Thoreau in jail—or the rest of us outside?

Thoreau was not a churchman because he thought the churches of his day too convention-bound—and perhaps he was right.
Yet in his book *Walden* he speaks often of God.
He explains that he went to Walden Pond to live the simple life because he wanted to get just those answers that you and I seek:

> "I went to the woods because I wished . . . to front only the essential facts of life and see if I could not learn what it had to teach, and not, when I came to die, discover that I had not lived . . . . "

At another time this amazing man commented:

> "If a man does not keep pace with his companions perhaps it is because he hears a different drummer. Let him step to the music which he hears, however measured or far away."

Any man or woman who accomplishes anything worthwhile must have the courage to be different, even to be regarded as strange, because they are marching to the drumbeat of a Different Drummer and they are not afraid to be out of step.

Abraham Lincoln was one who listened to the Different Drummer, and not to the vindictive voices of his advisers.

Stephens, Phillips, and Beecher were among Lincoln's contemporaries who were echoing the cry "Crush the South . . . ."
"Stamp out the whole slaveholding aristocracy . . .
Make them pay to the last acre of land,
the last vestige of power,
the last drop of blood."

But the great man upon whose furrowed brow the responsibility rested, heard a Different Drummer . . .

"With malice toward none, with charity for all, let us strive on to finish the work we are in, to bind up the nation's wounds . . .
to do all which may achieve and cherish a just and lasting peace among ourselves and with all nations."

What is the verdict of today?
Whose words are remembered and repeated—
Lincoln's or Stephens'?

Woodrow Wilson was another.

As a son of the manse, he knew how to listen to the voice of God, and he was not afraid to take a position that other men, hearing no distant drumbeat, delighted to ridicule.

When Wilson went to Paris after the first World War, his consuming passion was to work out a peace on a just and righteous basis.
Someone sneered that Wilson talked like Jesus Christ.
Could there have been a greater compliment paid to any man?
But it was not intended as a compliment.

In our day—as in Wilson's—there are many who are not at all certain that they want to be like Christ.
Most of their opinions of Him are formed out of puerile ignorance and a tangle of mistaken conceptions.

Yet Christ Himself would be the first to tell you that this is a central issue you need to face honestly—
before you dare call yourself a Christian.
Jesus never deceived anyone about the cost of following Him.
Over and over He asserted that what He was offering was hard,
that a man had better sit down and count the cost before deciding to become one of His disciples.
He offers a cross—not a cushion.
He recruits men—not weak-kneed boys.

And He would have stern words for the minister who pleads with people to join his church,
as if they were doing the church a favor . . .
who sets the requirements for church membership so low that people can fall over the threshold.

Yet Jesus did not ask us to be different just to make life hard.
He was thinking of our happiness when He said:

"Woe unto you, when all men shall speak well of you . . . "
(Luke 6:26).

Why . . . "Woe unto you"?
Isn't it all right to be thought well of?
Isn't popularity a fine thing?

Yes, popularity is pleasant.
I like it as much as you do.
But the truth is, no man can have any convictions
or stand for any principles,
or stick to any standards at all,
and be liked by everyone.

Jesus put it this way:

"How on earth can you believe while you are forever looking for each other's approval and not for the glory that comes from the one God?" (John 5:44).

It always amazes me the way people come to church, participate fully in the prayers and rituals, nod in agreement during a sermon on faith and prayer.

Yet if the same people were sitting socially at home that
Sunday evening talking about the problems of our time—and
if someone said impulsively, "Let's pray about this"—there
would be a most uncomfortable silence.
The one who suggested prayer would be considered a little
strange—different.
We preach about having faith and vision—yet when somebody shares a daring dream with us,
    presents us with an exciting and thrilling vision, we think
he is a bit peculiar.

We hold up certain ideals, and when in society a young man
or a young woman takes a stand for these ideals, even to the
point of making the rest of us uneasy, we think that he or she is
an oddball.

We say that we believe that God can lead people, and that His
guidance is available in everything . . . .
Yet when certain people try to seek His guidance in planning a
vacation
    in picking a college
        or in selecting friends,
we conclude that they are strange.

There is another reason why Jesus said,

    "Woe unto you when all men speak well of you."

As our fear about others' approval grows, our freedom
shrinks.
We can see this at its most extreme in the totalitarian state.
The totalitarian state cannot exist unless it is composed of de-
individualized persons.
There the citizen gives up one of Christianity's most outstand-
ing characteristics: the freedom of choice.

It is literally true that only in God's will do we have the chance
to find ourselves, to be persons.
Therefore, only in God's will do we have real freedom.
Today the world has a desperate need of people who are
willing to be different.

In Bernard Shaw's play St. Joan, some soldiers are talking
about the "Maid of Orleans."

One of them says, "There is something about—the girl . . . .
Her words and her ardent faith in God have put fire into me."
His captain replies, "Why, you are almost as mad as she is."

And the soldier stubbornly goes on, "Maybe that's what we
need nowadays—mad people.
See where the sane ones have landed us."

If it is sanity that has brought the world to its present state . . .
    if it is sanity that has produced the social order in which we
    live . . .
then I for one am willing to give madmen a chance.
I believe we need people who are different.

All those who have carried civilization forward have been
angry men—grousing in the public parks and the marketplaces,
nailing denunciations up on public buildings.
They knew they were in a conflict and they took the wrongs in
society—yes, and the wrongs in the church—
    terribly to heart.

We need such people who will carry their faith into the office
                                into Congress
                            into society
                        into the school
                    into the home . . .
people who will be different even if it will cost them their
social popularity
    their economic fortunes
        or their very lives.

But one does not get that kind of faith except by a personal
friendship with Jesus Christ.
Then He will tell you what to do.
    You will be sure of your ground.
        With His hand on your shoulder, you will have no fear of
        the opinion of other people.

Easy? Of course it is not easy.
I think too much of the youth today to offer you a sugar-coated
Christianity.
That would betray my Lord.
It would also not be worthy of your great potential.

If I can read the signs of the times at all, you are more than a
little satiated with softness,
   with having everything handed to you,
   so that you know the value of nothing.
You have contempt when the church contents itself with glad-
handing.
Deep in your hearts you look with longing toward the
heights.
You know that there will be rugged terrain
                panting lungs
             aching legs
but also the cool, clean upper air and the exhilaration of
gaining the summit at last,
   of achieving vision and perspective.

God's marching orders always involve sacrifice and courage.
The drumbeat of the Different Drummer calls for bravery.
It is not for dancing.
It does not appeal to the blood—but to the heart of a person.
It calls for will and sacrifice.
It is a stirring drum, and they who hear it are always in a
minority.

Those who answer it may perchance hear the words of a new
Beatitude . . .

   "Blessed are they who are thought strange, for they have
   taken the gospel to heart."

OUR FATHER, when we long for life without trials and work
without difficulties, remind us that oaks grow strong in
contrary winds and diamonds are made under pressure. With
stout hearts may we see in every calamity an opportunity, and
not give way to the pessimism that sees in every opportunity a
calamity.
   This we ask in Jesus' name and in His strength, Amen.

The Risk of Reach

I t was an afternoon in the early summer; there was a strange quiet on the battlefield.

In the bright sunshine, the air was balmy and had a breath of garden in it.

By some grotesque miracle, a bird was singing somewhere near at hand.
On the firing step, with his rifle lying in a groove in the parapet, stood a private soldier in field-gray, his uniform stained with mud and blood.

On his face, so young yet strangely marked with the lines of war that made him look old, was a wistful faraway expression.

He was enjoying the sunshine and the quiet of this strange lull in the firing.
The heavy guns had been silent—there was no sound to break the eerie stillness.

Suddenly a butterfly fluttered into view and alighted on the ground almost at the end of his rifle.
It was a strange visitor to a battleground—so out-of-place—so out-of-keeping with the grim setting
     rifles and bayonets
    barbed wire and parapets
   shell holes and twisted bodies.

But there it was—a gorgeous creature, the wings like gold leaf splashed with carmine,
swaying in the warm breath of spring.

As the war-weary youngster watched the butterfly, he was no longer a private in field-gray.

He was a boy once more, fresh and clean, swinging through a field in sunny Saxony, knee-deep in clover
>>buttercups
>>and daisies.

That strange visitor to the front-line trench recalled to him the joys of his boyhood, when he had collected butterflies.
It spoke to him of days of peace.
It was a symbol of the lovelier things of life.
It was the emblem of the eternal, a reminder that there was still beauty and peace in the world—that somewhere there was color and fragility
>and perfume
>and flowers
>and gardens.

He forgot the enemy a few hundred yards across no-man's-land.
He forgot the danger and privation and suffering.
He forgot everything as he watched that butterfly.

With all the hunger in his heart,
with the resurrection of dreams and visions that he thought were gone, he reached out his hand toward that butterfly.

His fingers moved slowly, cautiously, lest he frighten away this visitor to the battlefield.
In showing one kind of caution, he forgot another.
The butterfly was just beyond his reach—so he stretched, forgetting that watchful eyes were waiting for a target.

He brought himself out slowly—with infinite care and patience—until now he had just a little distance to go.
He could almost touch the wings that were so lovely.

And then . . . ping . . . *ing* . . . *ing* . . . *ing* . . .
A sniper's bullet found its mark.
The stretching fingers relaxed . . .
>the hand dropped flat on the ground . . . .
For the private soldier in field-gray, the war was over.

An official bulletin issued that afternoon said that
>"All was quiet on the Western Front . . . "

And for a boy in field-gray it was a quiet that no guns would
ever break.[17]

There is always a risk—when you reach for the beautiful.
When you reach out for the lovelier
    finer
  more fragrant things of life—
there is always a risk—and you can't escape it.

The risk is what makes the Christian life exciting.
  It is thrilling—make no mistake about it.
    It is an adventure.
As long as we live in this world, there will always be a risk in
reach.

But there are many in our time who are abnormally afraid of
that risk of reach.
They are afflicted with a modern disease.
The psychiatrists have ponderous names for the sundry pho-
bias that afflict us poor humans . . .
and the names are as terrible as the disease.

Agoraphobia is the fear of open spaces . . .
while claustrophobia is the fear of being shut in . . .
and acrophobia is the fear of heights.
There are many people who are afraid to climb . . . and they
will not leave the ground . . .
  to get out on the roof of a building
    or up in a tower
      or on a mountain.
To be up on any elevation and look down makes them dizzy,
  affects their sense of balance,
    strikes terror into their hearts.
They are afraid of that which is high.
They have acrophobia.

But acrophobia is not only the fear of high monuments
                        mountains
                and flights in airplanes.
        It may also be the fear of high ideals
                  high thoughts
                  high ambitions.

There are timid souls who avoid high places because they are
afraid . . .
But then there are others who avoid high ideals because they
are content with low ones.
There are persons who do not have high ambitions because
they are lazy.
Altogether there are a great many people afflicted with acrophobia.
Are you?

Not enough of you today are hitching your wagons to stars.
You think it enough to couple a trailer to your car.

Jesus remarked upon those who sought the small and shallow
things of life,

> "Verily, I say unto you, They have their reward"
> (Matthew 6:2).

That is, they got what they went after, and that is all they will
ever get.
That is what they deserve.

They take a tin thimble to the ocean and scoop up a few drops,
for that is all they can get into a thimble.
It isn't the fault of the ocean they did not get more . . .
that they did not plunge in and swim in the ocean's immen-
sity.

The tragedy of this age is that people with minds to think and
souls that are hungry are so afraid to reach up and seek the
things that are high.
What a tragedy that personalities in this glorious twentieth
century are afflicted with acrophobia!

The night sky does something to the star-gazer.
One does not remain the same after seeing a sunset,
   or gazing into the heart of a flower,
      or watching the tiny fledglings in a nest.

There is a silent uplifting importation from the Absolute.
It does us good to look up and see Orion driving his hunting
dogs across the Zenith . . .
Or Andromeda shaking out her tresses over limitless space.

It enlarges the self to have studied great architecture . . .
   to know great art—the reds of Titian
         the sunsets of Turner
         the seas of Winslow Homer . . .
to have felt the spell of epic deeds . . .
to have swung to the rhythmic pulse of Homer . . .
to have trembled with the passion of Romeo
   or the tenderness of Francis of Assisi.

To have wrestled with Kant's categorical imperatives,
   the whirring of angels' wings in Milton's *Paradise Lost*,
to have been swept away on the surge of music in Beethoven.
To have engraved upon the heart the prologue to John's Gospel,
to march with the majestic affirmations of the Nicene Creed.

It does something inside a man.
It stretches him mentally,
   stirs him morally,
      inspires him spiritually.
He is a bigger man—sweeter, nobler, higher,
                richer than he was before.

The uplift of adoration brings the humble but blessed beholder to the threshold of a worship which miraculously transforms him just by beholding.

Out of the horrors of the second World War came an expression of such worship—a poem written by a nineteen-year-old flyer who met his death serving with the Royal Canadian Air Force. His father was an Episcopal rector whom I knew in Washington.
Pilot-Officer John Gillespie Magee, Jr., called his poem "High Flight. . . . "[18]

"Oh, I have slipped the surly bonds of earth,
And danced the skies on laughter-silvered wings.
Sunward I've climbed, and joined the tumbling mirth
Of sun-split clouds—and done a hundred things
You have not dreamed of—wheeled and soared and swung
High on the sunlit silence. Hov'ring there,
I've chased the shouting wind along, and flung

My eager craft through footless halls of air.

"Up, up the long, delirious, burning blue,
I've topped the windswept heights with easy grace
Where never lark, or even eagle flew—
And, while with silent, lifting mind I've trod
The high untrespassed sanctity of space,
Put out my hand and touched the face of God."

The Christian is to seek the things above—to seek them
   as the needle seeks the pole . . .
   as the sunflower seeks the sun . . .
   as the river seeks the sea . . .
   as the eagle seeks the ceiling of the world.

That was why Paul pleaded with the first-century Christians
to set their affections on things above . . .
          high things
          lofty concepts
and "not on the things of the earth."

But it is so difficult for us to transfer our affections, for we have
fallen in love with toyland
   and our playthings have become so dear.

It is so difficult for us to believe the truth: that this life is but a
preparation for a greater and more glorious one to come . . .
and that if we would only believe,
   if we only had enough faith and the right kind and were
   seeking the "things above . . . "
all our real needs—earth's trinkets for which we strive so
desperately—would be provided for us.

Once and for all, we must put out of our minds that the
purpose of life here is to enjoy ourselves
          to have a good time
         to be happy
        to make money
and to live in ease and comfort.

That is not what life is all about.
You were put here for a purpose, and that purpose is not
related to superficial pleasures.

No one owes you a living—not your parents, not your government, not life itself.
You do not have a right to happiness.

You have a right to nothing.
I believe that God wants us to be happy—but it is not a
                    matter of *our right*, but of His *love and mercy.*

The time for drifting
     or sleeping
  or wishful thinking
or daydreaming is over.
The state of our world today makes that a very dangerous
pastime.

This generation of young people and all of you who are
sensitive to what is going on around you, are called to a
supreme adventure.
There is a great stirring in society.
The upheavals of life and the revolutions of multitudes across
the world in desperate motion are indications that our world
can never be the same again.

So do not ever underestimate what you can do. You have the
courage to cast off your acrophobia
     and to dream big
   and to aim high—
if you do it with God's help.

Two years before I left Scotland, I had a small part in a remark-
able demonstration of what youthful vision combined with
Christian faith can accomplish.

Bert Patterson was a medical student in Glasgow University,
very much in love with Nessie Knight.
They had been friends through high school.
They were wholesome young people, interested in life and
eager to invest their personalities to some noble end.
Both belonged to a group of about twenty of us who went
around together.
We played football and cricket.
The girls had a hockey team.
We went to picnics together . . . took hikes . . .

Normal young people—fond of life
full of fun
with some of the virtues and most of the faults of young
people anywhere.

At last Bert graduated . . .
secured his medical degree and volunteered to go to Africa
as a medical missionary.
Before he left, he and Nessie were married.
Leaving his wife at home, he then went out to establish the
Scotch Presbyterian Medical Mission at Sulenkama, Africa.

Bert knew there was nothing in Africa for him but a grass hut
and a tremendous need.
He determined to build a hospital
a dispensary
and a compound
before he could ask Nessie to come out to help him in his
work.

To those of us who were left behind there came the challenge
to do what we could to build that hospital and dispensary for
them in Africa.

Bert had gone out like a happy warrior to tramp the high road
of service and sacrifice . . . .
Surely there was something we at home could do.

Money was scarce . . .
Mission committees were hard up . . .
The churches were giving all they could, but there were
so many needs.

Now Nessie was quite small, but her heart was big, and she
had the spirit of a giant.
She organized us into a dramatic club to raise the money
needed to build the hospital.
She was director and coach,
organizer and leader
of one of the craziest, maddest, and most thrilling ventures
with which I have ever been connected.

We decided to present two plays by Sir James Barrie—*Quality
Street* and *Dear Brutus.*

We determined to present the plays in one of Glasgow's downtown theaters—the Coliseum—and to hire it for a week.

It was a fantastic sort of thing, I must admit, to think that a gang of twenty young people could hire a theater for a week, and do a good job of presenting such challenging plays . . .
>   to do it in such a way as to raise enough money to build a
>   hospital in Africa.

Nevertheless, I can only tell you what happened.

Sir James Barrie presented to us an autographed copy of the plays that they might be auctioned and the money applied to the fund.

Sir Horace Fellowes, a noted conductor, not only agreed to let his orchestra play, but he himself came on the opening night to conduct.

Each one of us frantically sold tickets for weeks before the production.
We enlisted all our friends in schools and in offices,
>   in restaurants and in picture houses,
>   in university and church,
>   in the stores and in the tramcars.

We secured the help of the newspapers.
There was something about the whole mad enterprise that captivated our fathers and mothers.

Suffice it to say that the plays were successful beyond our dreams.
The young people acted as if they were inspired, and who can say they weren't?
And every night for a week hordes of people came to the Coliseum theater and caught the spirit of it all, so that in the end enough money was sent out to Bert to build his dispensary and a compound—a place for him to work and live.
And Nessie went out to Africa at the close of the year to join him in God's work.

Nor does the story end there.
The next year Nessie's sister, Jean, directed another of Barrie's plays, *Mary Rose*, and played the lead herself to raise enough money this time to build a hospital.

One of the Glasgow newspapers in telling the story called Bert
and Nessie "pilgrims of the Lonely Way . . . . "
But I wonder if their way is so lonely after all!

Pilgrims of the Lonely Way. . . Pilgrims unafraid to reach . . .
They are in good company.
There are great people who walk beside them—a rich fellowship dedicated to hard labor and austere lives in far-off places.
But the excitement
    the joy
        the adventure
            the deep inner satisfactions
of those who dare to reach sky-high more than make up for
any loneliness.

For no way can be lonely if it is the way Christ walks . . .
No way can be lonely if it is the way to which He calls you.

O UR FATHER IN HEAVEN, give us the long view of our work
    and our world.
    Help us to see that it is better to fail in a cause that will
ultimately suceed than to succeed in a cause that will ultimately fail . . . .
    May Thy will be done here, and may Thy program be
carried out, above party and personality, beyond time and
circumstance, for the good of America and the peace of the
world.
    This we ask in Jesus' name, Amen.

Our Friend, the Enemy

T o most moderns, the devil is either a swear word
                    or an allusion to archaic folklore.
Nowadays the devil has become a clown in pantomime . . .
                    and hell a sardonic jest.

Quite in the mood of this gay, spoofing approach to the
subject is the now-famous book *The Screwtape Letters*, written
by the Oxford don C. S. Lewis.
The book is a series of letters from a senior devil, Screwtape,
to his underling and apprentice, Wormwood.

Wormwood has been given the assignment of seeing to it that
one average, middle-class Englishman never makes it to the
Father's house.

But underneath the blithe, sparkling façade of the book, there
are deep philosophical and spiritual insights.
Mr. Lewis wrote *The Screwtape Letters* not just as a humorous
exercise, but for a reason.

He had important things to say:
That there is a Dark Power in our world . . .
That this Evil Power has intelligence and wit . . .
                    was created by God . . .
                    was once good . . .
                    and went wrong.
That on this earth there is a war to the finish between God and
this Evil Power . . .

That we human beings are never so much in danger,
                    or please the Evil Power so much,
as when we do not believe that he exists, or refuse to take him
seriously.

"I know someone will ask me," Mr. Lewis writes in another
place, " 'Do you really mean, at this time of day, to reintroduce
our old friend the devil—hoofs and horns and all?'

"Well, what the time of day has to do with it I don't know.
And I'm not particular about the hoofs and horns.
But in other respects my answer is, 'Yes, I do . . . . ' " [19]

In so doing, Mr. Lewis places himself squarely back into the
stream of Jesus' teaching about the evil in our world.
In at least forty-three separate references recorded in the
Gospels, Jesus spoke of this Evil Personality, giving him a
variety of names:
    Satan . . .
      the Devil . . .
        the Enemy . . .
          the Adversary
          Tempter.

A loving heavenly Father is never the author of evil, Christ
insisted.
He attributed to this Dark Power all disease
                    pain
                depravity
          sin
            and death.
Hence the devil is one to be taken seriously indeed.

One does not take lightly the one responsible for a face eaten
by leprosy with a gaping hole where the nose has been . . .
    Or screaming children laid on the fiery arms of idols . . .
      Or the lust for world domination that reduced hundreds
      of thousands of men to the level of animals through
      slavery . . .
      Or the big business of prostitution.

If what Jesus had to say about the devil is true, then he is
something more than an idea for a Halloween costume.
But if what Jesus taught about the Evil One is merely superstitious nonsense, then how could we take authoritatively
anything else Christ said?

In Christ's eyes the stakes here are desperately high:
                  your immortal soul and mine,
where we shall spend eternity—either in the Father's house or
lost from ourselves, our Maker, and our fellows.

Jesus warns us that the devil's techniques are insidious.
In our time we have heard a great deal about infiltration.
But the Communists did not invent it.
It started back in the Garden of Eden when a snake slithered
his way into Paradise . . .
    and this technique has been used ever since.

There is no more perfect illustration of the way infiltration
works than the Old Testament story of "Little Sunshine" or
Samson.

Any young person would have admired Samson.
He was a powerful physical specimen . . .
    Head and shoulders above his companions . . .
        He had the easy grace of a born athlete . . .
and the wit of a toastmaster.

He loved life
    and practical jokes
        and laughter.
He was a born leader.

He had an open face, laughing and honest, a charm of personality which purchased for him indulgence rather than discipline from his parents—the discipline that might have saved
him.

His mother and his father had been told before his birth that
theirs was to be an extraordinary child, blessed with great gifts
of body, mind, and spirit.
And so, in full anticipation of the radiant energy which would
brighten their home, they named their son "Little Sunshine"
or "sun-man," for that is the meaning of *Samson*.

And then, as the child Samson grew, another even more
wonderful gift was added to the talents with which he had
been born:
    the Spirit of the Lord came upon him.

    "And the Spirit of the Lord began to move him at times in the
    camp of Dan between Zorah and Eshtaol" (Judges 13:25).

Even from the point of view of Samson's companions, rare
and awesome powers began to stir in him . . .

not only unparalleled physical strength,
> but also the ability to sway men,
>> to lead them.

And along with all this, there was his joy at being alive and young, with the world at his feet.

He became the romantic outlaw
> the benefactor of the downtrodden
>> the people's hero fighting the common enemy—the Philistines.

God was in the glory of this young man exulting unashamedly in splendid strength and developing muscle.

"Then went Samson down, and his father and his mother, to Timnath, and came to the vineyards of Timnath: and, behold, a young lion roared against him.

"And the Spirit of the Lord came mightily upon him, and he rent him as he would have rent a kid, and he had nothing in his hand . . . " (Judges 14:5–6).

Can you imagine what strength it would take for a man to subdue a lion with his bare hands?

And then we have a touch that makes Samson seem lovably modest:

" . . . but he told not his father or his mother what he had done" (Judges 14:6).

His father had always disliked braggarts.
Besides, most mothers are not fond of their darlings fooling around with lions.
Better to keep that quiet!

Then Samson deliberately chose an insulting weapon with which to swat Philistines:
> the jawbone of an ass.

Quite indifferent to the odds against him, he dove into a free-for-all fracas, with the final tally at one thousand Philistines.

So he goes cavorting through the pages of the book of
> Judges . . .
>> full of riddles . . .

playing tricks . . .
and practical jokes
with the firebrand stunt the craziest of all.

"Little Sunshine" caught three hundred foxes,
tied them together in pairs by the tails, with a lighted
firebrand knotted in the tails.
Then he turned the crazed animals loose into the enemy's
ripening cornfields . . . vineyards . . . olive orchards.

The tale must have traveled from mouth to mouth as rapidly
as the fire had spread.

Samson was now a giant in the community
the hero who won every contest
adored by the children
admired by the aged
envied by the other young men
worshiped by the girls.

He could do no wrong—or could he?
We are not told when his downfall began, but it is not difficult
to piece the story together.
Was there ever a male hero who was not tempted by the
seductive young thing?

One common desire of youth then, as now, was to be popular
to be sought after
admired
complimented
invited here and there.
No one knows this better than the devil, for it was he who
planted these seeds in the hearts of youth.

For any of us—as for Samson—the temptation is to put ourselves first, at the center of life,
to play at being god.
"I want what I want . . . "
My will—or God's will.

In this case, God had a great plan for Samson:

" . . . he shall begin to deliver Israel out of the hand of the
Philistines" (Judges 13:5).

"Little Sunshine" was meant to swat Philistines, all right, but
for a better purpose than personal glory.

More than that, he was meant to be a Nazirite . . .
   His body was to be kept clean of strong drink and sensual
   indulgence . . .
   No razor was ever to touch his head.

But the human will is always free.
God will force no man to obey Him, nor will He shield any
man from temptation.
The sin is not in being tempted but in yielding.
This is our battleground, where every human being faces a
decision between God and the devil.

So Samson was tempted.
He saw a woman in Timnath, a daughter of the Philistines,
and he took it into his head that he wanted her for his wife.
His parents protested and pleaded, but the pattern had been
set years before . . .
They had never been able to resist their child's willfulness;
                            they could not now.

The devil came to Samson in a woman's guise; he often
has . . .
   he often does.
Samson married the girl, and it was a pathetic travesty of a
marriage, because God was not in it.
Read the story for yourself in Judges.

So Samson lost his first battle with temptation—and we can be
sure that it *was* a battle.
For God, having blessed Samson with unusual gifts, needed
him.
There had to be a tremendous battle within, particularly that
first time.

But after the first giving-in to temptation, our defenses are
weaker the next time.
We have handed over our wills to this Evil Power,
   fraternized with him like the friend he pretends to be.
He has won control.
His sly suggestions infiltrate . . .

then contaminate . . .
then dominate.

"Then went Samson to Gaza, and saw there an harlot, and went in unto her" (Judges 16:1).

And so the man who with his bare hands had torn a lion limb from limb was victim of a snakebite in the tall grass of sensual indulgence.

The argument that desire alone is sufficient excuse for conduct is a philosophy as old as sex.
The unbridling of passion . . .
the exaltation of sexual pleasures torn from the context of life
and worshiped as the god of happiness—
this rationale has been given a fresh Freudian face in our century; otherwise there is nothing "modern" about it.

The temptation is always to purchase popularity by joining the crowd around the bargain counters of hell, when in exchange for an irrecoverable,
fragile,
precious thing—purity—
the devil will offer the cheap, glittering baubles with which his hooks are baited.

But the truth is that the devil has no bargains.
"Take what you want, Samson.
We can settle up later. . . . "

One of the devil's tricks is this:
When we choose evil, usually we get what we want at once and pay for it afterward.
When we choose good we have to pay for it first before we get it.

Most of us have found this out with as simple a matter as examinations in school.

If you chose good grades and a degree with honor, you had to pay months ago with hard study,
the giving up of some pleasure and recreation.

But if you chose to have a good time, you began that long ago, and you have had your fun.

You did not pay then, but you are paying now in your frantic,
last-minute boning for your exams, and your paying is not
over yet.
There will be further deferred payments later in your life.

Make no mistake about it.
This Evil Personality is very real and very subtle.
He is real to me; I know him well.

He wants to persuade us to choose the things that we do not
have to pay for right away.
Usually they are cheap and sordid things.
"You want it," the devil says. "Charge it.
I understand. I'm your friend. Take what you want."

But the bills always come due.
And what is more, they are not all presented to you.
Payments must also be made by those close to you, bound to
you through all eternity by ties of blood and bonds of love.
In Zorah, Samson's parents would worry . . . and hope . . .
                    and pray . . . and finally grieve.

There were other women after the harlot, and finally Delilah.
Samson was still trifling with the devil's baubles.
He thought he could handle them, only to find, when it was
too late, that he had flirted with temptation too often.

The story moves on.
    The scene changes.
        The music moves into a minor key.

Samson, his massive head in Delilah's lap, says, "I will go out
as at other times before, and shake myself . . . "
And then as you read, you catch your breath,
for the next words are so simple,
                    so terrible . . .

    "And he wist not that the Lord was departed from him"
    (Judges 16:20).

The Spirit of the Lord had been pushed out of a man's heart.
No man can serve God *and* the devil.
Samson had long since made his choice, had clasped the
serpent to his heart.

He had had his fun; now was the day of reckoning.

The Philistines had him at last, and there was no shaking them off this time.
The repeated yieldings to temptation had sapped Samson's vital strength.

"I will go out as at other times. . . ."
How often we have heard it: "I will pull myself together."
Ah, but this was not as other times:

" . . . the Philistines took him, and put out his eyes, and brought him down to Gaza, and bound him with fetters of brass; and he did grind in the prison house" (Judges 16:21).

Bound and blind in the prison of the Philistines was Samson—
the hero meant to deliver his nation from their hands.
The true nature of the Dark Power was out in the open now.
A wrecked manhood
an empty shell of a person
God's great plans all awry
a broken heart
gaping sockets where shining eyes had been.

But in his darkness "Little Sunshine" remembered the man he might have been . . .
He thought of the God he had abandoned . . .
And once more he prayed to that God:

"O Lord God, remember me, I pray thee, and strengthen me, I pray thee, only this once, O God, that I may be at once avenged of the Philistines for my two eyes" (Judges 16:28).

It was the last cry of a desperate man.
"Remember me . . . only this once . . . ."

Some part of his old strength returned to him.
Three thousand of the enemy were gathered in a great pillared hall.
They had sent for Samson to make sport of him.
So, groping his way, he found the two key pillars of the house,
bowed himself with all his might,
and in a thunder of crashing beams, collapsing masonry, and screaming men and women, the house fell.

The tragedy had come full circle.
The story ends with a sob . . . .

"So the dead which he slew at his death were more than
they which he slew in his life" (Judges 16:30).

Now we begin to see why Jesus, who loves us
                        and wills the good things of life for us,
wants us to know the true nature of the Evil Power with whom
we temporize.

Then is one like Samson lost forever to his Father's house,
                                    his Father's love?

We cannot know.
The one thing we do know is that—according to Jesus—
we can count on no blessed oblivion in death.
For Samson, as for all of us, the curtain comes down,
                            only to rise again.

Jesus warned us over and over that a lifetime of setting self-
will up as king . . .
    of making the wrong choices . . .
                inevitably leads down the broad road to hell.

He spoke of "the outer darkness" . . .
                "the lake of fire" . . .
                    "the everlasting fire" . . .
Not, as we might expect, so much to the murderers, the
prostitutes, or the outcasts . . .
            but to the scribes and Pharisees
        to His own disciples
    to the church people
  to the scholars and intelligentsia . . .
to them He had a great deal to say about hell.

You may not like it.
You may not believe in hell, but there it was, in repeated
references—on the lips of this "gentle Jesus, meek and mild."

The twentieth-century sophisticate is inclined to say conde-
scendingly, "Isn't all this merely a relic of a dark superstitious
past when bogeymen were conjured up to frighten children
into being good?

"If there is a God, He couldn't possibly permit such a place.
I cannot imagine it . . .
    I cannot entertain the thought . . .
        Therefore I won't."

I remember in a humble restaurant in a poorer quarter of
Atlanta, Georgia, seeing a card underneath the glass on the
counter. The card said:

    "Because you don't believe in hell is no sign you ain't going
    there."

Despite its crudity and bad grammar, there is an underlying
truth in that homely observation.
Far too often we moderns are tempted to think that just
because we reject an idea, it therefore ceases to be.

Certainly we need not discuss a literal hell.
I am not concerned that you believe in a burning pit,
                a boiling cauldron,
           the devil with a forked tail,
           the smoke and the flames.
Personally, I think hell will be more terrible than that!

Suppose a soul passes through the curtain of death without
the purging work of Christ—still soiled—with a record of
                          crime
                        iniquity
             sin and degradation.

Suppose that through all eternity he has to witness the playing and the replaying of his record upon earth . . .
Or to use another figure of speech, as though he were in a
motion picture house, seeing the same pictures over and over
again.
Would not that be hell?

We are told in the Bible that the inhabitants of hell . . .
those members of the lost legion . . . will be murderers
                idolators
            whoremongers
          sorcerers
       liars.

Now the lust to kill or to inflict pain
> to abuse sex . . .
>> to crave drink
>>> or narcotics . . .
these things are of the spirit, make no mistake.
They are spiritual urges.
We sin in the flesh . . . yes, but of the spirit!

These are sins of desire . . . and we desire, not with our body,
but with our spirits.
We desire with our souls, do we not?
The body supplies the vehicle of consummation . . .
> the means of gratification of a base urge.

When the clock chimes for us, we leave the body behind, and
it returns to the dust whence it came.

But the soul . . . what of it?
It goes on, we are told—the unsaved soul to join the lost legion
. . . to swell the ranks of the hopeless outcasts.
It goes on—with its longings
> its cravings
>> its lusts and passions—
>>> on behind the curtain.

Suppose then, these damned souls still have their desires and
lusts . . . their passions and their cravings . . . gnawing—
eating—burning constantly at their personalities,
and they have no bodies with which to gratify them?
Would not that be hell?
What could be more terrible than the thought of those lost
souls completely turned over to the base passions which they
had deliberately chosen in life?

I think that in this connection the Old Testament injunction:
    "Choose you this day whom ye will serve" (Joshua 24:15),
or in the New Testament:
    "No man can serve two masters . . . God and mammon"
(Matthew 6:24), has a deep significance.

Let me remind you that God does not send anyone to hell.
He permits the soul a choice . . . and if a human being has
chosen to gratify the lusts of the flesh rather than the longings
of the spirit . . .

that soul may have to be left with that choice!

What have you chosen?
What are you choosing—day by day?

The proof of how real Jesus knew hell to be is that He came to earth to save us from it . . .

"For this purpose the Son of God was manifested, that he might destroy the works of the devil" (I John 3:8).

In other words, the reason that the God-Man came among us to live a while on the planet Earth was to fight to the finish the Evil Power.

Christ gave His life to make sure of victory.

He was willing to be scourged . . .
            lashed with leather thongs studded with steel . . .
willing to be spat upon,
                smitten,
                    humiliated . . . .
He was willing to be nailed to the cross with huge nails driven through His hands and feet.

He was willing to endure such pain as we cannot imagine . . .
                    willing to burn up with thirst . . .
Willing to die suspended between earth and heaven . . .
Willing to be separated temporarily from His Father . . .
Willing to go even into hell itself.

"He was dead and buried and descended into hell . . . "
Millions in churches throughout the world repeat this every Sunday in the Apostles' Creed.

How? Why? In what way did Jesus go into hell?
It is Peter who gives us some clues in his first epistle.
Jesus' work of redemption on the cross would not be complete if it included only those who were living,
            or even those who would live in future centuries.

What of those—like Samson—who had lived before?
They must hear the good news too.
They must have their chance to embrace belief.

So, says Peter, during those three days, Christ's living Spirit went and preached "to them that are dead . . . " (I Peter 4:6).

They, too, must know that Jesus has offered us a way out . . .
the opening of our wills and hearts and minds to His cleansing,
    the giving of our lives to His safekeeping,
        the acceptance for ourselves of what He did for us on the cross.

Even in this, our wills are free to accept or reject.
But let us soberly consider the price we shall pay if we reject Christ's love.

He is the only One who can deal with our sins,
the only One who can open our inner eyes to perceive the tricks of the devil within us,
    the only One who can supply us with the strength to resist temptation,
        the only Friend who will never deceive us.

Others promise us sins excused
                        discounted
                    denied
                explained away.
But only at the foot of the cross do we ever experience the beautiful divine contradiction of *sins forgiven*.

Here is the greatest miracle of all!
    that God loves men even in their hate . . .
        that His heart yearns for us even in our indifference . . .
            that His pardon and His grace are waiting for us even though we may feel no need of either . . .
                that God, for Christ's sake, is willing to forgive sinners such as you and me.

W E CONFESS, O LORD, that we think too much of ourselves, for ourselves, and about ourselves.

If our Lord had thought about Himself, we would not now
have the liberty in which and for which we pray.

If the great men whom we honor for their part in building
our nation had thought about themselves, we would have no
free republic today.

Help us to see, O Lord, that "I" is in the middle of sin; that
when we think too highly of ourselves we may never be used
of Thee in Thy service for all mankind.

In Thy name, we pray. Amen.

Book V

The First Easter

By suffering for our sins on the cross,
Christ Jesus has paid the penalty for us.
With His own blood, He has written "Paid"
across the ledgers of heaven.

To Peter Marshall, the compass needle of Christianity pointed inevitably to Resurrection morning. He lavished his best thinking, his most careful preparation, and all his gifts for sermonizing through the years on his Easter messages. In these messages, his ability to paint a picture in words, to enable his listeners to see and hear and feel an incident, rose to its greatest height.

After Peter's death I found in my possession 96 Easter manuscripts from eighteen years and four months of preaching. In reviewing these sermons covering the events of Passion Week, I quickly found myself caught up in drama—sheer, engrossing drama, at times tender, at times terrible. And always I found myself moved by Peter's ability to enlist the emotions on the side of faith.

Thus *The First Easter* enfolded itself, and is reproduced in this section in its entirety. My only part in it was to shape from the many sermons Dr. Marshall's recreation of each scene as event followed event, and to edit the material only where necessary to weave it together.

Here, then, is Easter—the triumphant morning of Christianity—seen through the eyes and described from the heart of one man.

C. M.

W hat is this mysterious, strange, joyous influence that
seems to permeate everything at this time of the year
. . . that lingers, like a sweet perfume, delicate and clean, to
touch us all with its magic?

It is an intriguing thing . . . intangible, yet real.

We feel it . . .
   sense it . . .
      thrill to it.

There is more to it than bunny rabbits
    and colored eggs
        and gay new clothes.

Easter is more than a celebration
    because the sap is rising in the trees . . .
        and the bare branches are slipping bright green rings
        on bony fingers . . .
    and blossoms are turning wood and garden into fairyland.

Easter is more than a spring festival.
So far as the church is concerned, the message of Easter is
contained in the declaration
                "Christ is Risen!"

Did the Lord really rise from the dead?

   Is it true that He is alive?
     Was that tomb in Jerusalem really empty?
      Can we believe it?
Do we believe it?

Either we are dealing here with flaming truth or the hideous
falsehood of the Christian gospel.
It is important that we know which.

For if the Resurrection is a fact, then the events that took place
in the city of Jerusalem between the 14th Nisan and the 16th
Nisan in the year 3790 or—as we now record time—between
April 7 and April 9, Anno Domini 30, are the most important
and significant events in history.

What did happen?

Hear that story as it is given us . . . .

It was night.

Outside in the streets of Jerusalem, shadows fled before
a full moon rising over the pinnacles of the Temple.
Time was ebbing towards its close—and its beginning—
the cleft that would for the rest of recorded history mark it
                    Before Christ . . . After Christ . . .

A sinister silence beat in upon the heavy hearts of a group
of twelve men gathered in an Upper Room.
They knew that something dreadful was about to happen and
they were apprehensive.
This was the last night of Jesus' life on earth.
He had looked forward to this occasion—
                    having His own apostles—
              His chosen friends—
              His intimate companions
for three years grouped around Him in the fellowship of the
Last Supper.

He had Himself made the arrangements for the supper.
"Look for a man carrying a pitcher of water," He had told
His disciples.
That in itself would be an unusual thing
    for it was the women who usually carried the water.
The man would lead them to this Upper Room, perhaps in the
home of John Mark's father—a guest room built on the flat roof
of the house

Pillars supported a roof closed in with curtains, and
the curtains billowed and swung in a cool evening breeze.
A lamp hanging from the ceiling cast flickering light.

The men were reclining on couches around a low
U-shaped table.
At the Master's left was Simon Peter . . . at His right, John.

A quiet voice spoke:
        "With desire I have desired to eat this passover
        with you before I suffer. . . ."

Bronzed hands took a loaf of bread . . .
  gave thanks for it . . .
    broke it . . .
      "This is my body which is given for you:
      this do in remembrance of me. . . ."

The Last Supper was to institute a memorial—the loving
desire to be remembered.

Christ relied upon homely symbols—
  a piece of bread,
    a cup of the juice of the lowly grape—
to recall Him to future generations.

He knew that we would be in constant danger of
forgetting Him . . .
Therefore He enlisted sense on the side of faith and trusted
to these simple everyday memorials for the recalling
to our treacherous memories of His undying love.
      "This is my blood of the new testament [a new
      agreement] which is shed for many for the
      remission of sins. . . Drink ye all of it. . . .
      But I say unto you, I will not drink henceforth of
      this fruit of the vine, until that day when I drink
      it new with you in my Father's kingdom."

Strange words with which to institute a sacrament.
What did He mean?
The words that fell from His lips that night are standing
evidence of Christ's own estimate as to where the center of
His work lies—
  We are to remember His death.
Never did He ask that we should commemorate His birth . . .
Not once did He request that any of the wonderful deeds
He performed should be immortalized . . .
Only this—His last and greatest work—
          the work of redemption.

This was to be His memorial—a cross—to remind us that
God's love for us is a love
  that hate cannot nullify
    and death cannot kill.

Already, days before, He had told His apostles:
>"Behold, we go up to Jerusalem . . . the Son of
>Man . . . shall be mocked, and spitefully
>entreated . . . and they shall scourge him, and
>put him to death; and the third day he shall rise
>again. . . ."

Outside the night was silent, as if all Jerusalem held its breath,
feeling the approach of the storm.
Like sequins, the lights of the city appeared
>>twinkling one by one.
And an indigo sky grew darker and darker.
One by one the city's noises were silenced.
But in the room itself there was noise, for the disciples
were quarreling.

Their argument had started earlier in the day as they had
walked to the supper.
Then they had divided into smaller groups, so as not
to attract too much attention as they gathered for
the evening meal.

Because there were no servants to bathe their feet and because
they had been arguing about who was to be chief among
them, nobody had made any gesture of ceremonial washing.

They had walked past the earthenware pitcher of water at the
door and had taken their places around the table—angry
>>argumentative
>>sulking
>>cross
>>tired.

We can imagine them stretching out their robes so as to cover
their feet—trying to pretend there was nothing wrong—when
everything was wrong.
They had looked like sulky schoolboys.
Who wanted to stoop to do a slave's work?

Now, during the supper, Jesus rose and took off His
outer garment.

Then He took a towel, girded Himself, poured water into
the basin and began to do the menial thing that not one
of them would do—
He began to wash the disciples' feet.

And He did it because He was the Son of God.

That lowly loving deed expressed in all its loneliness
the glory and humility of His own heart.

Did the apostle John tell us of this incident so that we might
understand that those who shared the Last Supper with Jesus
of Nazareth were no plaster saints?
These were ordinary men—quite like you and me—
     subject to nerves and temper
          to pettiness and self-centeredness.

John makes a very significant statement in telling of this
incident. He says:
          "Jesus knowing that the Father had given all things
          into his hands, and that he was come from God, and
          went to God; he riseth from supper . . . and be-
          gan. . . ."

To reveal His death by signs and miracles? No.
To show His authority by displays of superhuman power? No.
To act like an all-powerful dictator? No, no.

Christ, knowing who He was, having come forth from God,
knowing that He was going to God, began to "wash the
disciples' feet."

The glory of Christ's life on earth was not the ethereal glory of
the supernatural . . .

No—but rather the simple fact that He loved us,
     that He loved unlovely men and women
with a love that goes on loving—and goes on loving—so that
nothing can ever defeat it . . .
Nothing can ever break it down.

"Having loved his own which were in the world," adds John,
"he loved them unto the end."

Then Christ again took His place at the table.

All eyes were upon Him.
And a look like shadows blotting out the sun crossed
the Master's face.
> "Verily, I say unto you, that one of you shall
> betray me. . . ."

The apostles were shocked.
Peter blurted out, "Lord, surely it isn't I?"
And one by one they all asked, "Lord, is it I?"
> "He it is, to whom I shall give a sop, when
> I have dipped it."

Judas was sitting second from the Master on the right,
with John between them.
Jesus had known all along that Judas had been plotting.
He knew that Judas had gone to the chief priests some days
before and had offered to help them arrest Him.
For Caiaphas, the high priest, had long since decided
that this Jesus of Nazareth must be gotten out of the way.

So Christ took a piece of bread and, dipping it in a bowl of
haroseth, handed it to Judas.

And slowly Judas rose to his feet.
He strode towards the stairway, then pausing
with one hand on the heavy curtains, he turned
and faced Christ.

An awful look passed between them—
> sorrow on the face of the Master . . .
> determination, strain, evil on the swarthy face of Judas.
Then he turned and was gone.
The curtains swung behind him.
There was silence.

And John adds, "And it was night. . . ."

The eleven men who were left were very quiet.
The voice of Christ was very soft and low—
tender with farewell.

It was now only a matter of hours until Christ and His disciples would be separated.
He wished to fill those last hours of fellowship with the tenderest and most significant of His teachings.

The most sacred
  the most tender
    the most heartfelt emotions
are those expressed at the end of the letter. . . .

The tenderest caress comes just before the parting.
The softest word just before the conversation is ended
                     before the train pulls out
                       before we turn away.

We seem to catch the quiet intimacy of that fellowship.
Unforgettable words of parting and comfort were spoken by Jesus to His friends.
Jesus has written them out for us:

> "Little children . . . . a new commandment I give unto you, That ye love one another; as I have loved you. . . . By this shall all men know that ye are my disciples. . . .

> "Let not your heart be troubled. . . . In my Father's house are many mansions: if it were not so, I would have told you. . . .

> "I will not leave you comfortless: I will come to you. . . .

> "I am the vine, ye are the branches. . . . Abide in me, and I in you. . . .

> "These things I have spoken unto you, that in me ye might have peace. In the world ye shall have tribulation: but be of good cheer; I have overcome the world. . . ."

Overcome the world? When the One who spoke was so soon to fall under the power of Caesar?

Yes, for in reality we must remember that Jesus could have escaped the cross.

No one compelled Him to go to Jerusalem on that last journey.
Indeed, His friends and apostles urged Him not to go.

Watch Him in the bitter hours that lie immediately ahead,
   time after time taking the initiative in deciding His own fate.

Christ had begun His ministry by telling His apostles that the
Son of Man must suffer many things.
Must—there was no other way.
It was for that purpose that He had come into the world.

> "As Moses lifted up the serpent in the wilderness,
> even so must the Son of man be lifted up; that
> whosoever believeth in him should not perish, but
> have everlasting life."

There was Light in the little room that night.
But beyond the light lay a death-ridden world . . .
   in the midst of the military might that was Rome
         where life was cheap . . .
   in the philosopher's porticoes of Athens
         where the mind found no hope . . .
   in the dangerous living of the great shipping centers of Asia
   Minor to the disease-infested alleys of old Jerusalem—
Men feared death, dodged its hideous grasp, could nowhere
find respite from their fear.

But here was something new . . .
Here was One facing death—not afraid, but confident . . .
   already triumphant . . .
   already speaking about seeing His friends again . . . about
   never leaving them . . . .

Strange words . . . about being with them to the uttermost
parts of the earth and to the end of time.

How? Why? Because He alone knew the Father's eternal
purpose for what it was—the determination once and for all
to destroy the power of death—
once and for all to deliver men from their lifelong bondage to
the fear of death.

Within a matter of hours, Christ Himself was to become the
instrument by which the Father would—for all time—make
death not a wall . . . but a door.

The Last Supper was over.
And when they had sung a hymn, they went out into the
dark and deserted streets.
It was almost midnight.
Past the Lower Pool and through the Fountain Gate
they walked slowly, moving in little silent clusters.
For a time the narrow cobblestone street, banked high in
the middle, led beside the Brook Kedron.

The group moved up the hill
towards their favorite rendezvous—
        a garden called Gethsemane.

Here in the deep shadows of the night, moving along in the
deeper shadows of the trees, they halted.
A few lights twinkled on the hill opposite, but most of the city
was asleep, for it was now after midnight.
They could see the Temple, its spire tipped with gold,
glistening in the moonlight.
And from the ramparts of the Fortress Antonia they could
hear a Roman sentry calling his watch.

As they stood there looking across the valley at the holy city,
they wondered at the strange turn events had taken.
They remembered the reechoing shouts of the people . . .
        the glad Hosannas . . .
        and the crown that had been refused.
Some of them were thinking of how Judas had left their
fellowship to move out into the darkness.
They were wondering where he was and what he was doing.

The eleven could not know that the betrayer had already
agreed to Caiaphas' offer of thirty pieces of silver—
    the cost of a slave, it was—
Or that Caiaphas was even then moving under cover of the
velvet night to seek audience with the Roman procurator . . .
        "If the Nazarene is captured this night, will you
        agree to sit in the Tribunal to condemn him
        on the morrow?"

The group moved on into the garden under the gnarled

old trees.
The odor of the olive presses clung to the still night air.

And now there was a period of waiting, as though the Master
deliberately waited for some rendezvous with destiny—
His apostles knew not what.

Once again He could easily have escaped; yet He did not.
There was plenty of time, so much time that the weary
apostles—propped against the olive trees—fell asleep.

While they slept, Christ prayed . . .
   kneeling under the little gray-green leaves that gleamed
   white where the moonlight filtered through.
Was there then no way, no other way? . . .
      "Father, all things are possible unto thee; take away
      this cup from me. . . ."
"This cup" . . .
Often Christ had seen the bodies of the crucified hanging on
the hill outside the Gennath Gate . . .
Sometimes He had heard their moans and their curses,
seen them writhing in their final agony.

Jesus of Nazareth was a man—a real man.
Every bit of His manhood shrank from such an end.

And Luke tells us:
      " . . . being in an agony he prayed more earnestly:
      and his sweat was as it were great drops of blood
      falling down to the ground."

Already He was living the pain of it.
Could ultimate triumph come in no other way?
Human sin—man fleeing God—was capable of dreadful
deeds.
Of course . . . but must He be the One to taste every depth
that sin could devise . . .
     misunderstanding
    betrayal
   desertion by friends
  expediency
weakness
  callousness

deliberate cruelty
　　excruciating pain
　　　death itself . . .
in order to prove finally and forever that no evil is any match
for the Father?

The worn face glistening with sweat—so young in time—
　　grown so old in understanding . . .
　　　bowed in final surrender. . . .

　　"Nevertheless, not what I will, but what thou wilt."

The stillness of the garden was suddenly broken by the low
sound of voices . . .
And now a flickering torch came into view . . .
　　　　　　　　and another
　　　　　　　　and another.
Surely this was a procession.
There were soldiers. . . .
Twigs crackled under their feet and they stooped low as they
passed under the olive trees.
Someone in front carried a swinging lantern.

A nondescript mob it was—a rabble of indiscriminate
ruffians—the hangers-on of the Temple . . .
　　　　soldiers
　　　Temple guards
　　　Temple doorkeepers
　　little priests with big ambitions . . .
who had laid aside their rings of heavy keys . . .
exchanged their brooms for staves and spears and blud-
geons—armed to the teeth, determined to capture the most
peaceable One who ever walked upon the earth.

Out of that sickening crowd there stepped a familiar figure.
It was Judas, a smile upon his face.
"Hail, Master," he said . . . and kissed Him with a kiss that
must have burned Christ's cheek.

Thus identified, Christ was seized . . .
　　　bound with ropes . . .

His hands manacled
His arms tied to His side.

The disciples, too, were caught in the trap.
After a moment's hesitation, some of them seemed to gain
courage, to think of fighting in defense of their Master.

One asked, "Lord, shall we smite with the sword?"
And Peter—not waiting for the answer—drew from the folds
of his cloak a short sword . . .
    more like a dagger . . .
and recklessly struck a vicious blow at the nearest enemy.

It happened to be the high priest's servant, whose name was
Malchus—and the blow severed his right ear.

But when Christ saw what Peter had done, He quickly
commanded him to put up his sword:
    "They that take the sword shall perish with the sword."

The method of Peter was the sword . . .
The method of Christ was a cross . . .
Peter sought revenge . . .
Christ sought reconciliation.

Peter cried, "Give me a sword, and we can advance
the Kingdom."
Christ cried, "Give Me a cross, and I, if I be lifted up, will
draw all men unto Me."

And so they led Him away as a butcher might drag a steer
to the slaughterhouse.

Simon Peter had seen the last flickering torch disappear
round the turn of the path that wound down the hill. . . .
Only once in a while could the lights of the procession be seen
through the trees—like giant fireflies.

The murmur of voices died away,
    the crackling of twigs
        and the rustling of dislodged stones through the grass.
There swept over Peter the realization that his Master had at
last been captured and was marching away to die.

The icy fear that gripped his heart was a startling contrast to the flaming courage with which he had drawn his short sword a few minutes before, for this was a different Peter.

He realized that he had blundered, and that he had been rebuked.
Disappointed and puzzled, he could not understand the calm submission with which Christ had permitted them to bind His hands and march Him off.

Realizing that he stood alone in the deserted garden, Peter stumbled blindly down the trail, heedless of the twigs that lashed his face and tore at his robes.

Stumbling on down the hill, instinctively hurrying to catch up with the others, and yet not anxious to get too close, he followed down to the foot of the Mount of Olives, across the Brook Kedron, and back up the hill to old Jerusalem, still asleep and quiet.

The procession made first for the house of Annas, into which they escorted Jesus.
The heavy door creaked shut behind Him, and when Peter approached timidly, it was to find John standing there.

John persuaded the girl stationed at the door to let them in and, as they slipped past her, she scrutinized Peter and said to him:
    "Art not thou also one of this man's disciples?"
He said, "I am not."

Perhaps she felt that she could speak to Peter.
Perhaps she felt sorry for him, seeing the hurt, wounded look in his eyes and the pain in his face.

Who knows what was in her mind?
Perhaps she had seen the Master as they led Him in and felt the irresistible attraction of the Great Galilean.

Perhaps in that brief moment, as they had crowded past her, *He had looked at her.*
If He had—then something may have happened to her, within her own heart.

Her faith might have been born,
A fire kindled by the spark the winds of strange circumstances
had blown from the altar fires in the heart of the Son of God.

Perhaps she wanted to ask Peter more about the Master.
Perhaps she would have said—had Peter acknowledged Him:
>"Tell me the sound of His voice.
>Is it low and sweet, vibrant?
>Tell me of some of His miracles.
>Tell me how you are sure He is the Messiah.
>What is this salvation He speaks about?
>How can we live forever?"

Maybe these questions would have come tumbling in a torrent
from her lips . . . who knows?

But whatever she meant, whatever her motive for asking
the question,
>"Art not thou also one of this man's disciples?"
Peter denied his Lord and said: "I am not."

We can only stand aghast at Peter and wonder if the strain
and the shock have destroyed his memory.

Simon, surely you remember the first day you saw Him.
>Andrew and yourself floating the folded net . . . His shad-
>ow falling across you as you worked.
Don't you remember His command, His beckoning finger, the
light in His eyes, as He said: "Follow me, and *I will make you
fishers of men*"?

Peter, don't you remember?

And that night when Nicodemus came into the garden
looking for the Master . . .
Don't you remember how he crept in with his cloak pulled
up over his face?
Don't you remember how he frightened you, and how the
Lord and Nicodemus talked for hours about the promises?

Don't you remember the wedding in Cana where He turned
the water into wine?
Don't you remember the music of His laugh and the Sa-
maritan woman at Sychar?

Don't you remember these things, Simon? . . .

And now they brought the Lord from Annas to Caiaphas, and the soldiers and the Temple guards mingled with the servants in the courtyard.

Because the night was cold, they had kindled a fire in the brazier, and Peter joined himself to the group and, stretching out his hands, warmed himself at their fire.

Peter was glad to join the hangers-on huddled around the blaze, for the morning air bit sharply, and he found himself shivering . . .
It was a kindly glow of warmth.

Coarse laughter greeted every joke and they discussed the things such people talk about:
the prowess of the garrison's chariot drivers
the gambling losses of their friends
the new actor from Antioch at Herod's court
the additional water tax just levied
the latest gossip from Rome.

Peter was not paying much attention to their conversation until one of the soldiers nudged him and said:
"Thou art also of them."
And Peter said, for the second time: "Man, *I am not.*"

Peter, you must remember . . . surely . . . it must be that you are afraid.

Your brave heart must have turned to water.
Surely you cannot have forgotten . . .
Many a time . . . crossing the lake in boats like your own,
with its high seats
its patched sails slanting in the sun
and its thick oars?
Remember the night He came walking on the water, and you tried it, and were walking like the Master, until your courage left you . . . your faith gave way?

Simon, has your courage left you again?

Have you forgotten the pool at Bethesda and how you laughed when the impotent man rose . . . rolled up his bed

threw it over his shoulder
and went away leaping in the air and shouting?

Ah, Simon, you spoke so bravely . . . and now here you are.

For the next hour or so they merely waited.
What was keeping them so long?
They little knew the difficulty of getting witnesses to agree.
They little knew that sleepless men, with tempers raw and
irritated, were trying to find some reason they could submit
to Pilate that would justify their demands for the death
of Jesus.

After an hour had passed, there joined the group a soldier
who had come out of the palace.
As he greeted his friends in the circle, his eye fell on Peter.
He scrutinized him very carefully, and Peter, feeling the
examination of the newcomer, looked around as the soldier
asked: "Did not I see thee in the garden with him?"

One of his friends joined in:
    "Certainly—he's one of the Galileans.
    Just listen to his accent."

And the soldier stubbornly went on: "I am sure I saw him in
the garden, for my kinsman, Malchus, was wounded by one
of them who drew a sword . . .
And if I am not mistaken—it was this fellow here."

Then Peter, beginning to curse and to swear, said:
    "*I know not the man.*"

He used language he had not used for years.
It was vile . . . even the soldiers were shocked.
They all looked at him in amazement.

They did not appear to notice the shuffling of feet, as soldiers
led Christ from Caiaphas to Pilate.
Perhaps they did not make much noise.
They were tired, worn with argument and talk, so they were
very quiet.

The group standing round the fire was silent, shocked at the
vehemence and the profanity of Peter's denial.

It was a torrent of foulness, but it was his face that
startled them.
It was livid
     distorted
   eyes blazing
   mouth snarling like a cornered animal.
It was not a pleasant sight, and they kept silent.
It was a silence so intense that the crowing of a distant cock
was like a bugle call . . .

Immediately, Peter remembered the Lord's prophecy:
   "Before the cock crow twice, thou shalt deny me thrice."

Like a wave there swept over him the realization of what he
had done.
All of a sudden he remembered what Jesus had said and, with
tears streaming down his face, he turned away from the fire.

Through a mist of tears he saw ahead of him the stairway that
led to Pilate's palace . . .
And by a terrible Providence, it was just at that moment that
Christ was being led up the stairs to appear before Pilate.

The Lord had heard!
The Lord had heard every hot, searing word . . .
The Lord had heard the blistering denial . . . the foul
   fisherman's oaths . . .
He—He had heard it all!

Christ paused on the stair, and looked down over the rail—
   looked right into the very soul of Peter.
The eyes of the two met . . . at that awful moment.

Through his tears all else was a blur to Peter.
But that one face shone through the tears . . .
   that lovely face
     that terrible face
        those eyes—sad, reproachful, tender . . . as if they
        understood and forgave.

Ah, how well he knew Him, and how much he loved Him.

The world seemed to stand still, as for that terrible moment,
Peter looked at the One he had denied.

We shall never know what passed between them.
Christ seemed to say again:

> "But I have prayed for thee, Simon,
> Satan hath desired to have thee,
> But I have prayed for thee."

Simon's tears now overflowed and ran down his cheeks—
            hot and scalding tears they were—
And with great sobs shaking his strong frame, he spun round
and rushed out to where the cool morning air might fan his
burning cheeks.

He fled with his heart pounding in his breast, while the
Nazarene walked steadily to meet the Roman governor.

> "Then assembled together the chief priests, and the
> scribes, and the elders of the people, unto the palace
> of the high priest, who was called Caiaphas,
> And consulted that they might take Jesus by subtilty,
> and kill him.
>
> "But they said, Not on the feast day, lest there be an
> uproar among the people."

Why did the religionists of Jesus' time want to kill Him?
Why was Caiaphas in particular anxious to get Him out of
the way?
What was the charge against the Nazarene?

The Sadducees were the religious elite of the day.
Not only was Caiaphas, the present high priest, a Sadducee,
but he was also the son-in-law of Annas, now an old man,
whom he had succeeded in that office.
Now that Palestine was under Roman jurisdiction,
even the high priest was a Roman appointee.
But so crafty a politician was Annas that Caiaphas was the
seventh member of his own family to receive the coveted
appointment.

Both were wealthy men.
The Temple—the religious domain over which they pre-
sided—was also a financial empire.
By a rare financial strategy, they had made it so.

Annas and Caiaphas controlled the market in the Temple porch, where sacrifices were sold to pilgrim worshipers and Roman money was exchanged for the statutory half-shekel required as a temple offering.

The priests determined the rate of exchange and made money shamelessly.

Moreover, they drew rent from the ground on which the sellers of animals for sacrifice put up their stalls and stacked their dove cages.
The people knew this and resented it, but what could they do? What can the general populace ever do about taxes that eat up the fat of the land?
An income equivalent to about a million and a half dollars a year was flowing into the Temple treasuries.

Jesus knew all this; it was common knowledge.
No wonder His indignation was aroused, especially when this evil was carried on in the name of worship of the living God.

The most scathing words He ever uttered were spoken against the men who perpetrated this wholesale theft.
The scathing words had come to the ears of Annas and Caiaphas.
For many months they had had spies reporting back to them on the itinerant preacher.
Exactly how dangerous was He?
The day came when the Nazarene strode into the Temple court and overthrew the tables of the moneychangers.
That dynamic figure had stridden about among the merchants, unafraid.
The folds of His robe falling away from His right arm had revealed powerful muscles.
Angry priests had stood helplessly by,
    muttering threats in throaty growls. . . .

The moneychangers had screamed in frenzy
    as they had groveled among the filth to retrieve their coins
    that had rolled in a hundred directions.
And the pilgrims who had been bled white all these years had laughed and added their own shouts of encouragement.

Minutes later an observer had run to tell the servant of the high priest.

But Caiaphas was afraid of the common people and dared not intervene.
For the popularity of this Jesus was largely with the common folk.
Stories of His wonderful works were everywhere.

The beggars in the streets talked of them . . .
They were discussed by the drivers of the caravans at every stop . . .
And the stories lost nothing in the telling.

It was said that He healed the blind. . . .
There were cripples who had thrown away their crutches . . .
There was a current story about a little girl who had been dead and had been restored to her father . . .
And now the latest story—
    the one about Lazarus, a prominent citizen, indeed a wealthy man of Bethany, being brought back to life. . . .

Caiaphas had secretly checked and rechecked.
That task had not been too difficult, because Bethany was so close.

He had been unable to find anyone to refute the story—
             It was so odd!
        Enough to make a man uneasy—
With such power and a growing following, anything could happen.

No wonder the chief priests and the Pharisees got together and asked:
        "What shall we do? for this man doeth many mira-
        cles. If we let him thus alone, all men will believe on
        him; And the Romans shall come and take away both
        our place and nation."

Caiaphas was the one who suggested a solution.
Only the Romans could execute a death sentence.
Surely it was useless to settle for less.
Nothing else would finally silence the Galilean.

Therefore the crux of the problem was to find a charge against
Jesus that would satisfy Roman law.

The high priest well knew that if the true Messiah should ever
come, there would be two immediate results . . .
    The political supremacy of Rome would be challenged
    by revolt. This would mean Rome's suppression of the
    revolt by violence,
                and
    The Messiah, if accepted by the people, would usurp
    Caiaphas' own position and power.

Did not this Jesus claim to be the Messiah?
Then this was the perfect charge. . . .
So Caiaphas argued to the priests:
    "It is expedient for you that one man should die for the
    people, and that the whole nation perish not.
    From that day forth, they took counsel that they might put him to
    death."

And now, with Judas' help, it had come.
The Nazarene,
    His hands bound with ropes,
    His face and beard matted with blood from the blows of the
    soldiers . . .
stood before him.

The court had been hastily convened in the middle of the
night.
Some of Caiaphas' colleagues might have been drowsy and
half-asleep at that time, but the high priest was
thoroughly alert.

For hours he had been busy getting word to the
seventy members of the Sanhedrin . . .
    trying to round up men who would testify against Christ.
Haste was important.

The members of the Sanhedrin sat on stone seats in a
three-tiered semicircle.
Some seats were vacant; it was still an hour before dawn.

Witness after witness came forward.
But the witnesses could not agree among themselves
and the prisoner refused to say anything.
As soon as one spoke against Jesus, another contradicted
and a great tumult broke out.

Caiaphas grew red in the face with mounting frustration. He
had already risked much to bring Jesus to trial:

It was illegal for the Temple guard, acting under the orders
of the high priest, to arrest the prisoner.
The arrest should have been made spontaneously by
the witnesses.
It was clearly against the law to try a capital charge
at night.

Finally Caiaphas, having utterly failed with his witnesses,
knew that nothing that had been said could give the color of
justice to the sentence of death.
He rose from his seat and walked over to where he could look
down into the calm face of the prisoner.
If witnesses could not condemn Him, he must try to get Him
to condemn Himself.

Turning to the Nazarene, the judge addressed Him:
"Answerest thou nothing to the things which these witnesses say against thee?"

But Jesus held His peace.
The silence angered the high priest.
He seemed ready to explode.
The jewels on his robes sparkled and flashed in the light from
the bronze lamps, as his eyes flashed anger.
And then, with all the authority he could crowd into the
words, Caiaphas put to Jesus the solumn Jewish oath of testi-
mony:

"I adjure thee by the living God. . . ."

When a question was put like that to a loyal Jew,
it was an offense not to answer.

Caiaphas was asking a question that really mattered—

a question that required an answer clear-cut, like
chiseled marble—
And the question rang out through the assembly:
> "I adjure thee by the living God, that thou tell us
> whether thou be the Christ, the Son of God?"

Priests and rabbis
  scribes
    Pharisees and Sadducees
      learned men of Israel . . .
They all knew what the question meant.

They sprang to their feet in the excitement, craning forward to
catch the reply.

Would the Nazarene reply?
If He kept His silence, then the Sanhedrin would have no
choice but to release Him.
His life hung on His answer. . . .

Once again Jesus took the initiative on His road to the cross.
He would answer!
His voice rang out.
There are three versions of His reply in the Gospels!

Mark writes it: "I am."
  Matthew writes it: "Thou hast said."
    Luke writes it: "Ye say that I am. . . ."

The meaning is the same.
There was no doubt in the mind of the high priest as to what
Jesus' reply signified.
At last he had triumphed.

He swung round on the assembled rabbis, tearing his robe
from top to bottom, according to custom.

His voice shrill with victory, he shouted:
> "What further need have we of witnesses?"
The charge of blasphemy had been established.
It was sufficient.
The Sanhedrin had no choice but to impose the solemn sen-
tence:
> "He is liable to be put to death."

The Roman procurator, Pontius Pilate, was not in the best of
moods.
He did not relish having to rise at cockcrow to try a case.
These Jewish people over whom Caesar had sent him to rule
four years earlier were a difficult, turbulent race.
The army of occupation was forever trying to keep the lid on a
smoldering volcano.

Pilate had a soldier's contempt for religion.
Of course, it was true that he was superstitious—
    some unexpected event . . .
    some omen . . .
    a dream . . .
    the pronouncement of some oracle . . .
    the voice of a soothsayer in the marketplace . . .
    the cast of the dice . . .
These could cause him to tremble.
But as for religion . . .
Well, he had seen many religions—
    in Egypt and Persia, through Asia Minor and Macedonia—
And they all seemed alike to him.

No prayers and mystic rites could stand up against the Roman
legions.

As for him, give him a legion of hardy veterans . . .
                        shining armor . . .
                        flashing spears . . .
                        trusty swords . . .
And a fig for all the religions in the world!

Yet these religious Jews baffled him—irritated him.
He had tried putting them down by force.
There had been the affair of the money he had taken from the
sacred treasury to better Jerusalem's water supply,
and the bloody revolt that had followed.
And that incident of the votive shields
in the Herodian palace. . . .

Yes, he had tried riding roughshod over their prejudices.
And the moment he had touched their religion, they had risen
defenseless as sheep but as angry as wolves.

It was all so illogical and absurd!
Such may well have been his thoughts as he strode through
the outer door of the Praetorium toward this unpleasant early-
morning hearing.

The Roman paused at the head of the marble staircase.
With cool scrutiny he regarded the crowd before him.
On his shaven face with its keen eyes there was just a trace of a
sneer, for he had been told that the Jews had ceremonial
objections to treading the stones of the Gentile palace lest they
be made unclean for the Passover.
So he, Pilate, must go out to them.

Grimly, he gathered his purple-bordered toga over his arm
and strode down the steps.
The seething mass of humanity before him seemed centered
around one solitary Man who was being thrust forward.
Pilate's first impression was that He was perfectly harmless.
He looked Him over with the eyes of a trained soldier.
He looked first for a sign of weapons . . . There was none.

The prisoner was dressed in a simple white robe,
                    open at the neck,
    wrinkled and soiled from rough handling.
His hands were bound behind His back.
Pilate then looked for confederates or friends of the prisoner.
There were none.

Many of the faces before him were livid.
The crowd looked like a pack of snarling animals.
The Roman governor raised his baton as a signal that the trial
could begin and asked:
"What accusation bring ye against this man?"

The reply was insolent . . .
"If he were not an evil-doer we should not have delivered him
up to thee."

Once more Pilate looked at the prisoner.
An evildoer?
If the Roman was any judge of men—
    and he prided himself on that—
this prisoner was no vicious character.

"Take him away," he said, turning to go back into the palace.
"Take him away and deal with him according to
your own law."

Now a veritable howl went up . . .
"It is not lawful for us to put any man to death."

Ah, so that was what they wanted . . .
The blood-lust was in their eyes.
He knew now what the Jews wanted of him—to make conven-
ience of his rank and position . . .
But woe be to him if he blocked their intentions.

Pilate hesitated.
Once more his eyes rested on the prisoner.

His was the only calm face in that seething sea—
and what a face it was!

There was something in the eyes . . .
in the set of the mouth . . .
something about the bearing that was different—
strange
compelling.

There came to the Roman governor an instinctive desire to
get away from the crowd,
to be alone with this Man and speak with Him face-to-face.

So he turned and strode back into the palace and sat down
upon the dais.
Then he gave command that the prisoner be brought before
him.

Quietly and with stately mien, Jesus—the chiliarch of the
Twelfth Legion beside Him—walked across the mosaic floor
until He stood in front of the powerful Roman, and turned His
deep, searching eyes upon him.

Outside of the narrow pointed windows the sound of the
impatient murmuring of the crowd was wafted into
the Judgment Hall.
Pilate paid no attention.
His hands rested on the gilded carving of the bisellium.

His eyes narrowed as they stared moodily at the white-robed figure before him.

For a moment there was silence.
Then Pilate's involuntary question surprised even himself:

"Art thou the King of the Jews?"

A faint smile came over the face of Jesus . . .
"Sayest thou this of thyself, or did others tell it thee concerning me?"

It was the first time that Pilate had heard the Man's voice.
He did not say so, but it was the prisoner's deportment that had made him involuntarily associate kingliness with Him.
"Am I a Jew?" he asked contemptuously.
"Thine own nation and the chief priests have delivered thee unto me. Tell me—what hast thou done?"

A faraway look came into the eyes of Christ.
He seemed to be seeing into the far distances.
He had done many things in three short years.

He had never hurried;
yet He had been conscious of time fleeting.
And He had warned His disciples that the night cometh when no man can work.

Yet the seed had been sown.
Eleven men had been impregnated with the gospel.
The increase would come in due time.
His task was almost finished now.
Only one great act remained, and it was moving swiftly towards its climax.

What had He done?
No crime certainly—no political misdemeanor.
Had He not told John's messengers:
" . . . the blind receive their sight, and the lame walk, and the lepers are cleansed, and the deaf hear, and the dead are raised up, and the poor have the gospel preached unto them."

That was something . . . .
But Pilate would not be interested in that.

So He said gently:
> "My kingdom is not of this world: if my kingdom
> were of this world, then would my servants fight,
> that I should not be delivered to the Jews: but now is
> my kingdom not from hence."

Pilate persisted:
> "Art thou a king then?"

"Anything less like a king—judged by his own standards—
could hardly be imagined," thought Pilate.
The prisoner stood before him alone,
without a single person to plead His cause.
He stood there arrayed in a plain, seamless, soiled robe, the
dress of a peasant.
Here at any rate was no king whom Caesar need fear.
> "My kingdom is not of this world," Jesus had said.

His Kingdom did not belong to the same order of things as
Caesar's kingdom.

Therefore, the two could never come into collision.
His Kingdom was a repudiation of all political aims.
It was a flat denial of the insinuations made by the priests that
the Nazarene was plotting treason.

But it was an assertion that claimed kingship of some sort . . .
So Pilate probed further . . .

> "So thou art a king then?"

And Jesus nodded.

> "Thou sayest. . . . To this end have I been born,
> that I should bear witness unto the truth. Every one
> that is of the truth heareth my voice."

Pilate seemed a little weary of the interview.
He had learned what he wanted to know—
   this man was harmless.

> "What is truth?" he asked.

Then, without waiting for a reply, he rose and went outside to
give his answer to the impatient Jews.
He held up his baton for silence.
In a ringing voice he said:
"I find no fault with this man."

The chief priests were now more angry than ever.
They spat out their accusations . . .

"He stirreth up the people.
He teacheth throughout all Jewry,
beginning from Galilee to this place. . . . "

The word *Galilee* leaped out at Pilate.
He saw a possible loophole . . .

"Is this man from Galilee?"

When the priests answered in the affirmative, he said firmly:
"Then send the prisoner to Herod.
I cannot try this case. It is not in my jurisdiction."

And Pilate thought that he had dismissed the matter,
was well rid of an embarrassing issue.
The New Testament narratives leave no doubt that
what Pilate most wanted was to find a way to release Christ.

But Christ before Herod was a greater enigma to the Jewish
ruler than to the Roman.
Herod expected to see Him do some tricks, for the stories of
His miracles had long since been trickling into the court.
The Jewish king was eager for a command performance.

But Jesus stood, silently eloquent.
He had nothing to say—nothing, that is, to Herod.
So Herod sent Him back to Pilate.

The howlings for His death now became even more vehe-
ment.
And Pilate, supremely weary now of the whole matter, sat,
chin in hand, on his curule chair—
the cobalt-blue chair of judgment under the
movable canopy—
gloomily watching the yelling mob.

At that moment, a cohort bowed before him.
"Sire, an urgent message . . . "
And he handed the Roman a thin wax tablet.

It was a message from Pilate's wife—Claudia.
Pilate frowned, because never before had Claudia interrupted
him in the midst of a hearing.
Ordinarily, she would have not dared.
The message was the more urgent for its brevity:

> "Have thou nothing to do with that just man:
> for I have suffered many things this day
> in a dream because of him."

Pilate's thoughts went back to the night before . . .
    the nocturnal visit of the high priest. . . .
Claudia had questioned him after the high priest had left.
Husband and wife had quarreled a bit . . . .

> "It isn't really like you—a Roman—to agree
> to a man's death ahead of time.
> I have seen this Man in the streets of Jerusalem,
> watched Him once for minutes on end from my litter.
> He seems harmless enough. I don't like this affair."

Pilate had slipped out that morning at cockcrow without
waking Claudia—
Now this—the Roman procurator's hand trembled a bit.
Dreams made him uneasy.
Warnings *could* come that way.
Perhaps Claudia was right after all. . . .

Pilate leaned forward intently in his chair.

> "Ye have brought this man unto me, as one that
> perverteth the people: and, behold, I,
> having examined him before you, have found
> no fault in this man touching those things
> whereof ye accuse him:
>
> "No, nor yet Herod: for I sent you to him; and lo,
> nothing worthy of death is done unto him.
>
> "I will therefore chastise him, and release him."

But the whole multitude burst into a shout,

> "Away with this man! If you release any,
> release Barabbas."

Pilate shouted, "Barabbas is a robber and murderer.
What harm has this Jesus done?"

But the mob would not listen.
Prompted by the priests, they shouted, "Crucify . . .
crucify . . .
crucify. . . ."

In a chant that beat with unreasoning insistence
and rose and fell like the waves of an angry sea.

The procurator could scarcely make himself heard.
He stood outwardly patient,
  his lips curling,
    and an ugly look in his eyes. . . .

> "Would you have me crucify your king?"

That enraged them the more. . . .

> "We have no king but Caesar."

Desperately Pilate tried once more.
He held up his baton. . . .
> "I know it is your custom to have a man released at
> your Festival. There is nothing in this Jesus that
> deserves death. If it will please you, I shall scourge
> Him and let Him go."

But the mob would not have it so.
Then the voice of Caiaphas rose high and clear
above the clamor:

> "Any man who sets himself up as a king is a rebel
> against Caesar. . . ."

The clear insinuation was, "Do you want me to get word back
to Rome that you have encouraged rebellion against Caesar?"

And now Pilate motioned for Jesus to be brought closer to the
curule chair.

In some strange way this Nazarene had impressed him.

Perhaps it was the look in His eyes.
It was something that made Pilate feel uncomfortable.

Of course the Roman governor had seen many zealots.
He had grown accustomed to them.
Down from the hill country they would bring an insurrec-
tionist . . . with blazing eyes . . . wild, twitching mouth . . .
Or men with pinpoints of fire for eyes . . .
    and hatred smoldering for the emblems of Rome . . .
Or some poor devils caught in the toils of religious bigotry.
He used to watch them in a detached way with a sneer
in his heart.

But this was different.
He had spoken to this prisoner, and it made him
the more uncertain.

He had a curious feeling that Claudia was right; there was
more in this than met the eye.
Surely he was enough of a politician to find some loophole,
some way to handle this curious case.

He addressed himself to the prisoner:
        "Whence art thou?"

But Jesus only looked at him straight in the eyes
and said nothing.
The silence puzzled Pilate.
The prisoner had talked to him inside the Judgment Hall.
Why not now?

        "Speakest thou not unto me? knowest thou not
        that I have power to crucify thee, and have power
        to release thee?"

It was almost as if Pilate were saying,
"Only say the word, and I shall release thee.
Only tell me that thou art no insurrectionist. . . ."
And so, once again, Christ could have escaped the cross—
        But He would not. . . .

And so Jesus answered—slowly—clearly—

"Thou couldest have no power at all against me,
except it were given thee from above: therefore, he
that delivered me unto thee hath the greater sin."

Christ's words did not irritate Pilate.
He squared his shoulders, all the more determined to find a
way to release the Nazarene.

But now the sea of humanity before him
took up the cry again . . .
"Crucify
"Crucify
"Crucify . . ."

The tumult was beyond all control, and a guard of soldiers
moved nearer Pilate—just in case—
But he waved them back, and spoke to an attendant who
hurried inside.

Pilate stood there waiting, unable to hide his contempt.
The prisoner before him was pale and very tired, swaying a bit
on his feet.
The Roman looked over His head to the priests—
seeing the hate in their eyes
hearing the savagery of their shouting,
and he found himself wondering about their religion . . .
marveling at any religion that would permit them
to behave like this.

By this time a servant returned bearing a basin of water and a
towel.
Pilate, unable to make himself heard at all now, wanted to
dramatize something.
Deliberately, in sight of them all,
slowly he washed his hands . . .
slowly dried them.

Now the tumult gradually died.
Then he stepped forward and said clearly and deliberately:
"I am innocent of the blood of this just man.
See ye to it!"

And with loud shouts of triumph, the people yelled:

"His blood be on us and on our children."

Pilate shuddered involuntarily.
He had tried . . . he could tell Claudia he had tried.
Perhaps, by washing his hands, he had dispelled the evil
omen.

His last act, before turning Jesus over to be scourged and crucified, was to write the inscription to be put over His cross . . .
    in Latin
  in Greek
and in Hebrew:

    "Jesus of Nazareth, King of the Jews."

When Caiaphas saw it, he remonstrated:

    "That is no accusation. People will not understand.
    Do not write 'King of the Jews,' but, 'He said I am
King of the Jews.' "

But Pilate answered bitterly, almost spitting out each word:

    "What I have written I have written."

And from a distant courtyard there came the sound of
a flagellum, into which had been fastened bits of lead and
glass and bone and chain, striking again and again the bared
back
of the Nazarene.

The little man Judas had followed the crowd to the courtyard
of the Fortress Antonia.
Slinking, keeping well to the fringe of the screaming mob, he
had watched with mounting horror the sequence of events.
When the farce of a trial had finally reached its climax
and Judas had heard the mob shouting:
    "His blood be on us and on our children,"
he had gathered his robes about him, and turned fleeing.

How could he have known it would turn out like this?
He had so hoped that his action would force the Master's
hand,

force Him to go ahead and establish His earthly
kingdom . . .
But crucifixion? Not *that!*

The thirty pieces of silver in the leather purse dangling around
his waist seemed to be burning his thighs.
This was now blood money.
Somehow, some way he must get rid of it. . . .
He raced through the narrow twisting streets towards the
Temple, dodging people and donkeys as he went.
Once he almost collided with a man carrying a basket of figs,
and the man swore loudly at his retreating figure.

In the Temple he asked a doorkeeper to see the chief priest.
"Through that room and along the colonnade to the right,"
the doorkeeper said.
Then, noting Judas' wild eyes, "No, wait—let me see—"
but already the wild one was racing towards the colonnade.

Judas burst into a room where some of the elders
were assembled.
His hands clutched convulsively at the moneybag swinging
at his waist.
His eyes were bloodshot.
"I have sinned," he said.

Eyebrows went up; there were questions in the eyes.
The elders noted that this strange man was panting.

"I have sinned in that I have betrayed innocent blood. . . .
You know—Jesus of Nazareth. He had done nothing amiss . . .
I did not know that. . . ."

Shoulders shrugged.
Sardonic smiles appeared on some of the faces.
    "Jesus of Nazareth? Oh, yes—that one.
Well—what is that to us? See thou to that. . . ."

Judas could not believe what he had just heard.
Then the truth dawned on him . . .
The fate of Christ was already out of the hands of these men;
moreoever, they didn't *care* . . .
The Master was going to die after all . . .

There was nothing he could do about it. . . .

With trembling hands he seized the coin purse and opened it.
Slowly he counted out thirty pieces of silver.
Once again he looked questioningly into the eyes of the elders
standing before him.
He saw only amusement—
With a contemptuous gesture Judas flung the silver at them
                              right into their faces.
They ducked the shower of silver, and the coins fell to the
marble floor, rolling in all directions.
Then Judas turned and fled from the room.

The little man did not stop running until he was outside
the city gates.
A picture kept flashing before his eyes—he brushed his hands
before his eyes but it would not leave.
It was Jesus' face at that moment when he, Judas, had
kissed His cheek.

"Friend," He had said gently, "wherefore art thou come?
Why have you done this?"

"Friend," that was what He had said. "Friend—why have you
done this?"
                    It broke Judas' heart . . .

His plan had failed.
Everything was smashed . . . his dreams . . . his hopes . . .
                    his life—everything.

There was nothing left—now.
Only one way out. . . .

A few hours later the body of Judas was found
swinging crazily from the branch of a tree on the precipitous
heights overlooking the Valley of the Hinnom.
He had died before the Master.

An orange morning sun was rising higher and higher over the
City of David.

Pilgrims and visitors for the feast were pouring in through the gates, mingling with merchants from the villages round-about,
> shepherds coming in from the hills,
> hucksters leading their laden camels in single file,
> donkeys standing sleepily beneath their burdens in the dappled sunlight.

The narrow streets were crowded.
There were the aged, stooped with years, muttering to themselves as they pushed through the throngs.
There were children playing in the streets, calling to each other in shrill voices.

And beggars raising sightless sockets to the sky,
> tapping sticks on the cobblestones
> demanding alms in nasal voices.

From every balcony and latticed window came
> the sound of voices
> scraps of laughter
> rude voices, bargaining.

There were men and women carrying burdens . . .
> baskets of vegetables
> of green almonds and sweet lemons
> casks of wine
> water bags.

There were cloth merchants with their bales.
Fruiterers were arranging their stalls in narrow bazaars striped with sunlight.
Tradesmen with their tools seemed out-of-place in the holiday atmosphere.

It was not easy to make one's way through the crowd.

It was especially difficult for the procession that started out from the governor's palace.

At its head rode Longenius, the Roman centurion in charge of a half-maniple of the famous Twelfth Legion.
He seemed a typical Roman, scornful alike of child or cripple who might be in his way.

Before him went two legionnaires, one of them carrying a board atop a pole on which had been printed the charges against those to be executed.
The legionnaires were clearing the crowd aside as best they could, with curses and careless blows.

The procession moved at a snail's pace.
The soldiers tried to keep step.
The centurion's guard evidently did not relish this routine task, which came to them every now and then in the governing of this troublesome province.

The sunlight glanced on the spears and helmets of the soldiers.
There was a clanking of steel as their shields touched their belt buckles and the scabbards of their swords.
Between the two files of soldiers staggered three condemned men, each carrying a heavy bar of wood with its crosspiece, on which he was to be executed.

It was hard to keep step, for the pace was slow, and the soldiers were impatient to get it over.
Left . . . right . . . left . . . right . . .
In sharp clipped commands they urged their prisoners on.

The crosses were heavy, and the first of the victims was at the point of collapse.
He had been under severe strain for several days.
He had eaten little and had not closed His eyes for two days.
Moreover, the lashing with the flagellum had taken the last bit of His strength.

The carpenter followed them, with his ladder and his nails, and they all moved forward out of the courtyard of Pilate's palace towards the Gennath Gate.

The orange sun was hot.
The sweat poured down the face of Jesus, and He swayed now and then under the weight of the cross.
A depression had fallen on the soldiers, and they marched in silence, as if reluctantly.

A group of women went with the procession, their faces half-hidden by their veils, but their grief could not be hidden.
Some were sobbing . . .
   Others were praying . . .
      Others were moaning in that deep grief that knows not
      what it says or does.

Some of them had children by the hand and kept saying over and over . . .
   "He gave my child back to me . . .
   How can they be so cruel?
   I know He healed my child—
   What harm could there be in that?"

And there were men, too, who followed as closely as they could—men who walked with the strange steps of those to whom walking was unfamiliar.
They were the cripples He had healed.

Others carried sticks in their hands—sticks that once had tapped out their blind tattoo along the city streets and the sun-hardened trails of Judea.

They did not use their sticks now, although once again they were blind . . . blinded by tears.

Once when the procession halted for a moment, Jesus turned and spoke to them, but they could not hear Him for the shouting of the rabble.

Most of the crowd hardly knew what was going on.
They did not understand.
They caught the infection of the mob spirit.

They shouted to the first of three victims.
That one had an absurd crown on His head,
   twisted from a branch of the long-thorned briar.
It had lacerated His scalp and caused blood to mingle with the sweat.

They shouted at Him, until roughly pushed aside by the soldiers, and then, in some cases, they began to shout at the soldiers.

It was an ugly situation as the procession went slowly along this way that will forever be known as the Via Dolorosa.

Meanwhile—Simon of Cyrene was approaching the city gate.

He had just arrived in Judea, and was about to enter the holy city as a pilgrim for the festival.
He had spent the night in some village just outside, and, rising early that morning, had bathed and dressed himself carefully . . . with a tingling excitement because soon he would be in Jerusalem.

The wonders of Jerusalem, that exiles had described, he would now see with his own eyes.
The sounds of the holy city which lonely hearts heard in their nostalgia . . .
> Noises that seemed to be whispered by the restless surf of distant seas, or heard in the moaning of winds that traveled far . . .
These he would hear with his own ears.

Yet he tried to keep calm, and as he set out on the short walk that lay between him and the city, he was very thoughtful.

He walked along the winding path that sometimes ran through the fields . . .
> sometimes along narrow roads between hedges where there was the fragrance of pomegranate trees and honeysuckle . . .
> sometimes along the tortuous course of the dried-up river bed where the earth was cracked with the heat of the sun.

Sometimes it wound up the jagged hillside to twist down among the giant boulders and huge rocks behind which many a robber might hide.
He walked along beside the tall rushes, where he frightened coveys of birds that flew wheeling, diving . . .
And he walked through the divided crops, ripening in the sunshine.

He could hear the sheep bleating on the inhospitable hillside, while the morning sun climbed higher and chased away the mists that lay in the hollows, trailing down into the ravines like tulle scarves.

As he walked along, he was thinking of the Temple and its glories, the history of his people and the worship of his fathers . . .

Already he could see ahead of him the domes of the Temple gleaming gold in the sunshine, could hear the pigeons that had their nests in the cupolas and gables,

And he thought of his own city looking from her height over the blue waters of the Mediterranean.

Then as he neared the city gate he began to hear shouting that grew louder and louder.

There seemed to Simon to be a sort of chant running through the noise . . .

a refrain that men's voices made clearer and clearer until he thought he could recognize the word

"Crucify

crucify

crucify. . . ."

They met right at the city gate . . . Simon of Cyrene and the crowd.

He found that the procession was headed by some Roman soldiers; he would recognize them anywhere . . .

the insignia on their shields . . .

and their uniforms . . .

He could tell a legionnaire when he saw one.

He had little time to gather impressions, and as for asking questions, that was impossible.

He could not make himself heard in all the rabble.

The noise and confusion with its sinister malice made Simon shudder.

Simon was aware of two moving walls of Roman steel.

There was something strange about it all but, before he could understand it, Simon was caught up in it—sucked into the procession, and swept out through the gate again.

Simon was excited, afraid . . . .

He was puzzled and ill-at-ease.

He scanned face after face quickly, looking for some light of pity . . .

of friendliness
of welcome . . .
But he found none.

He felt the drama of the situation, the cruelty of it . . .
And its horror crept over him like a clammy mist—and he
shivered.

He was captured by the procession, stumbling along tightly
wedged in the very heart of the crowd.
Then he noticed that there were three men who staggered
under the weight of crosses of rough, heavy wood on which
these unfortunates were going to die.

Each man was bent beneath the burden he carried, and perspi-
ration moistened his drawn face.
One of them was strangely appealing, His face arresting.
Simon felt his gaze returning again and again to that one face.
He noticed that blood was trickling down from wounds in the
brow.

On His face there was a twig of long-thorned briar, twisted
around in the shape of a crown and pushed down cruelly on
His head.

Simon watched with beating heart as they shuffled along,
fascinated by the look in those eyes.
He could see nothing else.
Everything was forgotten, even why he had come to Jerusalem.

This public execution had driven everything else from his
mind.

Forgotten for the moment were the Temple and its services,
    messages he brought from friends far away . . .
        things he had been asked to get . . .
Everything was forgotten as he watched this Man carrying the
cross.

And then *He* looked up! His eyes almost blinded by the blood
that trickled down from under that grotesque crown that was
on His head . . . .
Why didn't somebody wipe His eyes?

And as Simon looked at Him, He looked at Simon . . .
And the eyes of the two . . . met!
How did Christ know what was in Simon's heart?
What was it that made Him smile, a slow, sad smile that
seemed to still Simon's wildly beating heart and give him
courage?

The look that passed between them Simon never forgot as
long as he lived, for no man can look at Jesus of Nazareth and
remain the same.

As these two looked at each other, the Man with the cross
stumbled, and the soldiers, moved more by impatience than
pity, seeing the Nazarene was almost too exhausted to carry
the cross any further, laid hands on Simon and conscripted
him to carry it.

He was the nearest man.
He was strong.
His shoulders were broad!

Simon's heart almost stopped beating; he tried to speak, but
no words came.
A few minutes before, he had been a lonely pilgrim quietly
approaching the holy city.
And now, there he was in the midst of a procession of howling
men and women, walking between two moving walls of Roman steel, and carrying on his shoulder a cross on which
someone was going to die!

The look of gratitude and love that flashed from the eyes of
Jesus as Simon lifted the load from those tired, bleeding
shoulders did something to the man from Cyrene, and in an
instant life was changed.

Simon never could explain it afterwards—how it happened!

There are moments of spiritual insight that defy the limits of
syntax and grammar.
There are experiences that can never be poured into the molds
of speech.
There are some things too deep for words.

But all at once he saw the meaning of pain . . .

understood the significance of suffering . . .
The meaning of prayer was unveiled . . .
   and the message of the Scriptures.
He saw prophecy take form and live before him.
He remembered words of the psalmist and the prophets of
old, words that until now had been without sense or meaning,
but now . . . he saw . . . and understood.

And so the crowd came to Golgotha, a hill shaped like a skull,
outside the city gates, where two great highways, the Sa-
maria-Jerusalem road and the Joppa-Jerusalem road, con-
verged upon the city.

Only as the nails were driven in did the shouting stop.
There was a hush.
   Most of them were stunned . . . horrified . . .
Even the hardest of them were silenced.

Mary, the mother of Jesus, closed her eyes and stopped her
ears; she could not bear the thud of the hammer.

Simon of Cyrene from time to time wiped away his tears with
the back of his hand.
Peter stood on the fringe of the crowd, blinded by hot tears
that filled his eyes, while his very heart broke.

A group of soldiers took hold of the crossbeam and lifted it
slowly off the ground.
With each movement the nails tore at the shredded flesh in the
wrists of the Nazarene.
The cross swayed in the air for a moment and then with a thud
dropped into the hole prepared for it.

When the first spasm of pain had waned, Jesus opened His
eyes.
Over the heads of the crowd, He could see the city, tawny-
yellow, like a crouching tiger in the midday sun.

Nearer there was a hillside carpeted with anemone and cycla-
men.
For just a moment a gentle spring wind blowing across the
face of the suffering Man blew away the smell of blood and

wafted to Him the fragrance of flowers, and He saw a single lark circling high above the hillside.

But closer still a mad medley of fury surged below Him . . . .
There were eyes watching this Man on His cross . . .
   unbelieving eyes
     eyes with gloating in them
       other eyes that looked and never saw.

Faces were looking up at Him . . . convulsed faces,
   snarling, invective faces,
faces that through His pain-glazed eyes seemed to melt and run together.

Fingers pointed up to Him hanging quivering on the cross-gibbet . . .
   long bony fingers . . .
     mocking, accusing fingers—fingers of scorn and ridicule.

There was noise . . . confused noise that beat upon His ears with an added pain.
There was demoniac laughter that enjoyed suffering.
There was hoarse shouting that taunted and mocked.

From one side of Him there were sighs of pain and the soft moans of a dying thief, and on the other side blasphemies and curses terrible to hear.
There was weeping too, the crying of the women and the unashamed sobbing of men.

The wounded flower of Magdala was consoled by that lovely one who had once held Him in her arms, while the beloved John stood beside them.

The crowd hurled His own words back at Him, but they were barbs, dipped in venom and shot from snarling lips, like poisoned arrows.

     "He saved others; himself he cannot save.
     Yes, he healed the cripples.
     Yes, he gave sight to the blind.
     He even brought back the dead, but he cannot
     save himself."

They were willing now to grant the truth of His miracles.
Out of the mouths of His enemies comes this testimony to His
power—"He saved others" . . .

Yes, they were saved—those others . . .
   saved from the land of shadows
      saved from the caves of derangement
         from the couches of pain
         from the leprous touch of sickness
      saved from the enslaving grip of vice
   saved even from the jaws of death.
Yes, He had saved others—His enemies admitted it . . .

But now their taunt rose to its crescendo—

> "Perform a miracle now, Miracle Man! Come down
> from the cross, and we will believe thee.
> Aha, thou who wouldst build the Temple in three
> days,
> Thou hast nails in thy hands now . . .
> Thou hast wood . . . go on and build thy Temple.
>
> "If thou be the Christ . . . prove it to us . . . Come on
> down from the cross!"

They shouted until they were hoarse.
The noise was so great that only a few of them standing near
the cross heard what He said when His lips moved in prayer:

> "Father, forgive them, for they know not what they
> do."

One of the thieves, drugged and half-drunk, cried out to
Jesus:

> "Can't you see how we suffer?
> If you are the Sor of God, take us down from these
> crosses. Save us and yourself."

The thief cried for salvation—but only for salvation from nails
and a cross—not for salvation from himself and the hell that
his own deeds had wrought.
Then pain gripped him, and he began to curse and to swear,
blaming Jesus for the pain.

But the other turned his head so that he could see Jesus, and he said to his companion:

> "Dost not thou fear God, seeing thou art in the same condemnation? And we indeed justly; for we receive the due reward of our deeds: but this man hath done nothing amiss."

Then he said to Jesus, "Remember me when thou comest into thy kingdom."
And Jesus, His face drawn with suffering, but His voice still kind, answered:

> "This very day when this pain is over, we shall be together . . . thou and I . . . in Paradise."

And the man, comforted, set his lips to endure to the end.

The sun rose higher and higher.
Time oozed out slowly like the blood that dripped from the cross . . . .
Jesus opened His eyes again and saw His mother standing there with John beside her.
He called out the name of John, who came closer.
Strength was fast ebbing away; an economy of words was necessary . . . .

> "Thou wilt take care of her, John?" . . .

And John, choked with tears, put his arm round the shoulders of Mary.

Jesus said to His mother: "He will be thy son."
His lips were parched, and He spoke with difficulty.
He moved His head uneasily against the hard wood of the cross, as a sick man moves his head on a hot pillow.

The women beneath the cross stood praying for Jesus and for the thieves.
The centurion was silent, although every now and then he would look up at Jesus with a strange look on his face . . .
> puzzled . . . wondering . . . marveling. . . .

The rest of the soldiers had been playing knucklebones in the shadow of the crosses.

Agreeing that they did not want to tear Christ's tunic—or
seamless robe—they had tossed for it.
The Man on the cross would not need it again . . . .

Then, in the awful words of Matthew:

> "And sitting down they watched him there."

There before their eyes was being enacted the tremendous
drama of the redemption of mankind . . .
And they only sat and watched.

They were unwitting actors in the supreme event of which the
prophets had dreamed . . . .
They were witnesses, standing at the crossroads of history.
And they saw—*nothing!*

The sky was growing strangely dark.
A thunderstorm seemed to be blowing up from the moun-
tains and clouds hid the sun.
Women on the converging highways beyond the hill took
children by the hand and began hurrying back to the city.
People looked up at the sky and became frightened.
The darkening sun at noon caused bird songs to freeze in fear
as their melodies trailed off in the gathering shadows.
It was an uncanny darkness.

The shouting died away.
Now even the soldiers were silent.
They put away their dice. Their gambling was done.
    They had won . . . and lost.

Suddenly, Jesus opened His eyes and gave a loud cry.
The gladness in His voice startled all who heard it.
For it sounded like a shout of victory:

> "It is finished! Father, into thy hands
>   I commit my spirit."

And with that cry He died.
It was the ninth hour . . . .

Yes, "He saved others; himself he cannot save."
But they were wrong as well as right.
Could He not have saved Himself?

He might have followed the advice of His friends and avoided Jerusalem altogether at the feast time.
He might have left the Garden that night instead of quietly waiting there for Judas.
He might have compromised with the priests—and made a bargain of future silence with Caiaphas.
Had not Pilate almost pleaded with Him for an excuse, any excuse, for not sending Him to His death?

He might have made His Kingdom political instead of spiritual.
That would have pleased and silenced Judas.
He might have chosen the expedient.
As He Himself reminded Peter, He might have called upon twelve legions of angels to rescue Him and to show His great power.

Yes, He might have saved Himself.
He had the power; many ways of escape were available . . . .
But then He would never have been our Savior!

Had not Christ said, "I am the good shepherd: the good shepherd giveth his life for the sheep"?
Giveth His *life?* . . .

But could not our salvation have been consummated without that final price?
No, for when men sin to the uttermost, when sin sinks to its final degradation, no mere palliatives nor mild remedies can deal with it.

What then?
In a world where death by crucifixion was still possible no polite and perfumed half-measures could suffice.
A blood transfusion was necessary . . .
rich, red blood
human blood.
And if talk of blood offends us, let us remember that crucifixion would offend us, too.

Perhaps we need to be reminded that our religion is not all sweetness and light.

Christianity is much more than pretty pictures of Jesus among flowers and singing birds, moving with a smile among simple folk.
The gospel is much more than the Golden Rule . .
    much more than the Christmas story
        and the fair green hills of Galilee.

Christianity deals with reality,
    with life as you and I experience it.
For it recognizes that this is not always a pretty world.
It is a world in which dreadful things can happen.

The faith which is nourished and sustained by the Spirit of God faces frankly these human situations which often make our faith difficult.

More than that, Christianity has a cross at the very heart of it.
Leave out Calvary, and Christianity dwindles to a weak and empty cult—to a system of impossible ethics.

It would not be good news to preach that there was no sin in Jesus Christ
    therefore we ought to be like Him.
It is not good news to say that He did no wrong,
    therefore we too ought to be perfect.
It is not good news to say that He left us an example that we should follow . . .
These things are true—but they are not a gospel.
Christ did not come into the world merely to proclaim a new morality
    or a code of ethics
        or to set up a new social order.
He did not show men how to work out their own salvation by good deeds
    by charities
        or by trying to live respectable lives.

He came, He said, "to save that which was lost. . . ."
He came to save all those who were lost in the sense that they had lost their way . . . .

            "How think ye? If a man have a hundred sheep, and
            one of them be gone astray, doth he not leave the

ninety and nine, and goeth into the mountains, and
seeketh that which is gone astray?"

Never was there in Him condemnation for the lost . . . only
the desire to help the lost one back to the path . . .
   back to right relations with His Father . . .
      back home again.

Yet He well knew our human willfulness.
He knew that after making allowances for heredity and en-
vironment
         for education
      and example
   and the tyranny of habit
there is still a central shrine of freedom in every life.

There is a place where *we* do it, and no one else—
   where *we* are responsible for our own choices—
and we know it.

         "All we like sheep have gone astray;
         we have turned every one to his own way. . . ."

How would He deal with the iniquity
of our human willfulness? . . .

         "And the Lord hath laid on him the iniquity of us all."

         "Therefore I will divide him a portion with the great,
         and he shall divide the spoil with the strong;
         because he poured out his soul to death,
         and was numbered with the transgressors;
         yet he bore the sin of many, and made intercession
         for the transgressors."

Then there were the sick . . . .
"They that be whole need not a physician," He had said,
"but they that are sick"—
   the sinsick, the sick of mind, the sick of body.
And He who could not tolerate sickness or disease,
   in whom there was a passion for health and wholeness,
must somehow deal with that, too.

How should He do it? . . .

" . . . upon him was the chastisement that
made us whole,
and with his stripes we are healed . . . . "

And the last enemy, Death . . .
    that final fear lurking deep in every human heart . . .
That enemy, too, must be put down.

How should He do it?
Who but God could deal with all the sin of the ages . . .
    all the suffering of the flesh . . .
    all the sorrow of the heart?

None but God!

But not a God sitting on a gilded throne high up in the
heavens,
    not some ethereal, nebulous God floating about in space
    like a benevolent cloud . . .
    not some four- or five-dimensional deity created by a Greek
    philosopher . . .
But a God walking through your front door and mine . . .
A God who lives and feels and understands . . .
A God who can sympathize . . . who has explored the vast
treasuries of pain . . .

A God who knows what it feels like to weep . . .
A God who can remember the feeling of a tear trickling down
the cheek . . .

Someone utterly pure—in whom there is no spot
                              nor blemish
                              nor taint . . .
Someone willing to give Himself at whatever cost of pain and
suffering and death within this time process, and in the form
of the life that you and I know . . . taking shape—the body of a
man . . . the form of a servant . . .
    with a voice to speak to us . . .
        a heart to feel for us . . .
            eyes to weep with us . . .
            hands to bless and to be nailed to a cross.

    "Surely he has borne our griefs

and carried our sorrows; . . .
He was oppressed, and he was afflicted,
   yet he opened not his mouth;
like a lamb that is led to the slaughter,
and like a sheep that before its shearers
   is dumb,
so he opened not his mouth.
By oppression and judgment he was taken away; and
as for his generation, who considered that he was cut
off out of the land of the living, stricken for the
transgression of my people?"

The gospel message is simply that—that such a thing has
come to pass. . . .

This is the Good News the church has to proclaim . . .
that there is available for us today a Sin Doctor who will come
to you and to me and heal us, if we will but let Him into our
lives . . .
Whose gracious Spirit will mysteriously steal into our hearts
and show us the doorway to a new life. . . .

Thus the gospel is not something to do—
   but something done.
The gospel is not a demand—
   but a supply.
Not something you can do—
   but something that has been done for you.

And it happened at a certain point in time . . .
   on the brow of a hill shaped like a skull.
It was done for me—and for you—simply because He loves
us.

Had not Jesus said to His apostles that last memorable night
with them in the Upper Room . . .

   "Greater love hath no man than this, that a man
   lay down his life for his friends."

That is why a hideous cross has become the world's symbol of
blessing.

It was plain to be seen that the Nazarene was dead.

He had died after only six hours of suffering.
Long enough, surely . . .
Yet the Roman centurion who watched could not believe that
any crucified one could die in just six hours.
To make sure, one of the soldiers pierced Christ's side with a
spear, and the last remaining drops of His blood were poured
out.

Yes, He was dead . . .
There was no need to break His legs in an effort
to hasten the end.

During those last hours, John had tried over and over to
persuade Mary to leave—but she would not.
Her son was hanging there . . .

So long as there was a breath of life—no—she would
not leave Him.

But Mary herself was nearing a state of collapse.
When it was over, she flung herself on John's breast . . .
                              sobbing . . . quietly.
Then John lifted her up, put his arms around her shoulders,
and gently led her down the hill toward home.
And Salome, John's own mother, who had been watching afar
off with some of the other women from the outskirts of the
crowd, seeing the little tableau, left the others and came
running to help.

"That one didn't take long," the soldiers said, as they
prepared to fall in line and march back to their barracks.

"Dead so soon?" inquired Pilate, when Joseph of Arimathea—
a member of the Great Jewish Council—came to him to ask for
the body of Jesus.
According to Roman custom the body of an executed criminal
belonged to the relatives or friends, so that by his request
Joseph had now openly avowed his faith in the prophet.

This request surprised Pilate, for the Councilor was a rich
man and a distinguished one—not the usual type to
acknowledge himself as a follower of the Nazarene.

Not until the centurion, having been summoned, confirmed the statement that the Galilean was really dead, did Pilate grant Joseph his request.

In some haste—lest anyone else should meddle in the matter—Joseph, with Nicodemus to help him, then took down the disfigured body from the cross.
Gently they wound it in strips of clean linen eight feet long with spices between the layers—as was the custom of the Jews.

And as their hands busied themselves with the sad work, words from the prophet Isaiah came winging their way into Joseph's mind.
He had learned them as a child in the synagogue . . . had often recited them to the elders.
How strange that he should remember them at this moment . . .
   as if they had a special significance . . .
     as if—as if—they were meant for him . . . .
        " . . . And they made his grave with the wicked
         and with a rich man in his death,
       although he had done no violence,
         and there was no deceit in his mouth. . . ."

And Nicodemus was remembering, too, remembering that night when he had laid aside his work for the Sanhedrin, turned down the lamp, and gone out under the stars to ask questions of the Galilean. . . .

"For all the rest of my life," he thought, "whenever the wind moans or tugs at my robes—I shall be remembering that musical voice:

      "The wind bloweth where it listeth, and thou hearest the sound thereof, but canst not tell whence it cometh, and whither it goeth: so is every one that is born of the Spirit."

And now He was dead. . . .
Nicodemus was tortured by the knowledge of all the things he might have said while Jesus lived.

So many things he might have done. . . .

"Now," he thought, "it is too late."
And as he looked at the still face of his Friend, unashamedly he watched his tears making little smudges on the white linen.

Then Joseph and Nicodemus carried the body of their Lord to a newly made tomb in the Councilor's garden—a tomb which he had had hewn out of the rock for himself.

After the Sabbath they would arrange for a burial with proper ceremony.
All they could do at the moment was to make sure of a decent provisional burial without interference on the part of
the priests.
It would be enough to roll a great round stone to the door of the sepulchre, for the evening star was already shining . . . and no more work could be done until the Sabbath was over.

The two men—and the women, Mary Magdalene, and Mary, the mother of Joses, who had followed at a distance to see where the body of their Master was being laid—went away very silent . . . very sad. . . .

On the morrow the Roman governor was told that a group of priests and Pharisees sought audience with him.
Pilate undoubtedly suspected that even yet he was not finished with the matter of the Nazarene—and he was right.

The priests remembered only too well Pilate's mood when they had asked that the inscription for Christ's cross be changed . . .
So they selected the most softspoken and diplomatic member of the group and thrust him forward as their spokesman:

"Sire, we remember that Jesus, that deceiver, said while he was yet alive, 'After three days I will rise again.'

"Command therefore, we pray you, that the sepulchre be made sure until the third day, lest his disciples come by night, and steal him away, and say unto the people, He is risen from the dead: so the last error shall be worse than the first."

The priests irritated Pilate.

He thought of having washed his hands in the golden bowl such a few hours before . . . "I am innocent of the blood of this just person: see ye to it. . . ."

But somehow he had not been able to wash his hands of it. The case kept coming back and back. . . .

He leaned forward in his gilded chair and wearily passed his hands across his eyes.

Then he almost roared at the priests:

> "No! I will not send a Roman guard. That's nonsense. . . . The man is dead. What care I what his disciples say? You have your own watch. Make it as sure as you can . . . Now—go your way—"

And he waved his arm for the priests to be escorted from the audience chamber.

So—in the ironic words of Matthew:

> " . . . they went, and made the sepulchre sure, sealing the stone, and setting a watch."

It was still dark. . . .

Through the deserted streets of Jerusalem three men were hurrying, almost running towards the residence of the high priest.

In the courtyard a slave lifted a torch to see their faces. . . .

"See Caiaphas now? At this hour? Impossible . . .

You will have to wait until the dawn at least."

An hour-and-a-half later the three men reported to Caiaphas that the tomb of the executed Nazarene—which they had been sent to guard—was empty.

Caiaphas was at first puzzled, then angry, then thoughtful . . . for the men had no explanation.

Repeated questioning could not shake their story . . .

No—they had not gone to sleep . . .

There had been a strange stirring in the garden . . .
They had thought they had heard something . . .
Investigation had found the tomb empty—
That was all—

Caiaphas requested that the men tell their weird story again
later on that day to the elders meeting in plenary session. . . .

> "And when they were assembled with the elders,
> and had taken counsel, they gave large money unto
> the soldiers, saying, Say ye, His disciples came by
> night, and stole him away while we slept.
>
> "And if this come to the governor's ears, we will
> persuade him, and secure you.
>
> "So they took the money, and did as they were
> taught. . . ."

Meanwhile the despair and disillusionment in Simon Peter's
heart were complete . . .
despair over the shamefulness of his own denial . . .
disillusionment over the fate of Jesus of Nazareth.
For Peter and the other apostles had hoped that this One
would redeem Israel.
Now all hope was gone: Christ was *dead* . . .
hailed as King on the Sabbath before . . .
dead like a common thief on Friday.

"I go fishing," Peter said to the others.
What else was there to do?
Life had to go on, be picked up where they had dropped it
when, at the imperious call of a Stranger, they had
abandoned their fishing nets and left everything to
follow Him.

Perhaps away from Jerusalem with its bitter memories, they
could forget.
Perhaps with the sea wind once again fanning
their cheeks . . .
with the rough nets sliding through their fingers . . .

with the feel of the tug of fish
they could forget a certain Face
  a Voice with music in it
    a Smile . . .
      Perhaps. . . .

The women, too, who had ministered to the little band of
apostles, were just as despairing—only, as women will, they
were trying to work out their grief in a different way.

They had watched from a distance as Joseph of Arimathea and
Nicodemus had hastily anointed the body of Jesus.
At the first possible moment they would complete
the anointing. . . .
So before light dawned on the Sabbath morning Mary Magdalene, Salome, the mother of James the Greater and of John,
and Mary were on their way to the tomb where Jesus' body
had been laid.

As they walked in the half-light, they were preoccupied with
one problem . . .

> "And they said among themselves, Who shall
> roll us away the stone from the door of
> the sepulchre?"

But even as they pondered . . .

> " . . . when they looked, they saw that the stone
> was rolled away: for it was very great. . . .

> "And they went out quickly, and fled
> from the sepulchre; for they trembled and
> were amazed. . . ."

What did it mean?
Someone had tampered with Jesus' tomb.
Perhaps His body had been stolen. . . .

But the women were so frightened that they did not wait
to investigate.
They had only fled. . . .
Mary Magdalene, being younger than the others, outran
them.

But ere she had reached the road, she met Simon Peter and
John—Simon had planned to pay his last respects before he
left for Galilee.
Breathlessly Mary blurted out:

> "They have taken away the Lord out of the
> sepulchre, and we know not where they have
> laid him. . . ."

The two men were shocked; they too started running, but
John outran Peter.
And when they stooped down and saw what was in the
sepulchre, they believed.
Believed *what*?
Not, as Mary thought, that Jesus' body had been stolen—
But that Jesus of Nazareth was alive!

John and Peter, as they went into the grave in the garden that
first Easter morning, did not know *what* to think—until they
saw what was inside the grave—
And then they believed.

The inside of the tomb revealed something that proved the
Resurrection.
What was it?
Let us turn to the narrative again and read carefully:

> "Then cometh Simon Peter following him, and went
> into the sepulchre, and seeth the linen clothes lie,
> And the napkin, that was about his head, not lying
> with the linen clothes, but wrapped together in a
> place by itself. Then went in also that other disciple,
> which came first to the sepulchre, and he saw, and
> believed."

In this connection, it is well for us to remember that the stone
was rolled away from the door, not to permit Christ to come
out, but to enable the disciples to go in.

Notice what it was they saw.
They saw the linen clothes lying, not unwound and carefully
folded, as some people appear to think—
 not thrown aside as is a covering when one rises from bed,

but lying there on the stone slab in the shape of the body.

True, the napkin had been removed and folded, but the grave-clothes were lying there, mute but eloquent evidence that a living organism had come out.

The grave-clothes lay like the shriveled, cracked shell of a cocoon, left behind when the moth has emerged and hoisted her bright sails in the sunshine . . .
Or, more accurately, like a glove from which the hand has been removed, the fingers of which still retain the shape of the hand.

In that manner, the grave-clothes were lying, collapsed a little, slightly deflated—because there was between the rolls of bandages a considerable weight of spices, but there lay the linen cloth that had been wound round the body of Christ.

It was when they saw *that*, that the disciples believed.

The Greek word here for "see"—*theōrei*—is not to behold as one looks at a spectacle, not to see as the watchmaker who peers through his magnifying glass.
It means to see with inner light that leads one to conclusion.

It is perception
  reflection
    understanding—more than sight.
Do you *see?*

It is to see, as one who reasons from the effect to the cause.
And when John and Peter reasoned from what they saw in the tomb, they arrived at the conclusion
    the unshakable
  unassailable
 certain conviction
that Jesus Christ had risen from the dead.

But Mary Magdalene, still weeping, lingered at the edge of the garden.
Along with the other women, she had come to find a dead body . . . and had been shocked to find the grave empty.

She thought it had been broken open—grave-robbers, per-
haps.
She did not know . . .
She could not think clearly.
Only one thought seems to have absorbed her soul—
    the body of the Lord had been lost . . . she must find Him!

She ran as never before back toward the empty tomb, with the
speed and unawareness of time and distance that grief or fear
or love can impart. . . .

> "But Mary stood without at the sepulchre weeping:
> and as she wept, she stooped down, and looked into
> the sepulchre . . . She turned herself back, and saw
> Jesus standing, and knew not that it was Jesus.
>
> "Jesus saith unto her, Woman, why weepest thou?
> whom seekest thou?"

And John tells us that she thought He was the gardener.
She fell at His feet, her eyes brimming with tears—her head
down—sobbing, "Sir, if thou hast taken him hence, tell me
where thou hast laid him, and I will take him away."

To her tortured mind there was a gleam of hope that perhaps
the gardener, for some reason known only to him, had moved
the body . . .
She was red-eyed . . .
She had not slept since Friday . . .
There had been no taste for food . . .
She had been living on grief and bereaved love . . . .

> "Jesus saith unto her, Mary."

His voice startled her . . .
She would have recognized it anywhere.
She lifted her head with a jerk . . . blinked back the tears from
her eyes and looked—right into His eyes.

She knew . . . her heart told her first and then her mind . . .
She saw the livid marks of the nails in His hands and looking
up into His face, she whispered:
    "Rabboni!"

The loveliest music of that first Easter dawn is the sound of
those words echoing in the garden . . .
　　His gentle . . . "Mary . . . "
　　and her breathless . . . "Master!"

Mary had come prepared to weep—
　　Now she could worship.
She had come expecting to see Him lying in the tomb—
　　She had found Him walking in the newness of
　　resurrected life.

So much had happened in those last few days.
To Cleopas and his friend, the week that had closed seemed
like a terrible dream.

Event had followed event in a swiftness which had left no time
for meditation.
As the two men walked along the winding road to Emmaus, it
was of these things they spoke.

There had been Christ's entry in triumph into the holy city.
To all of them, it had seemed that—at last—their Messiah
would enter into His own.
Surely, the days of Roman occupation would now soon be
over. Exactly when the Messiah would announce Himself and
declare their independence, they did not know.

Joyously, the multitudes thronged around Him, awaiting the
good news.

Then, swiftly, there had been woven around the Nazarene a
net of intrigue—soon to be drawn tighter and tighter.

There had been that night when Judas had turned on his heel
and left the Upper Room to keep his treacherous rendezvous.
There had been Jesus' strange words of dismissal, as He had
watched Judas disappear into the night.

Then the scene that followed in the Garden
out on the hillside . . .
Would they ever forget it?

In the silence of the night, Jesus prostrate in prayer . . .
        the bright Syrian stars seeming to fill the sky . . .
        the gnarled olive trees casting grotesque shadows . . .
        a swinging lantern coming up the winding path . . .
    the rabble of Temple doorkeepers and Temple police, who
    had laid aside their brooms and their keys long enough to
    come out with Judas to arrest the Galilean . . .
How could they ever forget?

As Cleopas and his companion talked,
they became more and more engrossed.
Their words came pouring out in a torrent of recollection.

There had been the despicable kiss of Judas . . .
    the arrest itself . . .
        the foolhardiness of Peter with his little sword . . .
            the return to the city . . .
                Peter's blasphemous denial by the fire . . .
                the all-night vigil.

The rest was an agony of painful memories . . .
    the scourging of Christ in front of Pilate's palace . . .
        the bloodthirsty cries of the mob . . .
            the march to Golgotha . . .
                those awful moments
        when the sound of a hammer had echoed across the valley.

There had been the ravings and curses of the thieves on their
crosses . . .
    the strange, eerie darkness . . . and the earthquake . . .
And the death of Him whom they had learned to love, of Him
whom they had called . . . "Master."

So engrossed were the two men in these memories, that they
did not notice the approach of a Stranger.
Suddenly, there He was walking beside them.

And He said to them, "What is this conversation which you
are holding with each other as you walk?"

And they stood still, looking sad.
Then one of them, Cleopas, answered him,
    "Are you the only visitor to Jerusalem who does not know
    the things that have happened there in these days?"

And He said to them, "What things?"

And they said to Him, "Concerning Jesus of Nazareth, who was a prophet mighty in deed and word before God and all the people, and how our chief priests and rulers delivered Him up to be condemned to death and crucified Him.
But we had hoped that He was the one to redeem Israel.
Yes, and besides this, it is now the third day
since this happened.

"Moreover, some women of our company amazed us.
They were at the tomb early in the morning and did not find His body; and they came back saying . . . He was alive. . . ."

And He said to them, "O foolish men, and slow of heart to believe all that the prophets have spoken!
Was it not necessary that the Christ should suffer these things and enter into His glory?"

And He began with Moses and all the prophets and explained to them all the Scriptures that referred to Himself.

Thus did the walk of seven-and-a-half miles pass quickly.
And when they reached Emmaus, the sun was fast sinking behind the copper hills.

The shadows were long . . . soon it would be dark.

The two men begged the mysterious Stranger to spend the night with them, or at least to share their evening meal.
Still they did not know who He was.
Why?
Largely because Christ was the last Person these disciples expected to see.
Had they not seen Him die?
Had they not watched His head fall limp on His shoulders?

It had seemed so absurd to them as they had stood at the foot of the cross and remembered His words:

"Whosoever believeth in me, though he were dead, yet shall he live . . . and whosoever liveth and believeth in me shall never die . . ."

Then to see Him die—right there before their eyes . . . .

They had not been able to grasp the glorious truth that life
hereafter is not dependent upon the physical at all . . . is not
material but spiritual.
So the disciples imagined that Jesus of Nazareth could not
possibly be alive unless He were just as He was before . . .
    dependent upon the same material limitations that bound-
    ed their lives.

And so they sat down at last to eat their evening meal.
The Stranger stayed with them and, in the most natural way in
the world, gave thanks before He took bread in His hands.

There was something in the way He gave thanks . . .
    as He took bread . . .
        reached across the table . . .
            broke the bread with a characteristic gesture . . .
            and the folds of His robe fell back . . .
Perhaps they saw the livid red marks of the nails in His hand.
But whatever it was, in that instant they knew . . .
They knew!
And He was gone.

It wasn't possible!
It couldn't be . . .
But they had seen Him with their own eyes.
Then the women were right!
And they rose and ran—ran, not walked,
all the seven-and-a-half miles back to Jerusalem to tell the
other disciples the incredible news.

But they found some of the disciples completely unwilling to
believe what they were reporting.
Salome and Mary, the mother of James the Less and of Joses,
had been there much earlier in the day and had already told
them the news of the empty tomb.
Then Mary Magdalene had appeared—her eyes shining like
stars—saying . . .
        "I have seen the Lord!"

But these women were emotional creatures.
How could their testimony be accepted as credible?

        "And their words seemed to them as idle tales, and
        they believed them not."

Then Peter and John had appeared not only talking about the
empty tomb, but offering an explanation for it—
an explanation they could not, would not accept.
Resurrection? Impossible!
How could intelligent men believe *that?*

And now the breathless Cleopas and his friend with the same
words that Mary Magdelene had used . . .

> "We have seen the Lord!"

Seen a dead man? Impossible!
Had everyone suddenly gone crazy?

Thomas, one of the disciples, thrust out his jaw and stepped
forward.
He said what some of the others had been wanting to say . . .

> "I don't believe you . . . . What we've all been
> through must have temporarily unhinged your
> minds . . . . I would have to see the Lord for myself.
> Not only that, except I shall see in his hands the print
> of the nails, and put my finger into the print of the
> nails, and thrust my hand into His side,
> *I will not believe."*

It was eight days before Thomas got his proof.

Once again the disciples were gathered together,
Thomas among them.
Suddenly Jesus was with them in the room.
He singled Thomas out, smiled at him:

> "Reach hither thy finger, and behold my hands; and
> reach hither thy hand, and thrust it into my side; and
> be not faithless, but believing."

Thomas was all but overwhelmed.
Gone was all his blustering skepticism.
He fell to his knees . . . All he could say was . . .

> "My Lord and my God."

Simon Peter witnessed this.
There was now no doubt in his heart . .

Something tremendous had indeed happened.
The Christ who had been crucified was alive . . .
Life could never be the same again!

Yet something else troubled Simon, ate at him.
He was still nursing deep and bitter shame, still smarting with
the searing iron that had eaten into his very soul.

He had denied his Lord.
How could he ever face Him again?

Whenever Simon was deeply troubled, always he went back to
his nets.
"I go a-fishing," he would say . . . and this time six of his
friends decided to go with him.

There came the night when the men had worked hard and
had caught nothing.
As they rowed back towards shore, discouraged and in com-
parative silence, they saw Someone standing on the beach in
the early light of morning. The sea was calm—calm as a
millpond—and a light early-morning mist still clung to the
surface of the water.

"Children, have ye any meat?"

And when they replied in the negative, the voice called:

"Cast the net on the right side of the ship,
and ye shall find."

They had nothing to lose in following the Stranger's advice.
Over the side went the nets again, this time with success—
so much success that the nets were in danger of breaking.

They were now getting closer to the shore, and the mist was
beginning to lift.
They could see flames leaping from a fire on the beach, and
this mysterious Figure waiting for them to beach their boat.

"It is the Lord," said John, and that was enough for Simon.
Here was the opportunity for which he had longed—to tell the
Lord that he loved Him—to show how well he knew Him.

Without a moment's hesitation, he jumped overboard and waded ashore.

And then comes the loveliest record of God dealing with a penitent sinner . . . .
Its tenderness and understanding come stealing into our own hearts like the perfume of crushed flowers.

As they sat round the fire, cooking some of the fish they had caught and baking their loaves of bread on the live coals, Jesus suddenly turned to Simon . . . .

"Simon son of Jonas, lovest thou me
more than these?"

Simon was a little puzzled at the question:

"Yes, Lord, thou knowest that I love thee."

Christ looked him straight in the eyes . . . .

"Then—feed my lambs."

Then again He asked:

"Simon, son of Jonas, lovest thou me?"

Simon was a little hurt. Why would the Lord *keep* asking?

"Yes Lord, thou knowest that I love thee."
"Then—feed my sheep."

But when the question came the third time, light began to dawn for Simon.
For every one of Simon's earlier denials Jesus was now asking a pledge of love.
This was His way of making everything all right again.

When next we see Simon, he is Simon no more—
but Peter—the Rock.

We see him fearless and eloquent,
fire in his eyes
and his voice vibrant with conviction,
melodious with good news.

His own will has gone; his Master's will has taken its place.
Peter stands up and preaches the gospel of his crucified and
risen Lord.

Furthermore he is preaching it in Jerusalem, at the storm-
center of the enemies of the Nazarene.

Implicit in the whole situation is the fact that on the day of the
crucifixion the disciples did not ever expect to see Christ
again.
The Resurrection was the last thing they expected.
Their belief in it was not some fantastic idea, wafted in from
the swamps of fevered imaginations.
It was not some romantic wish out of their dream-house, not
the result of wishful thinking.
For it had come as a complete shock,
    unexpected
      bewildering.

There is no more adamant fact in the records than the changes
that came over these men.
Jerusalem had been anything but impressed with the way
Christ's disciples had conducted themselves during the arrest
and trial of the Nazarene.
His followers had certainly not been courageous.
In fact, they had all either fled to save their own lives
or followed at a great distance.

Peter was so fearful that he had even denied having known the
Nazarene.
Then after their Master's death, the band of disciples had
stayed in hiding with the doors locked—"for the fear of the
Jews."

Yet after that first Easter morning, we find these same men
    timid
      frightened
        ineffective
preaching openly, with no fear of anyone.

Their personal conviction rings like a bell through the pages of
the New Testament . . . steady and strong . . . .

> "That which we have heard with our own ears,
> seen with our own eyes, handled with
> our own hands, declare we unto you."

And of what were they so sure?
That Jesus Christ was alive—but no spiritual resurrection
this—not just the perpetuation of a dead man's ideas.

No, by a Resurrection they meant that on a certain Sabbath,
suddenly, at a given time between sunset and dawn,
in that new tomb which had belonged to Joseph of Arimathea,
there had been a fluttering of unseen forces . . .
   a rustling as of the breath of God moving through the
   garden.

Strong, immeasurable life had been breathed back into the
dead body they had laid upon the cold stone slab;
And the dead man had risen up
      had come out of the grave-clothes
   had walked to the threshold of the tomb
   had stood swaying for a moment on His wounded feet
and had walked out into the dewy garden alive forevermore.

It was so real to them that they could have almost heard the
whispered sigh as the spirit had fluttered back into the worn
body . . .
Almost catch a whiff of the strange scents that had drifted back
to Him from the tomb
   of linen and bandages . . .
      of spices—myrrh and aloes . . .
         and close air and blood.

Furthermore, they were saying these things in the same city
that had sought to destroy the Christ,
   right at the door of the stronghold of the priests,
      a thousand paces from the tomb where Christ had been
      laid.

Christ's enemies would have given anything to have refuted
their claims.
One thing would have done it—so simply.
If only they could have produced a body.
But they could not . . . .

So they tried everything else they could think of to silence
these fishermen, tax collectors, farmers, carpenters, shepherds, housewives . . .
   imprisonment
      threats
         scourgings
            stonings and death.
Nothing succeeded in silencing them.

There would come the time when Peter would actually stand
before Caiaphas and the Sanhedrin, as Jesus had done, and
nothing but flaming words of courage would pass his lips:

> "Whether it be right in the sight of God to hearken
> unto you more than unto God, judge ye.
> For we cannot but speak the things which we have
> seen and heard. . ."

Now it takes a very great conviction to change men so dras-
tically.
Nor do men persist in a lie or even a delusion, if every time
they insist on its truth, they are driving nails into their own
coffins.

Men do not invent a story, so that they can be crucified upside
down, as Peter eventually was . . .
   or have their heads chopped off, like Paul, outside the city of
   Rome,
      or be stoned to death—like Stephen.

A self-hypnotic illusion may sustain men for a time—
but not for long.
In the long run, an illusion does not build character strong
enough to stand great hardship, great persecution.
Only the bedrock truth can do that!

Moreover, men who are merely fooling themselves do not
become purposeful men
   well-integrated men with self-sustaining qualities of leadership . . .
as these erstwhile timid apostles became.

And here is something else—it was their continuing fellowship with their risen Lord through the years which became
the integrating
    guiding
        sustaining
power in their lives.

Through His Spirit they had guidance and strength. . . .
They had His wisdom.
    His peace
        and His joy.
They had boldness and courage and they had power . . .
    qualities that they had not had until after the first Easter
    morning.

They now felt that they were still in touch with Him . . .
    in a different way—yes—but in a more powerful way.
They knew that He was still with them, even as He had
promised. . . .

    "Go ye into the world and lo, I am with you always."

They felt that! They knew it!
The promises He had made to them before His death were
now fulfilled, and they (men like Cleopas and his friend) went
up and down in the land. . . .
They crossed the sea.
They shook the Roman Empire until it tottered and fell.
They changed the world.

This is the fact we in this twentieth century cannot ignore.

Through the nineteen centuries which have followed in every
land there have been men and women who have experienced
the same fellowship . . .
    who have felt the same power in their lives . . .
        who have had the same peace and inner serenity . . .
            who have had the same joy and the
            same radiant victory.

They were not crackpots, morons, nor lunatics.
Included among them were some of the greatest minds the
world has ever seen . . .

Some of the most brilliant thinkers
                    philosophers
                        scientists
            and scholars . . . .
They were not frustrated personalities who fled the world of
reality and found refuge in the dugouts of their own wistful
escapes from life.

On the contrary, most of them have been radiant souls filled
with an abiding joy, living to the full every golden hour, and
tasting the deepest joys of life.

Dismiss, as you will, the sentimentality, the hysteria and the
wishful thinking that may be born in times of crisis and
danger, there is still a residue of hard, stubborn testimony
from men who met Him during the second World War. . . .

For example, while they drifted on liferafts on the ocean . . .
who came home through dangerous skies "on a wing and a
prayer" . . . who met Him in the dog-watch of many a long
night in dangerous waters.

And you, too, may have that fellowship with the risen Christ.
Indeed, you will not believe the fact of the Resurrection for
yourself until the living Christ lives in your own heart.
When you have in your own life that sense of His nearness and
His power—ah, then, you too will *know!*

Your life today may be guided by Christ . . .
Your problems may be solved by His wisdom . . .
Your weakness may be turned into strength by His help . . .
Your struggles may become victories by His grace . . .
Your sorrows may be turned into joy by His comfort.

To you there may come the same wonderful changes that have
come to other men and women all down through the years.

This is the reality that can be yours—this comradeship with
the resurrected Christ through His Spirit is available now . . .
    To the man in the street . . .
        to the government clerk . . .
            to the anxious mother . . .
                to the confused schoolboy or girl.

This is the real meaning of Easter.
Forget the bunny rabbits and the colored eggs.
Forget the symbols of spring that so often confuse and conceal the real meaning of what we celebrate on that day.

No tabloid will ever print the startling news that the mummified body of Jesus of Nazareth has been discovered in old Jerusalem.
Christians have no carefully embalmed body enclosed in a glass case to worship.
Thank God, we have an empty tomb.

The glorious fact that the empty tomb proclaims to us is that life for us does not stop when death comes.
Death is not a wall, but a door.
And eternal life which may be ours now, by faith in Christ, is not interrupted when the soul leaves the body,
for we live on . . and on.

There is no death to those who have entered into fellowship with Him who emerged from the tomb
Because the Resurrection is true, it is the most significant thing in our world today.
Bringing the resurrected Christ into our lives, individual and national, is the only hope we have for making a better world.
"Because I live, ye shall live also."

That is the message of Easter

L ORD JESUS, may we never again think and act as if Thou wert dead. Let us more and more come to know Thee as a living Lord who hath promised to them that believe: "Because I live, ye shall live also."

Help us to remember that we are praying to the Conquerer of Death, that we may no longer be afraid nor be dismayed by the world's problems and threats, since Thou hast overcome the world. In Thy strong name, we ask for Thy living presence and Thy victorious power, Amen.

From Peter Marshall's Pulpit

Those we love are with the Lord, we believe, and the Lord has promised to be with us: "Behold, I am with you always." And if our loved ones are with Him, and He is with us, they cannot be far away.

Modern politics appear to be related to the art of conjuring . . . . The skeletons in the nation's cupboards are replaced by the rabbits that come out of the politicians' hats.

Evil forces may be triumphant for a moment. But they are always deprived of the results of their triumph. The conquests of their armies to date are hollow victories . . . . The flies have conquered the flypaper.

A definition is a prison, with its walls and bars and limitations. . . . But a story, as told by Jesus, is a sunrise that casts a golden light upon the truth which it contains.

from THE LOCKED DOOR

The Church has in her keeping the secrets of prayer and meditation and communion with the risen Christ, but sometimes she keeps them too long in the icebox of orthodoxy.

from HUNGRY SHEEP

Along with our higher education has come a sort of national debunking contest. It is smarter to revile than to revere; more fashionable to depreciate than to appreciate . . . .

We have failed to realize that when we deny the existence of great men, we are denying the desirability of great men.

from A TEXT FROM LINCOLN

No problem which any married couple can have is beyond solution if they are willing to get down on their knees together and ask God what to do about it. It is not a question of what the husband wants— or what the wife wants—but always, what does God want?

from THE ELECT LADY

All that death can do, it did to Christ. Our Lord felt the chill of it: He died—alone. But He did for us what we are not able to do for our loved ones . . . He explored the basements of death to the very bottom . . . and came back to tell us to be of good cheer.

from QUO VADIS, AMERICA?

It is a fact of Christian experience that life is a series of troughs and peaks. In His efforts to get permanent possession of a soul, God relies on the troughs more than the peaks. And some of His special favorites have gone through longer and deeper troughs than anyone else.

from LIFE'S FRUSTRATIONS

The waters of the oceans of God's love do run up into the tiny bays of our unbelief . . . .

from REMEMBRANCE

Do you know the beauty in those small homely things?

> Sunlight through a jar of beach-plum jelly . . .
> A rainbow in soapsuds in dishwater . . .
> An eggyolk in a blue bowl . . . .
> White ruffled curtains sifting moonlight . . .
> The color of cranberry glass . . .
> A little cottage with blue shutters . . .
> Crimson roses in an old stone crock . . .
> The smell of newly baked bread . . .
> Candlelight on old brass . . .
> The soft brown of a cocker's eyes.

NOTES

Many favorite, well-marked books in Dr. Marshall's library were examined and compared with his manuscripts in an attempt to locate all instances of indebtedness to others. It was difficult, since he made oral acknowledgments in his sermons that did not appear in his sermon notes. For any debts of gratitude unacknowledged in these pages, I offer to the authors and their publishers most sincere regret and apology.

C. M.

[1] Dr. G. A. Buttrick, *Jesus Came Preaching* (Charles Scribner's Sons).

[2] This thought was first expressed in just this way, I believe, by Dr. Harry E. Fosdick in *On Being Fit to Live With* (Harper & Brothers).

[3] From the hymn "Have Thine Own Way, Lord" (Hope Publishing Co.).

[4] For many of the ideas in this sermon Dr. Marshall is indebted to Claude McKay, *Knowing Jesus Through His Friends* (Revell Company).

[5] *Ibid.*

[6] Dr. Leslie Weatherhead, *How Can I Find God?* (Revell Company).

[7] This direct quotation and the previous eleven lines are quoted from and based on *How Can I Find God?*

[8] Lines 13-18 on p. 57 and lines 10-21 on p. 58 are quoted almost verbatim from Dr. Leslie Weatherhead's *Transforming Friendship* (Abingdon-Cokesbury). Beginning with the twenty-seventh line on p. 59 through the twenty-third line on p. 60, the material is adapted and quoted from *Transforming Friendship*. The fifth paragraph on p. 61 is from *How Can I Find God?* by Dr. Weatherhead (Revell). Lines ten to sixteen, p. 62, are also quoted from *How Can I Find God?*

[9] From Dr. Loring T. Swaim's presidential address in 1942 before the American Rheumatism Association, published in Annals of Internal Medicine, July 1943, American College of Physicians, Philadelphia.

[10] From the column "Pitching Horseshoes" by Billy Rose, published by the Bell Syndicate. Reprinted by permission of *The Reader's Digest.*

[11] These paragraphs were also included in Fulton Oursler's book *Why I Know There Is a God,* Doubleday & Co., Inc., 1950. Used with permission.

[12] Starr Daily, *Recovery* (The Macalester Park Publishing Co., St. Paul, Minn.). Used with permission.

[13] From the hymn "I'll Go Where You Want Me to Go," The Rodeheaver Hall Mack Co., Winona Lake, Ind. Used with permission.

[14] From the hymn "Take My Life and Let It Be," words by Frances R. Havergal.

[15] From the hymn "Make Me a Captive, Lord" (Hope Publishing Co.).

[16] Paraphrased from C. E. Montague, *Rough Justice* (Doubleday & Company). Used with permission.

[17] Paraphrased from Erich Maria Remarque, *All Quiet on the Western Front* (Little, Brown & Company). Used with permission.

[18] The poem "High Flight," by Pilot-Officer John Gillespie Magee, Jr., R.C.A.F., is reprinted with the permission of his mother, Mrs. John Gillespie Magee.

[19] C. S. Lewis, *Mere Christianity* (The Macmillan Company).